A MOTLEY FOOL BOOK

Simple

Systems

for Beating

the Market

The Unemotional Investor

Robert Sheard

Simon & Schuster

 SIMON & SCHUSTER
Rockefeller Center
1230 Avenue of the Americas
New York, NY 10020

SIMON & SCHUSTER and colophon are registered trademarks
of Simon & Schuster Inc.

Designed by Meryl Sussman Levavi/digitext, Inc.

Manufactured in the United States of America

10   9   8   7   6   5   4   3   2   1

Library of Congress Cataloging-in-Publication Data
Sheard, Robert.
    The unemotional investor : simple systems for beating the
market / Robert Sheard.
        p.   cm.
    Includes index.
    1. Investments.   2. Stocks.   I. Title.
HG4521.S518   1998
332.6—dc21   98-6007
                                                            CIP
ISBN 0-684-84590-3

For my parents

For my partners

⬚ Contents

⌘ Foreword

We first made Robert Sheard's acquaintance in an online chat room in late 1994. Back then, Robert was a rather frustrated graduate student teaching English lit and identified himself with the AOL handle "RSheard." He quickly became a regular visitor to The Motley Fool in the months shortly after the debut of our service. Robert was polite, enthusiastic, and enjoyed answering others' questions, which he did with increasing frequency as he learned more about the stock market. At the outset Robert knew very little, but as has so often been the case with visitors to Fooldom, he learned a tremendous amount and he did it very quickly. That's the beauty of a good liberal arts education; it prepares you for anything you wish to set your mind to.

From the outset, Robert was clearly interested in the Dow Dividend Approach—a purely mechanical approach to value investing. We first discovered this method in Michael O'Higgins's book *Beating the Dow*, and we have elaborated it in each of our books *(You Have More Than You Think, The Motley Fool Investment Guide*, and *The Motley Fool Investment Workbook)* and it's been endlessly discussed and elaborated in our online domain **(www.fool.com)**. There, many Foolish tinkerers combined efforts to try to build a better mousetrap. And this book is one such fruit borne of that effort.

Fooldom's fascination with the Dow Dividend Approach revolves around the simplicity of the strategy and its mechanical nature, the two sine qua nons of what we call a "gadget approach." Gadgets are mechanical gizmos designed to simplify our lives, providing us with convenience, and in so doing saving us time. The same is the case for gadget approaches to the stock market and investing. The Dow Dividend Approach is a prime example, has historically outperformed the market, and will continue to enjoy enduring popularity in the Fields of Folly to boot.

But Robert's liberal arts education taught him to ask questions, always to keep investigating, and to search tirelessly for better or additional answers. That's the classic intellectual approach to take in this Second Age of Reason, where through the use of computers and mathematics human beings have learned more about the universe in one century than in all the previous ones put together. Robert has done his small part by simply asking, "Might we invent more gadget approaches like the Dow Dividend Approach that perform similarly, or better?" It was that question—that quest—that yielded Unemotional Value and Unemotional Growth.

Unemotional Value is our favorite twist on the Dow Dividend Approach, and following publication of our first book we ended up changing our popular Foolish Four approach to conform to Robert's Unemotional Value approach. The approach has been written about before, and receives more treatment at length in this book, so we need spend little additional time here elucidating it.

Unemotional Growth (UG) is a different story. This is a creature entirely of Robert's own creation, which makes it fascinating on its own. But further, it sports superior returns and greater diversification. However, it also brings with it less of a back-tested history and demands more active trading. Readers must weigh these factors before determining how appropriate UG is for them. Many may wish to treat the list of Unemotional Growth stocks simply as a superb "screen" from which to choose superior longer-term investments. Indeed, it's through UG that we first invested in companies like Coca-Cola, Nike, Tellabs, and Applied Materials, which we continued to hold past the appointed UG switch date. (Read the chapters dedicated to this approach and you'll understand what we're talking about.) Whether you wish to employ Unemotional Growth whole hog, as a screen for stocks, or not to employ it at all largely comes down to your degrees of experience and comfort, your tolerance for risk, and the amount of money you have (as trading commissions and market-maker spreads will eat into your profits).

Being gadgets, the approaches in this book remove emotion from the investing equation, a variable that too often troubles or even ruins investors, as Robert correctly asserts. It is this trait of course that Robert celebrates with the title of this book.

It must also be noted that any employment of a mechanical approach also necessarily removes decision-making and reason from the equation as well—your decision-making and reason come into play only at the beginning, if and when you make a commitment to use the approaches. It's for this reason that some Fools choose to use these approaches as screens—retaining the right to make their own decisions. In so doing, they also welcome back emotion (typically, greed and fear). But regardless, the companies one finds in these screens are typically great growth stocks, so don't play too much with fire.

Two things to note in closing. First, as Robert makes clear from the outset of the book, he was no "Wall Street gooroo" before coming to The Motley Fool to learn how to invest. Quite the opposite, in fact—which we consider an asset! That he is writing and publishing a useful investment book today demonstrates how accessible investing can be to those who wish to spend the necessary (but not inordinate) time getting to know the subject. Heck, we ourselves are no experts either, and would never presume to use the term. We agree with the minister who wrote, "The greater the island of knowledge, the longer the coastline of mystery." The more you learn, the more you have to learn, and the more you want to learn it. Yes, investing makes for a lifelong education, one that should be both pleasurable and financially rewarding. It is open to all, and the world should welcome further contributions to investment literature by similarly "inexpert" Fools.

Second, much of the work in this book came to fruition through the Foolish Workshop section of our Motley Fool Web site. It is accessible on the Internet at **http://www.fool.com/Workshop/Work shop.htm** and continues to offer Robert's daily write-ups along with a wide range of input from other Foolish investors. As is the case with many nooks and crannies of our online sites, the message board that undergirds this editorial work is also outstanding, and we encourage your participation!

Fool on!

—*David and Tom Gardner*

The Birth of a Fool

When I decided to embark on this project, I was thrilled to be writing a book, although if you had told me five years ago I'd be writing a book on the stock market, I'd have asked the bartender to start watering down your drinks. My pedigree is anything but typical for Wall Street and my career path five years ago was governed by literary theory rather than price/earnings ratios and dividend yields. I thought my first book was more likely to be a dry-as-dust version of my doctoral dissertation I blackmailed some university press editor into publishing so I could get tenure.

So when I started planning this book, the last thing I wanted to include was personal material about my background. Who was I to be writing about the stock market? And without the typical list of credentials (an M.B.A. from the Wharton School of Business, thirty years as a grizzled Wall Street veteran, or battle scars from the bear market of 1973–74 and the Crash of October 1987), who would listen to what I had to say?

Tom and David Gardner—the founders of The Motley Fool—insisted, however, that it is precisely because I come to the world of investing from the outside that I tell my own story. This book, after all, is for people exactly like me, who come from all walks of life, have careers in fields ranging from alfalfa farming to zymology, and who want to take charge of their own investments but are intimidated by the prospects of doing so and want someone to walk them through the entire process, step by step. It's the book I wish someone had written years ago when I was struggling to make sense of investing. So let me back up a few years and tell my own story—the birth of a Fool.

Six years ago, I was a Ph.D. candidate in English literature at Penn State University. I had just married another graduate student, also in the doctoral program in English, and I was settling in for a year of reading toward my comprehensive exams while my new bride, Cynthia, was recovering from a broken back suffered in an auto accident and writing her dissertation, having already passed her exams.

Over the course of the next two years, our entire world was changed by a series of events no one could have foreseen. In fact, any writer including them in a novel would have had his manuscript rejected for relying on melodrama. Lord Byron was right: " 'Tis strange—but true; for truth is always strange; stranger than fiction" *(Don Juan)*.

In November of 1991, I did manage to pass my exams, but, in retrospect, that was the least crucial event of the next two years. My wife's mother had pancreatic cancer diagnosed earlier that summer and the disease progressed rapidly. She died on Christmas Eve. Enough adjustment for one year, one would think, especially during graduate school. But onward.

In short order, two much happier events propelled our lives forward. In the spring, my wife became pregnant with our son. And, a few months later, she successfully defended her dissertation and graduated. Our next goal was Cynthia's job search.

In quick succession, Cynthia's father died suddenly, our son, Brenden, was born, and Cynthia was offered a position at the University of Kentucky. Dazed, we left Pennsylvania for the Bluegrass State. The plan was that I would try to teach part-time at either the University of Kentucky or another local college while writing my dissertation, and then we would do another job search if I couldn't secure a tenure-track position locally.

What does any of this have to do with investing? Not much, actually, other than to explain that in 1993 and 1994, I was on the treadmill toward a Ph.D. and a career in talking and writing about British novels. Because of the premature deaths of Cynthia's parents, we were also faced with deciding what to do with her parents' modest estate—a topic neither of us was prepared for, emotionally or financially.

We did what most young couples do when faced with a new job, home, and baby—we went house hunting. Interest rates were very low at the time and the housing market in Lexington was far more reasonable than the property values we had seen in Pennsylvania. For roughly what we were shelling out in rent for a tiny student apartment in Happy Valley, Pa., we could buy a house big enough to afford us both offices at home. So we invested a healthy amount of Cynthia's inheritance into the house and put the rest in three or four mutual funds. We didn't know anything about investing and weren't particularly interested in learning at the time. The logical alternative, or so we thought at the time, was to let a professional manage the money from the inheritance and we'd live out our lives in an ivory-tower paradise.

Over the next year or so, I taught part time at both the University of Kentucky and Georgetown College, but I was rapidly losing my enthusiasm for the profession. Between the miserable job prospects for new Ph.D.'s, the "publish-or-perish" mentality driving the humanities in silly directions, the students who would rather suffer unanesthetized root canals than read or write, and the hyperpolitical atmosphere that infects the profession, my reason for getting into higher education in the first place (my love of reading literature) was rapidly becoming a mirage. Enter The Motley Fool.

About the time I was getting despondent about my future in academe, I plugged one of those ubiquitous America Online promotional floppy disks into my computer. When I plugged the disk in, I fully intended to little more than fritter away the ten free hours and then cancel the service.

Call it chance, call it free will, what have you (appropriately, my master's thesis focused on chance, free will, and fate in the novels of Margaret Drabble, so perhaps it was a bit of each), but the first time I loaded the software and signed on to America Online, an icon with a Renaissance jester's face and a blurb linking Shakespeare and finance together appeared in one of the three slots where AOL highlights different forums. Not knowing my way around the service and being attracted to both Shakespeare and finance, I naturally clicked the button.

I still haven't recovered.

In those days (the summer of 1994), The Motley Fool was almost brand-new. What was once a print newsletter published by David and Tom Gardner, with their longtime friend Erik Rydholm, had evolved into a public message folder on Prodigy, then a message folder on America Online, and eventually a full-fledged forum on America Online. I stumbled across it shortly after its birth as an autonomous forum.

In those days, the forum consisted of only a handful of articles, a message folder or two, and a chat once a week, hosted by the Gardners. They were still running the business out of the back of David's home and were working insane hours as the forum exploded in popularity. But what hooked me almost immediately, before I even chatted with the Gardners or any other readers, was the original series of articles called "How to Invest What You Have: From $1 to $1 Million." The articles were short, irreverent, literate, hilarious, all the qualities I admired in writing and tried to convey to my writing students.

The entertainment value wasn't all that kept me enthralled, though. The information in those articles—straightforward, honest, practical information that anyone could use to start learning about investing—was the real hook. Nowhere else had I found information I knew I could use. I had glanced through a handful of the classic investing texts, those by Peter Lynch (of mutual fund fame as the manager of Fidelity Magellan), a few about Warren Buffett (one of the two richest men in America and a brilliant investor), and others, and while they were inspiring, I never felt that what I had learned helped me as an individual investor with a job outside professional money management. No companies are going to knock on my door and pitch me their success stories as they did for Peter Lynch.

The articles in The Motley Fool, though, launched me on an educational journey that continues today. After printing out those articles and poring over them again and again, I began to find other books to flesh out the approaches the Fools taught online. I attended every chat the Gardners hosted, until you could hear them groan all the way through cyberspace: "That Sheard pest is back. Quick, lock the door." I posted endless questions, seeking clarification about points I still didn't understand, and the Fools were gracious again and again with their all-too-precious time and their desire to teach.

In the end, it was the Fools' spirit of education and their ax to grind about the misinformation spread by the traditional money management industry that kept me coming back again and again, long after my ten free hours vaporized and I was "on the clock" at AOL's subscriber rates.

I obviously wasn't alone in my race to become Foolish. (In Folly, to be Foolish is the goal rather than to be Wise. The Foolish theme comes from Shakespeare's use of the Fool as the only character at court who could tell the king the truth without losing his head. As La Rochefoucauld put it, "Who lives without folly is not so wise as he thinks.") The forum was growing so rapidly as more and more Fools began participating that the Gardners couldn't keep up with the requests for information and the demands of a growing readership.

As the forum expanded, the Fools asked some of the earliest participants who were still around and had absorbed a certain measure of Folly if they'd join the staff on a volunteer basis and host a chat occasionally, or host a message-board discussion. The goal was simply to spread the message to as many readers as possible that, hey, if you can take a little time to learn the basics of investing, you can manage your own money and put the professional Wall Street Wisemen to shame with your returns. In October of 1994, then, my AOL bill threatening to outpace my salary as a lecturer, I gladly accepted the Gardners' offer of a volunteer position and became MF DowMan, my America Online screen name (for reasons that will become apparent later in the book).

Over the next seven months, I found I was spending more time on Folly than I was writing my dissertation, and having a great deal more fun. I learned as much as I could while hosting a chat for beginning investors to help them discover what I had learned. Interestingly, the hardest challenge in the early days of The Motley Fool was to get people to realize that under the facade of jesters' hats and Shakespearean punning, we were deadly serious in our message. Many new readers who would pop into one of our chat rooms would spend the greatest portion of their time trying to figure out when our sales pitch was coming. When they finally discovered the information we were providing was free (except for whatever they paid to America Online for their connection time), they went away thinking we might well be fools (little *f*).

After all, most people have precious little sense of humor when it comes to money matters, and here we were, clowning around, calling ourselves Fools and explicating the merits of being un-Wise. If nothing else, we were (and are) opinionated and out to put fun back into the dusty museum most people picture as the hallowed halls of finance.

As the end of the spring 1995 semester rolled around, I was in despair at the thought of another year of teaching for peanuts and having little or no hope of seeing my efforts pay off in the form of a tenure-track job after graduation. At precisely the same time, the Gardners contacted me to see if I'd be willing to give up academe to work for them as an editor and writer. It was an agonizing decision and I spent the better part of two minutes making it. Sew that belled cap to my forehead, boys, I'm a Fool!

Needless to say, there was some hand-wringing behind the scenes. I was asking my wife to have faith in me as I abandoned a professional goal I had held for a decade in favor of a new job where I sit at home (most of the time in what could hardly be called "professional" attire) and write and talk online about the stock market with people I can't see, employed by two guys who, at that time, were still in their twenties, and whom I had never met in person. And the real leap of faith? My checks were going to be deposited electronically! She saw a future episode of *60 Minutes* written all over this scenario. But she saw where I was heading emotionally in academics and supported me in my decision to follow a radically different path. It's been an incredible learning experience for me, not only in terms of investing and financial analysis, but also in the electronic medium that's revolutionizing how people communicate and share information that previously had simply not been available outside of an institutional context.

Since beginning with The Motley Fool, my focus has changed a number of times as the forum has evolved and my own interests and financial research have carried me down new avenues. Much of what you'll read about in this book grew out of some interactive collaboration between me, The Fool staff, and our ever-changing and growing community of readers.

To many of you, this rather personal story may seem entirely irrelevant in a book purportedly about investing in the stock market. My point in relating it, though, is that the knowledge one needs to invest well isn't highly specialized. It doesn't require an M.B.A. and professional grooming, courtesy of a Wall Street firm. In a very direct way, I'm living proof of that. My professional training was in how to interpret literature and how to interpret those interpretations, a spiral that can be as daunting as wading through financial statements to the uninitiated. Yet with some very pointed instruction and a minimal amount of independent study, I soon learned enough to manage my own investments well. From there, my personal research and model building (the subject of this book) blossomed out of some very basic principles.

Most new investors, and I still feel I'm a new investor at heart, fear uncertainty more than anything when it comes to investing. It's the single most powerful force keeping the professional fund managers in business. If investors can get over that fear of the unknown (and if you read this book, I guarantee you'll know enough that the basic uncertainty of managing your own portfolio will be removed), the actual act of managing one's own stock portfolio will be as unthreatening to you as balancing your checkbook each month. (Maybe less so; I've seen the way some people keep track of their checkbooks.)

Regardless of your experience with investing, then, know that you can do it yourself without having to become a professional in a daunting and completely foreign discipline—high finance. When you start to doubt whether you can do it—and if you are anything like the thousands of readers I've chatted with in e-mail and in online seminars (or chats), you will—just recall my own personal odyssey into the investment world. When the Gardners insisted I tell my story, I think the comment I heard was, Your readers need to know that if you can do it, anyone can. After pulling the darts out of my neck, I realized they had a very good point. I came to investing with no special training, no special gifts for financial analysis, only the desire to learn more and the excitement of finding an interactive forum that afforded me the opportunity to pursue my interests, both as a novice, and now as a writer and researcher.

If you ever need a personal cheerleader, read these introductory pages again and realize that building wealth is possible for all of us, no matter how much education you have, how much experience you've had, or how much money you start with. If you can look at two numbers and can tell which of them is larger, you've got the basic skills necessary to manage your own stock portfolio. The rest is just learning where to look for the right numbers to compare. That's precisely what I'll tell you, step-by-step, number-by-number, throughout this book. I'll walk you through the first day of your learning process, clear through to your first set of trades and beyond. If you're a complete tyro at investing, I've been there. And I've talked with thousands of other investors just like you and have answered the vast majority of questions you'll probably have along the way. I'll do my best to anticipate them throughout this book and cover the bases crucial to get you started in stocks. Congratulations are already in order, in fact. Simply by reading a book like this one, you've taken the first step toward financial independence. In short order, you'll be wearing a jester's cap and proudly boasting that you're a Fool. "I met a fool i' the forest, A motley fool" (Shakespeare, *As You Like It*).

A Note on How to Use This Text

I'm working from the assumption that you are likely to have had little or no experience at all in the stock market before reading this book. If that's not the case, please bear with me during sections that may seem obvious to you. One thing I've learned in the last two years, writing about these subjects online and chatting with readers in e-mail, is that each individual will bring to investing a range of experiences. For me, it's better to err on the side of repetition and take too basic a path than to assume the reader has already worked through certain issues and doesn't need help.

The outline of this book, then, is geared toward a first-time stock investor, or even someone one step earlier in the process than that, someone who is just trying to find out whether or not stocks are even the right way to invest. To that end, I've tried to lay out the information in a sequence that new investors may find helpful.

Even though I've arranged the book to follow what I think is a logical pattern for new investors, feel free to skip around in it or even omit parts you feel don't apply to you. While I'd like you to think of me guiding you as if I were your personal investing coach, I'm not going to be looking over your shoulder along the way. Take what you can and need from the book and make it your own. There may be several places in the book where you feel as if you've learned all you need to know to be comfortable with your investments. Feel free to stop right there and be content with that. There's no rule that says you must learn or attempt everything you'll find in this book. Incorporate what you need into your own world. That's the real goal of education. I have no doubt that one of you reading this will take what I've built here and expand on it or improve it to make it more useful. The only thing I ask of you in return is that you then share what you've discovered with other investors.

We've got the greatest investment club in history going in The Motley Fool, and a lot of the ideas in this book were fired in the flames of that communal kiln because of the remarkable ease of communication in that interactive medium. By sharing our ideas, working to test possibilities, banging into dead ends only to discover another avenue, we've been able to help hundreds of thousands of individual investors improve their returns and wrest control of their investments back from the Wall Street Wisemen. This book can get you started on the same journey I began not too terribly long ago. And even though Tom Gardner was joking (I think) when he said that if I can do this, anyone can, to some degree, that's the idea behind this book. I've learned how to manage my portfolio well in a short time; so can you, no matter where you're starting from or what you have to invest. You *can* build your own wealth. Fool on!

PART ONE

Stock Market Basics

Let's start with a simple question: Is this book for you? That may sound a little silly, since my editor expected a book suitable for everyone interested in the stock market (and who isn't?), but there are a lot of people for whom this book is not intended. So let's make that clear from the start.

This book is not for people wanting to get rich overnight. While the goal of investing is undoubtedly the creation of wealth—maybe even more wealth than you ever really believed possible—the approaches we'll be working with here are intended for use over a long period. There's no sure prescription for a home run in the financial world, and I won't even try to show you how to swing for one. What we're aiming for is a long investment career with lots of base hits instead of trying for that one lucky swing for the fences.

This book is also not for Wall Street Whiz Kids or financial wizards. Most of what you'll find between these covers will either be old news to them, or they'll assume (wrongly) that because the approaches I'm writing about are simple, they cannot be effective. In other words, sophisticated investors (especially those in thrall to the Wise) will dismiss me and my work out of hand. After all, they've read my introduction, too, and know full well I'm an outsider looking in on the financial world, not an insider with access to the mystical keys to Wall Street. My feeling is that the individual investor has no more need for the Wise than the Wise have for me. Sounds like a pretty healthy arrangement all the way around.

This book is for the *Everyman* investor. (In these more politically correct times, I realize that should read "Everyperson," but the fifteenth century was influenced by the Old English and gender-neutral definition of "man.") If you have an interest in managing your own portfolio, in building wealth gradually but effectively, in wresting control of your investments out of the hands of the mediocre mutual fund industry, and in getting better returns than you may have thought possible with an approach simple enough that a seventh grader can use it, this book is for you.

In my experiences with The Motley Fool, I've taught the principles and strategies included here to readers I've never met in person, who span the globe (literally), who range in age from preteen to nonagenarian, whose education levels span a similar range, and who have had little or no investing experience or have spent their investment career watching someone else handle their money when they entered the online forum. Like me, they had an interest but no experience, and weren't sure where to turn.

Perhaps the most satisfying aspect of my work with The Fool is hearing from people months or years after I have worked with them to learn the investment strategies included in this book. Most of their e-mails and letters discuss how much they enjoy the feeling of independence that they have now that they're confidently managing their own portfolios. Some even convey a touch of justifiable gloating in their tones as they compare their portfolio returns with those of the mutual funds they abandoned when they began investing in stocks directly. Not enough teachers get that tangible reward. In fact, it was all but absent when I was in academe. Today, it's a fairly common occasion when I hear from a former reader who is proud to report his or her success. Perhaps I'll hear from some of you in the future.

It's time to get to work. I assume that if you are still reading, you are interested in becoming your own investment manager and that what you want now is a little concrete information. The first thing we need to tackle is the definition of a stock itself. Just what is this stock market and how (in basic terms) does it really work?

There are essentially two major types of business structures regarding ownership of a company itself—private and public companies. Privately held companies are those that are owned by an individual or a fixed group of individuals and the ownership only changes according to their own wishes. For example, Irving and Marylou's I. M. Diner is 100 percent owned by Irving and Marylou, making it a private company. If their son decides he wants to be involved in the I. M. Diner, and Irving and Marylou decide to make him a partner, it's still a private company, owned exclusively by Irving, Marylou, and Irving Jr. There is no limitation on the size of a private company or the number of owners. Typically, this type of structure suits smaller businesses, though there are some quite large privately held companies in America.

Ten years down the road, however, the family business has grown. Irving, Marylou, and Junior own six I. M. Diners and all of them are *always* full of satisfied customers. Their diner is a major hit and now they want to expand into four more states and fifteen new cities. Problem: Virtually all of their financial resources are already wrapped up in the six current diners and they are hesitant to borrow the extra capital they need to start the expansion. What are they to do to capitalize on the craze for Marylou's Heart-Stopper Special Meatloaf? One possible answer is to "go public."

A publicly traded company is one that has raised capital by selling shares of stock, individual shares of ownership in the company itself. The company works with investment bankers who launch what is called an initial public offering (IPO). The owners and their investment bankers decide how many shares they will offer and what percentage of the company those shares will represent, as well as the approximate price per share, which is based on how much the company is worth and how much the company is trying to raise. The investment bankers (called the underwriters of the offering) then seek out interested investors to purchase the available shares of stock. The money raised from the initial offering goes to the company to finance its expansion plans, and then the shares of stock enter the open market.

Once a stock is publicly traded, the original private owners no longer have complete control over the company's ownership; that rests with the current shareholders. (Though many original owners retain enough of the new public stock—at least 50.1 percent of the shares—to keep control of the voting.) Nor does the company control how often or to whom those shares of outstanding stock are bought and sold. That function is taken over by the marketplace. Stocks that are publicly traded act to a large degree like any other publicly traded item in a marketplace. The stock market brings together (through the stockbrokers) individuals and institutions who either own stock and are looking to sell it for the best price possible, or who are looking to invest money in a particular stock and hope to find the best bargain.

The price of the stock for any given company, then, depends on the same market forces of supply and demand that dictate the movement of prices for apples or corn, Reggie Jackson rookie cards, or Joe Montana autographed sweatbands. When there are a lot of buyers clamoring for a small number of shares (or apples or sweatbands), the people who own that supply can command a higher price for the stock. Conversely, if you're trying to sell a stock and there is not a flock of eager buyers, you will probably have to settle for a lower price than you hoped for.

While the actual workings of the stock market can get very complicated, what with all the middlemen involved in the actual buying and selling transactions, the basic functions of the stock market work pretty much like any farmers' market in the country. Visit one and you'll see that Farmer Lotsocare has the best-looking melons you've ever seen because of his special blend of organic fertilizer and the tender attention he gave them. He also has a frantic crowd surrounding his booth trying to get the best melons before they're snatched away. Contrast that to Farmer Quicksale, who cut corners at every opportunity and has a melon crop that seems better suited to doorstop duty than as fare for your buffet table.

As the fair opens, the crowds around Farmer Lotsocare's booth will pay just about any price Farmer Lotsocare asks (within a reasonable range, of course) for fear that they will end up empty-handed if they don't. In the meantime, Farmer Quicksale's booth is deserted. Who would buy an inferior product when a superior one is available right next door? Such is the power of the marketplace. The only buyers Farmer Quicksale will be able to attract as long as Farmer Lotsocare's booth still has melons for sale are ones who simply can't afford the higher prices for the top-grade melons. But that means Farmer Quicksale is already having to mark his prices down to attract buyers. The supply is there, but the demand isn't evident at his original prices.

Once Farmer Lotsocare runs out of melons, though, the few buyers who were too late to get any of his prizewinning crop may then decide to check out the booth next door. With the memory of what could have been, though, those buyers are not going to pay the same price to Farmer Quicksale for his obviously poorer melons. They may buy a few just to have something for their tables, but they won't pay a premium price and they won't buy in the same quantity that they might have if Farmer Lotsocare had not run out of melons. Plain and simple, market forces of supply and demand determine the price for whatever the commodity is. And in this pure sense of the word "commodity," that's how the stock market works as well. (I won't be advising you to look to the commodity markets for your investments, though. Might as well head to Vegas.)

What drives the forces of supply and demand for stocks, however, is not as easy to see as what drives them for our two farmers. On the surface, it's not as easy to see which of two stocks is the better "melon," and that's where the techniques and strategies in this book come into play. You will need a way of thumping the melons to see which farmers are charging too much and which ones are offering you a bargain. Almost everyone who has ever invested has, at some point, run into the cliché "Buy low, sell high." Yet the actual task of determining those values can be extremely complicated. If it were a simple, guaranteed, and well-known process, every investor would be making a fortune in the market on every single investment. Obviously, that is not the case. What, then, drives the forces of supply and demand for stocks?

These forces are driven by many factors, of course, but the crucial distinction we need to make as investors is between long-term and short-term market forces. In the short term, almost anything can affect investor psychology. A rumor that the chairman of the board left his wife, embezzled the company's pension fund, and ran off to South America with his assistant is enough in the short run to knock a stock's price down. Remember that the interplay between buyers and sellers is what determines a stock's price. Would you want your investment strategy to depend on market rumors?

More relevant perhaps is a news story that affects how investors feel about a given stock. Several years ago semiconductor maker Intel was flying high. Everyone loved the company because it was dominating the personal computer market with its microprocessors. The stock was soaring. Then came the announcement that a flaw existed in its new top-of-the-line Pentium chip, which generated false results in certain very complicated mathematical computations. Wham! For a while, the stock price was hammered because of the fears that Intel might lose money on the new product, that a recall would devastate the company, that . . . well, you get the picture. A year or so later, with the Pentium problem solved, Intel's stock was again the darling of the market, making great gains and being touted as the one stock you *must* have in your portfolio by pundits far and wide. For now . . .

All of that, however, is in the short run, a period we at The Motley Fool are not nearly as concerned about as what happens over a much longer time frame. Over the long run, there's no doubt what drives the forces at work on a stock's price—the earnings a company records. There is a good reason "the bottom line" has come into our lexicon to mean "what everything boils down to." The bottom line, or how much a company earns in profits, is the factor above all else that will move a stock price up or down over time. Keep in mind, a shareholder is a part owner of the company and, therefore, "owns" a tiny portion of those bottom-line earnings. If the company is making a lot of money, it will take a higher price from a potential buyer to induce a shareholder to sell his share of the business. The stock price rises. The crucial nature of the company's earnings can be seen in a statistic that financial analysts watch constantly—earnings per share (EPS). This is simply a figure derived by taking the total earnings for the company and dividing that number by the number of shares of stock outstanding.

If you look at any of the great stock success stories over the last few decades, you'll find companies whose earnings per share have grown consistently, year after year. Let's just look at two examples from completely different industries: soft-drink giant Coca-Cola and computer software leader Microsoft. Over the last five years, Coca-Cola has had growth in its earnings per share on the average of 18.5 percent a year. That's a total growth rate for the five years of more than 130 percent. For one of the largest companies in the country, that's an impressive achievement in a seemingly stable and mature business. The earnings, though, continue a long-term trend for Coke that has led to terrific gains for shareholders over the years. Over the past decade (from the end of April 1987 to the end of April 1997), Coca-Cola's stock has generated annual returns of more than 30 percent a year. A $10,000 investment in Coke made in 1987 would have grown to more than $145,000 during that decade. Short and sweet: It's earnings, baby!

An even more compelling example is the history of Microsoft, the world leader in personal computer software operating systems. The Windows operating system all but controls the personal computer market today and the company has recorded terrific earnings. Over the last five years, for example, Microsoft's earnings have grown at an annual rate of 35.5 percent—a phenomenal performance for such a behemoth. As with Coca-Cola, shareholders who were a part of that phenomenal earnings growth profited handsomely. A $10,000 investment in Microsoft a decade ago would be worth over $420,000 today. The annual return on the stock during the decade has been better than 45 percent a year—another example of the incredible growth in earnings over a sustained period pushing the stock value to loftier levels.

The trick, of course, is identifying the Coca-Colas and Microsofts before the fact, not after it. I'll come to that later in this book, but, for now, we have some other ground to cover about why you would want to invest in stocks with all of the choices available to today's investors.

With all the possibilities available for your investment dollar today, it's not surprising that the task of managing your own investments can appear daunting, even overwhelming. That's why there are so many financial gurus out there offering to take control of your money (and charge you for the privilege). Gold, real estate, government bonds, corporate bonds, annuities, options, futures, commodities, mutual funds, unit investment trusts, certificates of deposit, money market accounts, international investments, your cousin Guido's "family business." Any one of these might get your investment bucks, but should they?

It is in the investment industry's own best interests to make the process of investing so complicated and intimidating that the average investor cannot or will not try to go it alone. "You need us," their advertisements cry out. "We are professionals, trained to make the most money for you (for a modest fee, of course), and you'd be a fool to try to do this for yourself." There was even an ad last year for a financial services company that showed a patient getting ready to perform brain surgery on himself, with antiquated surgical tools, no less. The implication, of course, is that you wouldn't try to perform brain surgery on yourself, would you? You're not qualified. It's a far stretch, though, to equate investing with brain surgery. Sure, investing requires some work, but beyond that, the comparison falls apart. Individuals are perfectly capable of managing their own portfolios, but every time one of us decides to take control of our financial destiny, it's money out of their pockets.

Where do you turn, then, now that you've decided managing your own investments is the way to go? Those 1,000 percent returns your neighbor's been bragging about in pork belly futures are pretty enticing. Or that penny stock your boss bought over lunch that doubled in three hours? (Penny stocks are extremely low-priced stocks, usually under a dollar a share, and represent the riskiest investments in the stock market. Your odds of making money in penny stocks are literally worse than your odds of making money in Las Vegas. At least in Vegas you can make back some of what you lost gambling at the buffet tables.)

For us at The Motley Fool, the only answer is buy and hold. We're looking for investors who are planning to leave their money invested for at least five years in common stocks. That, we believe, is where the money is. There are simply no two ways about it: the stock market has produced the best long-term returns of any legal investment vehicle. Bonds, gold, real estate, the buried can in Aunt Agatha's prize rose garden, none has been able to keep pace with the returns generated by the American stock markets over many years.

Let's look at some comparisons for different types of typical investments and talk about the magical properties of time and compounded growth. According to Ibbotson Associates, the average annual return for Treasury bills since 1926 has been 3.7 percent. Over the same period (nearly seven decades), the average annual return for corporate bonds has been 5.7 percent. And stocks during that seven-decade stretch? Common stocks returned an average annual return of 10.8 percent. Since the growth of your savings is what you're really interested in, let's put those returns into dollars to show how radically a few percentage points a year can change your long-term gains.

At 3.7 percent a year for ten years, a $10,000 investment will grow to $14,381. At 5.7 percent, the same $10,000 will grow to $17,408. At 10.8 percent a year, though, the same initial investment, untouched for the decade, grows to $27,887. In just ten years, the difference created by investing in stocks rather than one of the two other popular options would have been enormous.

Continue that growth over a lifetime of investing, though, and the differences are almost beyond credibility. After forty years at 3.7 percent, the original $10,000 investment will have increased to $42,771. With the 5.7 percent that corporate bonds have averaged, the original investment becomes $91,833. But achieving the return of 10.8 percent in stocks, the historical returns achieved for most of the twentieth century, the original $10,000 would grow to $604,770. That's a difference of 559 percent over the corporate bond investment and 1,314 percent over the Treasury bill investment. Which would you rather have after a lifetime of saving and investing?

Years	Treasury Bills 3.7%	Corporate Bonds 5.7%	Common Stocks 10.8%
5	$11,992	$13,194	$ 16,699
10	$14,381	$17,408	$ 27,887
15	$17,246	$22,968	$ 46,569
20	$20,681	$30,304	$ 77,767
25	$24,801	$39,983	$129,866
30	$29,741	$52,753	$216,867
35	$35,666	$69,602	$362,153
40	$42,771	$91,833	$604,770

It is true, of course, that investing in common stocks carries with it a certain measure of risk. Over any given period, stocks can go up or down, and there is no way to predict exactly when those changes will happen. (A slew of professional market timers try to jump in and out of the stock market, attempting to anticipate when it will go up or down in the short run. It's a sucker's bet, though. No one has a crystal ball over a short period of time, and the only way the average investor—or even the professional who's honest about all his gains and losses and costs—can make consistent profits that are better than the overall stock market returns is to invest for the long haul in a group of terrific companies and then ride out the peaks and valleys that come with all investments in stocks.) This book is not intended for those looking for a short-term timing system or a get-rich-quick scheme.

All of the strategies I discuss here are predicated on the assumption that you are willing to invest your money for a minimum of five years, preferably for a much longer period. The luxury of a long time horizon takes a lot of the anxiety out of investing. If your stocks are down this month (or even this quarter or this year), you're looking a decade or two down the road and it won't bother you overly much. If you expect instant returns and never to see a stock investment go down, you won't be happy with what I have to say. You have to become literally a stoic to make money in the stock market over a long period of time. When you're losing money, you can't be panicked into selling out. When things are going well, you can't be enticed into a silly gamble on something your barber has convinced you will revolutionize the industry. ("Hey, the stock's only trading at forty cents per share; you can really load up." They don't call it a haircut for nothing.)

The most exciting aspect of investing, though, is that with time, even the most modest investments can become significant. In part 2 of this book, I'll explain a simple investment approach that has recorded stunning gains of over 23 percent a year for the last two and one-half decades (since 1971). With that kind of growth and enough time, anyone who is willing to put away a portion of his pay each month can become a millionaire. An investment of as little as $2,000 (without adding a penny) can grow to $1 million in about thirty years at that rate.

Naturally, though, I'm assuming you plan to save and continue to invest over your whole lifetime, not just make a one-time investment of a couple thousand bucks and let it go at that. But isn't it nice to know that even starting from a very small amount, you can still build impressive wealth if you go about it the right way?

What about a retired investor? Should someone who is no longer in the workforce take on the risk of stock investments? The conventional wisdom you'll hear from most money managers and financial planners is that you should be either very lightly invested in stocks once you retire or, even more conservatively, out of stocks altogether. Given the average life span of Americans today, this is simply ludicrous. If you retire at age sixty or sixty-five, you may still have two or three decades of life ahead. If you expect your investments to last that long (because there's no guarantee Social Security will be there), the biggest threat over that time is inflation.

Let's compare a couple of scenarios for the retired investor at age sixty. Assume, if you will, that Retired Ralph has saved and invested throughout his working career and amassed a half a million dollars. (If this sounds impossible to you, keep reading. Over an adult lifetime, a $500,000 goal, even $1 million or more, is readily attainable if you are even moderately disciplined in your savings.)

Ralph is debt-free; he owns his house, has paid cash for his car, has no credit card balances (the financial bane of the average American today), and figures that between taxes and living expenses he can make do comfortably with $35,000 a year in income (7 percent of his current portfolio value).

If Ralph follows the conventional wisdom and puts his $500,000 in fixed-income investments that are guaranteed (government bonds, Treasury bills, or insured certificates of deposit through his bank), he might be able to get a return of roughly 6 to 7 percent, exactly what he needs to meet his spending needs. And he makes what he needs with no effort and doesn't take on any risk, right?

Not exactly.

If Ralph puts his $500,000 into a 7 percent bond, for example, he'll receive his needed $35,000 a year, but at the end of the year, he'll still have only his original investment of $500,000. After another year, that half million dollars will be worth less in real terms because inflation, even relatively low inflation such as we've enjoyed for the last few years, will take a hunk out of his buying power. If inflation runs at 4 percent a year, Ralph's original $500,000 is really only worth $480,000 the next year. After ten years, the value of his half million is cut by a third, down to $332,000. After twenty years, it's worth only $221,000. And on Ralph's ninetieth birthday? His $500,000 will really only be worth $147,000 in today's dollars. Of course, this means the annual "salary" he pays himself ($35,000) becomes worth less and less each year, too. The worst part of this scenario is that 4 percent inflation may be too optimistic. We've seen inflation much higher than that in recent times and there's no guarantee we won't again.

A fixed-income investment, then, while on the surface seemingly a safe place to invest your savings, carries hidden risks that can destroy your retirement savings and leave you in much worse shape than you ever feared on your retirement day. If you have to support yourself on your investments for twenty or thirty years beyond retirement, you have to be concerned with continued growth to fight off inflation's insidious effects, not just "staying even." The best way to invest for that growth? You're way ahead of me—the stock market, of course.

While all investments in the stock market do carry risk, with time and good planning on your side, it's still the best place to entrust your savings in order to achieve growth over many years. By riding out the weak patches and staying invested at all times in the best stocks you can identify, you can keep even a retirement portfolio, which you will pull money out of each year for your living expenses, growing indefinitely.

Let's take Retired Ralph's money out of this fixed-income portfolio and put it in a simple index mutual fund that will keep pace with the overall stock market. As I mentioned above, the annual average return for stocks since 1926 has been 10.8 percent, so we'll use that as our growth rate for Ralph. In year one, at that rate, Ralph's portfolio would grow from $500,000 to $554,000. Take out the $35,000 Ralph needs to live on, and the ending balance after the first year is $519,000. He's met his spending needs and yet he's still been able to add a little bit to his portfolio value.

The following year, his $519,000 portfolio grows to $575,052. Now to keep up with our hypothetical rate of inflation, let's increase the annual withdrawal Ralph makes by 4 percent. In year two, then, Ralph would pay himself $36,400, which leaves his portfolio with $538,652. So even after allowing for inflation, Ralph's portfolio continues to grow.

Let's carry this scenario out until Ralph's ninetieth birthday as a comparison with the fixed-income approach. After five years of annual gains at 10.8 percent a year and increasing Ralph's annual withdrawal by 4 percent a year to match inflation, his total portfolio is worth $601,661. After ten years, he's paying himself a salary of $49,816 a year (42 percent a year more than he began paying himself), and his total portfolio has grown to $720,881 (44 percent more than he retired with).

After twenty years, he's paying himself $73,740 a year and his portfolio's worth just over $1 million. And in Ralph's ninetieth year, after three decades of retirement, his annual "salary" is $109,153 (more than triple what he began paying himself) and his portfolio is worth $1.35 million. Not bad considering that he's spent the last thirty years traveling around the country playing all the best golf courses. (To get the big picture, see the thirty-year table on page 36.)

Do you remember what the fixed-income approach was worth after the thirty years? That's right—it was still worth only $500,000 and yielding only $35,000 a year.

Of course, neither the stock market nor inflation is as predictable as this example suggests. You could have rotten luck and start off your retirement years with a down year or two for the stock market. But as long as the amount you have to withdraw for living expenses is a small fraction of your total (my example was 7 percent of the total), you can ride out the weak patches without destroying your plan. In the past, when the market goes through these skids, it has often rebounded even more strongly in the following year or two.

Also, if you are able to live on a smaller percentage of your total portfolio than my example, your cushion for down times and your overall growth rate will be even larger. You might well retire with $1 million and only need $50,000 a year to live on (only 5 percent of your portfolio value). A market correction will be even easier for you to ride out under those circumstances.

The trump card for this approach, however, is that I've stacked the deck against the stock model by using the 10.8 percent historical

Year	Year Open	10.8% Gain	With-drawal	Year Close
1	$ 500,000	$ 554,000	$ 35,000	$ 519,000
2	$ 519,000	$ 575,052	$ 36,400	$ 538,652
3	$ 538,652	$ 596,826	$ 37,856	$ 558,970
4	$ 558,970	$ 619,339	$ 39,370	$ 579,969
5	$ 579,969	$ 642,606	$ 40,945	$ 601,661
6	$ 601,661	$ 666,640	$ 42,583	$ 624,057
7	$ 624,057	$ 691,455	$ 44,286	$ 647,169
8	$ 647,169	$ 717,063	$ 46,058	$ 671,006
9	$ 671,006	$ 743,474	$ 47,900	$ 695,574
10	$ 695,574	$ 770,696	$ 49,816	$ 720,881
11	$ 720,881	$ 798,736	$ 51,809	$ 746,927
12	$ 746,927	$ 827,595	$ 53,881	$ 773,714
13	$ 773,714	$ 857,275	$ 56,036	$ 801,239
14	$ 801,239	$ 887,773	$ 58,278	$ 829,496
15	$ 829,496	$ 919,081	$ 60,609	$ 858,472
16	$ 858,472	$ 951,187	$ 63,033	$ 888,154
17	$ 888,154	$ 984,075	$ 65,554	$ 918,521
18	$ 918,521	$1,017,721	$ 68,177	$ 949,545
19	$ 949,545	$1,052,095	$ 70,904	$ 981,192
20	$ 981,192	$1,087,160	$ 73,740	$1,013,421
21	$1,013,421	$1,222,870	$ 76,689	$1,046,181
22	$1,046,181	$1,159,168	$ 79,757	$1,079,412
23	$1,079,412	$1,195,988	$ 82,947	$1,113,041
24	$1,113,041	$1,233,249	$ 86,265	$1,146,984
25	$1,146,984	$1,270,859	$ 89,716	$1,181,143
26	$1,181,143	$1,308,706	$ 93,304	$1,215,402
27	$1,215,402	$1,346,665	$ 97,036	$1,249,629
28	$1,249,629	$1,384,589	$100,918	$1,283,671
29	$1,283,671	$1,422,308	$104,955	$1,317,353
30	$1,317,353	$1,459,627	$109,153	$1,350,474

growth rate. That's the annual average for the overall stock market for over seven decades. In recent decades, though, the rate has been several points higher each year, and with the strategies I'll teach you in this book, you should be able to outpace the overall market on a consistent basis. If you're able to earn 15 percent to 20 percent (dare we hope for more? Maybe), the advantage for stocks becomes even more dramatic. But for the sake of a baseline level of comparison, I've chosen the historical rate for the overall stock market.

You decide which risk is worse: the risk of a fixed-income investment, where there's no risk of losing money directly (unless the entire government collapses, unlikely as that is), but there's a loss each year to inflation; or the risk that the stock market will go down in the short run (which it is wont to do), but in exchange, you get the long-term growth that's only available in stocks. If the last seventy years are any indication of the future, even for a retired investor, the stock market is a better option than bonds and certificates of deposit as income-producing tools. Look at the results over time in Retired Ralph's stock portfolio.

If stocks are the best investment vehicles, then, what is the best way to go about getting into stocks? "I have absolutely no experience in the stock market and you're telling me to buy shares on my own? Wouldn't I be better off letting a professional stock manager do it for me?" That single very logical question has fostered one of the largest industries in America today—the mutual fund industry. And not only is it a huge industry, controlling billions and billions of dollars, it's also one of the most shameless industries in America, passing off industry-wide shabby performance as if it were doing investors a huge favor. Let me explain.

A mutual fund is a large cooperative group of investors who pool their investment money together and hire a professional money manager to make all of the decisions regarding what stocks to purchase, which ones to sell, and when. For a fee (a percentage of the assets the fund has under management), you hand all the responsibility for your investments over to someone else. In theory, it makes perfect sense. You have a career, a family, a life. What kind of time do you have to spend making these kinds of decisions? After all, the mutual fund manager is a professional, trained in financial analysis, with an entire team of market analysts and statistical wizards to help decide where to invest. Sporting an M.B.A. from a hot business school and working for a Wall Street powerhouse, your mutual fund manager is the best one to look out for your interests, or so the theory goes.

The problem is that mutual funds are compensated based on how much money they control in their fund, so to them, bigger is better. But the bigger a mutual fund gets, the harder it is to manage and continue to find good ideas for stock purchases. It's a great deal easier to manage a personal portfolio, or even a small mutual fund of anywhere up to $100 million, than it is to manage the mutual fund behemoths we see today. Fidelity's Magellan Fund, for example, had $53 billion under management, according to a recent survey. Can you imagine trying to invest $53 billion, given all the rules the Securities and Exchange Commission forces upon funds, governing issues like how much of any one company they can own? The manager has to buy hundreds of stocks just to find places to park all the money. In fact, when legendary investor Peter Lynch was managing the Magellan Fund, he was reported to have held positions in as many as 1,400 stocks at one time, just to find enough companies in which to spread around all that cash.

Because of their immense size, mutual funds have become victims of their own greed. The more they manage, the better their paychecks look. The cost of that enormous bulk, however, has been passed on to the individual investors pouring their savings and retirement accounts into these funds in the form of pathetic performance. Industry-wide, mutual funds have recorded a shameful performance for the last decade.

Thousands of these funds, though, are clamoring for your savings like crowds of kids for candy. And each one has an army of professional managers and researchers ferreting out the best opportunities for you. Only the best opportunities. Right? Only the best for you. Right? Looking out for your best interests every step of the way, right? Right?!?

Well . . . maybe not.

Two years ago, I did my own survey, sorting almost 6,000 mutual funds by three-year, five-year, and ten-year returns. Then I compared them with the benchmark that mutual fund managers try to beat every year—the Standard & Poor's 500 Index (a group of 500 of the most popular large stocks in America, representing a majority of the money being traded in stocks each day).

Ready for a shock? Of the 5,845 mutual funds, fewer than half have been in business long enough even to have three-year performance records. So those funds were dismissed from my survey at the outset. Of the remaining 2,615 funds, a paltry 510 managed to perform better than the S&P 500 over the previous three years. In other words, over 80 percent of the funds in the database lost money to the overall market's performance from 1992 to 1995. Ouch.

Well, I thought, maybe three years isn't indicative of an overall trend. I mean, these are paid professionals! So what about the five-year record? The number of funds with five-year records dropped to 1,936, but the percentage that lost to the market didn't change much: 79 percent of those funds fell short of the S&P 500, which averaged 10.8 percent for five years.

The ten-year survey was even more telling. Out of 780 funds with ten-year records, only 99 were able to beat the S&P 500 average return of 13.8 percent. A miserable 87 percent of the funds in the game for ten years lost ground to the overall market.

On a roll now, I put the group through a final test, wondering how many funds managed to beat the S&P 500 for all three periods. The grand total? Only 43 of the 780 funds with ten-year records beat the market in all three time horizons. Less than 6 percent. You still feel you're getting your money's worth paying those mutual fund fees?

Now, there are a couple of disclaimers I should mention regarding my original study. First, I included all mutual funds in the survey, not just funds that invested in common stocks. Some critics of my survey argue that it is not fair to expect bond mutual funds (or money market funds) to stack up against the benchmark for stocks, the S&P 500. To a certain extent, I agree with them that it's not likely that other categories of mutual funds will compare favorably with the stock market, but doesn't that also support the idea that stocks are where you should be investing in the first place?

Even if you exclude other types of mutual funds, though, the performance for the industry doesn't get much better. Over the last five years, more than 70 percent of all stock funds failed to keep pace with the Vanguard 500 Index fund (which is set up essentially to mimic the S&P 500 Index). If 70 percent of the stock mutual funds can't keep pace with the index that supposedly represents the overall stock market, what does it tell you about the industry itself? It tells me it's broken and has the wrong priorities. Yes, mutual funds are at a bit of a disadvantage in that they have layers and layers of SEC regulations under which they operate, governing everything from the number of stocks they must hold to limits on the amount of any single stock they may own. Some funds also operate under self-imposed investing guidelines and limitations. But the real problem with mutual funds is that they are simply too big. Instead of gorging themselves and growing as large as they can, the funds should be required to stop accepting investors well before they reach an un-manageable level. With as many funds as there are, the financial papers don't even start listing them in their mutual fund tables until they reach $100 million under management. I think that should be the level where they cap the funds, not the level where they begin coverage of them in the financial press.

America has a fascination with funds, though, and the retirement industry, which pours billions of 401(k) and 403(b) dollars into the mutual fund industry every month, forces a bloated monster to keep consuming as much as it can. Don't get me wrong; I don't for a minute believe that mutual fund managers are a poor bunch of investors—far from it. The problem is simply that they've set themselves an impossible task. And it's their own greed that makes them do it.

I fantasize about managing a mutual fund from time to time, believing that I could do a credible job of it. But it would have to be an independent fund, because I think to do the best job, the fund has to be small enough to allow the manager to stick to a reasonable strategy. As the fund gets larger and larger, the manager has to in-clude that many more stocks, and the returns for the fund come to resemble the market as a whole. With the really large funds, the managers buy so many stocks, they can't keep pace with the market simply because the more stocks you have to hold, the farther down the food chain of good ideas you must descend in order to invest all of the money. It's just the law of averages come to life: By the time your fund is a household name, you're in essence ingesting the entire food chain. Add in a handful of management and other fees (all those pros you have working for you—you're paying them, and they do cost plenty), and it's no wonder that even good fund managers lose to the stock market.

So the Sheard Mythical Modest-but-Reasonable Fund couldn't be a part of any of the large fund conglomerates. To be profitable enough for the Wall Street crowd, assets under management need to grow into the billions. The Sheard Mythical Modest-but-Reasonable Fund would have to be closed to new investors when it reaches about $100 million in assets under management, barely enough even to get listed in some financial newspapers. At $100 million, at least if it's invested in reasonably large stocks that are very liquid (that is, there are lots of shares in the marketplace and the volume of trading in the shares on any given day is high), the manager could build a portfolio of thirty to fifty stocks and have a fair shot at besting the overall market regularly. But human nature all too often gets in the way. If a $100 million fund brings in $1.42 million a year in fees (assuming the average expense ratio for the stock fund industry of 1.42 percent), a $1 billion fund is obviously more attractive to the *fund company*, even if it means a sacrifice in overall performance for the millions of investors who have been led to believe they can't invest their money on their own. I'm not holding my breath waiting for someone to knock on my door and ask me to manage a fund with the criteria I've laid out here. It goes against the financial companies' best interests to do so. That's what's wrong with the fund industry.

The individual investor, however, doesn't suffer under the same disadvantages in managing her own portfolio. She can pick only the very best stocks, anywhere from ten to twenty of them, and she can afford to be disciplined with her investing approaches. Not sticking to a winning strategy, either because you let emotions get in the way of your strategy, or because you start to tinker with the strategy without really knowing what the modifications might do, is the surest way to weaken your investing results. In the mutual fund industry it's called style shift.

If the Nascent Hyper Value Fund opens its doors with a strategy designed to focus on a specific angle to investing, say new and emerging small companies, and does very well for two or three years in a row, eventually new investors will throw money at the fund. What was a comfortable fund of $20 million or $30 million a year or two ago is now a bloated monster of $200 million or $300 million and bulking up quickly. So what does the fund manager have to do to maintain the good results he's been generating? He has to buy more and more companies, some of which begin to stretch the bounds of suitability for his announced management style. And, predictably, his fund's returns begin to sink back to the levels of most other too-large funds. Of course, his management fees keep rising, though, since he's paid not by how well his fund performs, but by how much money he manages, so he has no personal financial incentive to stay on track with a manageable level of assets. For the investor, it's the same old story. Bloated funds fall prey to style shift, which results in mediocre returns.

In the two years since my original survey of mutual funds—two extremely good years for stock investors, with a gain of 34 percent for the S&P 500 in 1995 and an additional 20 percent gain in 1996 —the comparison between the mutual fund industry and the benchmark index hasn't brightened much (for the individual investors, that is; the funds themselves are enjoying unparalleled growth in terms of money under management). I came by another survey on the cheap, however. Instead of sorting through a database of thousands of individual mutual funds as I had done two years ago, this time I let one of the investing magazines *(Money)* do the legwork for me. Their February 1997 issue, "The 1997 Ultimate Guide to Mutual Funds," sports an interesting banner:

3,424 FUNDS RANKED BY PERFORMANCE
FEATURING: The 1,204 funds that beat the '96 market

I suppose one could be excited that only 65 percent of the funds in their survey lost to their respective benchmarks in 1996. Certainly, they wouldn't trumpet such a performance if it weren't good news. Would they?

As I went through the tables of the *Money* survey, I narrowed the field first, only taking into consideration stock mutual funds. I didn't want to judge funds in other categories unfairly. (Although I strongly believe if you're a long-term investor, accepting lower returns in bonds or money market funds in the name of supposed safety is silly. If you really think bond funds are "safer" than stocks, ask investors in those funds how well they did in 1994. They are hardly loss-proof. And if you think money market funds are safe, calculate how much your returns are after inflation gets hold of your account.)

Money included funds that had been open at least a full year, were available to individual investors in at least twenty-six different states, and had a minimum investment requirement of $25,000 or less. There were 2,787 funds passing their screens. Of those, only 580 stock funds had been open long enough to register a ten-year return. Of those 580 funds with long-term records, only 107 were able to boast a return that bettered the ten-year return for the S&P 500 Index of 15.3 percent a year. A whopping 81.6 percent of all funds in the category (stock funds, mind you, not their beleaguered relatives, the bond and money market cousins) failed to beat the industry benchmark. Imagine that proficiency rating in any other industry! How many of you and your colleagues would be able to keep your jobs if four out of five of you couldn't perform up to expectations? For a whole decade? The really incomprehensible fact is that some funds actually averaged a *loss* for the decade and still have millions of dollars under management.

By now, I hope you can see why all of us at The Motley Fool hold the mutual fund industry in such contempt. Mutual funds should be one of the greatest financial instruments of the twentieth century. But for all the wrong reasons, they've become an embarrassment, and yet the industry is praised as a godsend for individual investors. It's no wonder that index funds (funds designed specifically to mirror a certain index in a purely mechanical fashion) have become so popular. If nearly 82 percent of all stock funds lose to the indices, stashing your savings in an index fund at least puts you in the top 20 percent of all funds over the long haul—the simplest of all investment approaches!

That's the beauty of index funds as the most basic investing plan of all. They're easy to invest in; the returns smash the performance of most of the managed funds in the industry; the turnover in the fund itself is very low (stocks are only replaced when the composition of the index itself changes), which means that the management fees are generally very low because there's no research or big staffing needs associated with them. (The average stock mutual fund in the *Money* survey carried a 1.42 percent annual fee.) Low turnover also means smaller taxable distributions. If you never went any farther up the ladder of investment sophistication than an index fund, who could blame you? With a long-term average annual gain of 11 percent, an index fund could take you from $25,000 to $1 million in just over thirty-five years. At the very least, then, start with an index fund. (This is an especially good plan if your employer's pension plan is administered through mutual funds only. Park that 401[k] money in an index fund, add to it regularly, and you're on your way to a fine retirement.)

But this book obviously wasn't planned with the intention of funneling you into mutual funds, even index funds. Think of the S&P 500 Index as a baseline alternative. If you can't beat it, you know it's there waiting for you in a simple format. You can always revert to it and still be proud of your portfolio returns. I'm writing this book, though, because I'm convinced that with just a little more time and effort (and believe it or not, not a great deal more), you can achieve even better returns consistently by investing directly in a portfolio of well-chosen stocks. You don't need an M.B.A. You don't need to pay Merrill Lynch or Fidelity Funds or an annuity salesman to do it for you. You are the person in the best position to do it, and I'm going to help get you there with the strategies outlined in this book. After all, you've already paid for this help to your local bookseller, no need to pay an expensive manager as well. (If you checked this out of the library, well . . . I suppose the citizens of your fair city footed the bill. Donate a new wing to the library when you retire and send them a holiday postcard when you get your beach house in Bimini.)

If you're still with me at this point, you've already taken the first step. You've made the decision, even if tentatively, to consider managing your own portfolio. Now it's time to take the first tangible step toward making your first set of stock purchases. I know, I know. You're anxious to get to the stocks themselves, but there's still one crucial area we need to discuss before you can plunk your money into Hewlett-Packard or Walt Disney. You need a brokerage account.

Brokers today extend along a long continuum of services and costs. It's important to find the right mix for your particular needs. Let me summarize (briefly) the different types of brokerage houses for you. The image of the traditional stockbroker evoked by the term today is what is generally considered a full-service broker. These are the huge Wall Street firms you've undoubtedly heard of even if you've never invested before: Merrill Lynch; Salomon Smith Barney; Morgan Stanley, Dean Witter, Discover & Company; Paine Webber. These full-service houses offer a wide range of services, many of which are geared toward institutions and the investment banking side of the business. For the retail side of the business, the part dealing with the likes of you and me, they have full-time extensive sales staffs. They offer portfolio management services, where they make all the buying and selling decisions for the clients. Many offer all-in-one asset management accounts, combining checking account, investment portfolio, and credit card into one product. In other words, they offer a lot of hand-holding for which the retail client pays a hefty price. The cost to make a single purchase of a stock, 200 shares of DuPont, for example, through a full-service broker might cost more than one hundred dollars. The commission scales vary depending on what other services you're using and how big your account is.

A tremendous conflict of interest exists for many of these brokers, however. For the most part, the brokers are primarily sales staff, not financial analysts. They're told what stocks to push and their job is to move whatever stocks the company wants moved. They're paid based on how much revenue they generate in commissions on trading activity. So their incentive isn't necessarily to do what's right for the client; it's simply to move the products through the system, often meaning excess trading (churning) for the clients. A year or two ago, *Smart Money* magazine ran a feature story about a broker who was seen as a star in the industry. He was driven, hardworking, and completely motivated by the system itself, which meant the more clients he convinced to buy and sell frequently, the more he made in commissions. His clients were just dupes to him, suckers he could count on to buy whatever stocks or bonds or slapped-together products the company wanted pushed so he could score another commission. Stock research? He didn't bother with it. He ignored the analyst reports, threw them in the trash, and just sold whatever was easiest to move to "churn 'em and burn 'em." The fact that so few people in the industry would see his attitude and behavior as despicable is why brokers are gaining fast on lawyers in the snake-and-shark-jokes department.

Another inherent conflict of interest in the brokerage industry is the dual nature of their business. Not only do these large houses serve the retail side of the business, through sales staffs and research departments, but they also serve the institutional and investment banking sides. Obviously, much of the big money in the industry is made on the investment banking side, where the brokers handle lucrative transactions for billion-dollar corporations.

Now put yourself in this situation. You're a stock analyst assigned to cover Atomic Fusion Industries. You think the company's in a bit of trouble because management has set the last three facilities glowing, has been spending cash right and left, and has only one client, the crumbling dictatorship of Southeast Crooksville. There's a problem, though. Your company is vying for the investment banking business of Atomic Fusion Industries. If you issue a research report with your real opinion of the company's stock—that it's basically a Chernobyl waiting to happen—what chance does your company have of landing Atomic Fusion's business?

So the analyst, pressured not to offend a potential (or current) client, issues a research report that rivals any of the politically correct silliness rampant today in higher education and rates the stock a "neutral." In the industry, this really equates to "You should have dumped this disaster six months ago and if you don't do so now, heaven help you." The scarcity of an actual "sell" rating on any stock is evidence of the depth of this conflict of interest. (My favorite lame euphemism is a stock rated "source of funds" instead of "Sell, you bonehead!") Expecting the brokerage industry to be completely aboveboard here is a bit like asking Congress to levy penalties on itself when it grossly exceeds the bounds of propriety. Who's going to hang a fellow legislator when your neck may be next in line? Brokers hate to make waves as much as anyone. Yet there you have the full-service industry's conflict of interest in its full glory. The brokers get a "neutral" rating on Atomic Fusion, do their best to unload whatever inventory they can, and who's left holding the glowing bag? The trusting, unsuspecting, retail customer who believes that his broker really has his best interests at heart.

Fortunately, there have been a few changes of late in the brokerage industry and some of the more egregious abuses of power over clients are being reined in. In fact, a number of the big houses are moving clients away from the models where "churn 'em and burn 'em" is so prevalent into management models where the broker's interests are more in line with the client's. In other words, compensation is tied to the size of the account, and thus portfolio growth, rather than simply based on the number of trades a broker can rack up. Foolish investors, though (and that's Foolish with a capital *F*), bypass this end of the brokerage spectrum altogether since it is the antithesis of independent management. We champion the do-it-yourself movement, especially when doing it yourself actually produces a better result than hiring a professional manager to do it for you, and charging you for the privilege of getting mediocre results.

Another type of broker has sprung up in the past decade or so to focus more on individual retail clients and less on the large institutional clients and investment banking. In general, these companies are referred to as discount brokers. Some of the more popular names in this category are Charles Schwab, Waterhouse, Muriel Siebert, and Fidelity. These companies tend to focus exclusively on the retail side of the investment business, that is, on the individual consumers and private money managers who purchase and sell stocks for individual clients. They're not generally in the investment banking business.

Their services are typically somewhat more limited than those offered by full-service brokers. They offer their customers the ability to get frequent stock quotes, news stories on individual stocks that come across the news wire services, and various asset management account services. Some even provide links to money managers if a client is interested, or offer a wide range of mutual fund options, such as with Schwab's One-Source service. They don't, however, hold clients' hands when it comes to the actual decision-making process. The client is responsible for all the investment decisions, whereas with full-service brokers, if the client signs a trading authorization form, the broker is often free to make any and all trades on his own.

Where the full-service broker might charge over one hundred dollars for a purchase of 200 shares of DuPont, a discount broker might charge anywhere from $40 or $50 or so, again depending on the broker and the arrangement with a specific client. (Some of the commission schedules look a bit like airfare schedules: "If you buy more than 100 shares but less than 200 of a stock with the letter *p* in the name and the Kentucky Wildcats are in the top five of the NCAA rankings, your commission is $60. If, however, your broker's wearing a red tie and the company is based west of the Mississippi, your commission is $75. Unless of course . . ." You get the picture?)

Many investors making their first foray into choosing stocks on their own will opt for the discount brokers, and no one can blame them. These companies are generally household names, they offer a wide range of services, and they provide a minimal level of support as you go through your decision-making process. But for most Fools, there's a better way to go, simply because by the time you're done reading this book, you'll be in a position to make all of your own decisions and you won't need any hand-holding from your broker. And if you're not using the extra services, there's absolutely no reason to pay for them. Welcome to the world of deep-discount stockbrokers.

Over the last few years, another new category of brokerage house has made it much easier and far less expensive for individuals with modest portfolios to manage their own stock market decisions—the deep-discount brokers. These companies are primarily just order takers, accepting orders from their clients and filling them. No frills, no extraneous services, very low costs. But for an investor who is making all of his own decisions regarding what to buy, when to buy it, and what and when to sell, why pay for the fancy digs of a full-service or discount broker and their full-time extensive staffs if all you really need is an order filled?

With the deep-discounters, you're in complete control of your own portfolio. A broker doesn't call you to "make suggestions" (read, churn your account so he gets another fat commission). You don't pay for a research staff you're not using. And you're not paying inflated commission costs. Today, some of the most popular deep-discount brokers charge from $8 to $15 per trade, hundreds of dollars less than full-service brokers charge for the identical transaction.

Are they safe? As long as you choose a broker that is insured through the SIPC (Securities Investor Protection Corporation), which is much like the Federal Deposit Insurance Corporation for bank deposits, your cash and securities are guaranteed against loss should the business fold, for example. Such insurance doesn't insure you against bad trading decisions, though. It just protects you against potential fraud. The SIPC insures your account up to a preset limit ($500,000—$100,000 of which can be cash), and then most brokers carry additional private insurance above that amount, usually up to several million dollars. So safety isn't a necessary concern.

A tremendous advantage of these deep-discount brokers is that their commission rates are often the same for every single trade, regardless of how many shares you buy or how much each share costs. They simply charge a flat rate per trade. For example, if you buy 10 shares of Nike at $50 per share, the commission is the same as if you bought 1,000 shares of Procter & Gamble at $110 per share. At a full-service or discount broker, you're often put into a sliding scale where your commissions go up with the dollar amount of each trade. A 1,000-share purchase of Procter & Gamble at $110 (a transaction worth $110,000) would cost hundreds at such a broker. At a deep-discounter, it could cost as little as $10. However, some deep-discounters do charge extra for very large orders, such as orders for 1,000 shares or more.

These no-frills brokers also eliminate the "odd lot" penalty. It used to be that one had to buy stocks in round lots, meaning at least 100 shares, and buying an odd lot (under 100 shares) would be more expensive because the broker would tack on a premium to execute such a small trade. Another vestige of the big-boy system done away with. With the flat-fee commissions today, odd lots are irrelevant to your commission costs. You'll pay the same on virtually every single trade.

The full-service brokers might try to con you into believing that they can get you better prices on your stock purchases, though, so they make up for the extra commission cost by getting you a lower purchase price. Don't believe it. Let's look at an example. Suppose you wanted to buy 100 shares of Merck & Co. Each stock actually carries two prices at any time—the bid and the ask. The bid is the price you could get right now if you were selling the stock. The ask price is what you will pay if you're buying the stock right now. The ask price is always higher than the bid, and the difference between the two prices is called the spread. The spread is pocketed by the specialist or market maker who brings the buyer's broker and seller's broker together, the broker to the brokers, as it were.

For stocks that are very large and trade a large volume of shares each day, the spread is usually very small because there's very little risk involved for the middleman. He knows that if he buys a bunch of shares in this sort of company, he can turn around and sell it to someone else easily. So he deals in volume and the spread he makes is relatively small on each transaction. If a stock is less liquid, there's more risk to the market maker, so the spread he pockets between the bid and ask prices is much higher, sometimes exorbitantly high. For the brand-name stocks I've been referring to, however, the spreads are minimal, often just an eighth or a quarter of a dollar per share.

The 100 shares of Merck you want to buy might have a bid price of $90 and an ask price of $90¼. Your purchase, then, would go through at the ask price and your total cost for the purchase would be $9,025 plus your broker's commission, let's say $10. Now even if the full-service broker were to get you the lower bid price instead of the ask price, your savings on that trade would be just $25. But the full-service broker's commission is so much larger than the $10 you would pay at the deep-discounter so there's no savings whatsoever. If the full-service commission were $125, for example, you're still better off with the deep-discount transaction, even though, in theory, the full-service broker got you a better price.

What's worse is that all of this example is just theory. I've yet to see any credible evidence that deep-discount brokers get worse prices on their trade executions. It's simply the old guard trying to protect its turf and realizing that a revolution is coming in the way stock market investing is carried out by individuals. As if the full-service brokers weren't frustrated enough, the New York Stock Exchange (the major American exchange) is moving away from pricing stocks in fractions (typically in eighths) and will eventually begin listing stocks in decimals. America's markets are the last major ones to make the switch to decimal pricing, but it's an important one for individual investors. Not only will the prices be easier to follow (quick, tell me how much ³/₁₆ is in decimal form), but it will also serve to reduce the spreads on most trades. Instead of the standard eighths (12½¢ intervals), stocks will soon be quoted in intervals of a nickel or a dime (for most stocks). And while a few pennies per share doesn't seem like much in isolation, some economists arguing for the merits of the switch have suggested that the savings for individual investors could total billions of dollars each year. A couple of billion a year and pretty soon you're talking real money!

What it all boils down to, then, when picking a broker is the question of what balance you need between services and what price you're willing to pay for them. For the investment strategies I'll discuss in this book, and for everything you'll discover in our online forum, the clear advantage goes to the deep-discounters. We may be Fools, but we're not stupid. If Winn-Dixie charges five times more for your favorite ice cream than Kroger charges (or vice versa), where are you going to pick up that carton of Pralines 'n' Cream?

A number of deep-discount brokers are currently available and more are appearing on the scene regularly. Rather than try to review them all, I'll summarize some of the basic characteristics most of them share. When you start choosing among them, it's a good idea to get a new-account packet from each one and read through all the fine print. Some will hide charges that you need to be aware of (such as transfer fees if you decide to close your account and take your business elsewhere, inactivity fees if you don't make any trades during a specific period, annual maintenance fees on IRAs, and the like). Most of these fees are disappearing as competition forces the brokers to drop them, but occasionally you'll find a stinker fee hidden somewhere.

Most of the deep-discount brokers offer trading on the Internet. In maintaining a Web site rather than a full office full of brokers and support staff, these deep-discounters have slashed their overhead costs and can make money based on the volume of trading rather than through steep commissions. The trade-off for the customer, however, is little or no personal service. These brokers are order takers, nothing else. A few deep-discounters will offer minimal services—delayed stock quotes, the occasional reprinted research report, perhaps even some nifty software you can download and use—but you won't get an opinion on whether you should buy Coca-Cola or Microsoft, and no one will be there to help you figure out if and when you should place a sell-stop order.

As far as fees go, you'll normally pay a flat fee per trade of somewhere between $8 and $15 with these brokers. Instead of basing the commission on the number of shares or the amount of money involved in the transaction, these brokers have chosen a one-size-fits-all approach. For the individual investor, it's a boon, not only because the prices are so low but because you'll always know what to expect as a commission. The price won't change on every trade.

These deep-discount brokers are in the best of the do-it-yourself tradition. If you are making all of your own decisions, can trade through the Internet (a few offer telephone trading as well, but usually at a somewhat higher price), and don't need any hand-holding, then a deep-discount broker is probably just right for you. You'll still get the quick and accurate executions of your trades you'd expect from any broker, but you're not going to be financing your broker's new ski chalet.

A number of deep-discount brokers are used by the readers of our forum. Here are the names and Internet addresses for several of them. Shop around for the best combination of commissions, fees, and margin interest rates to choose one that suits you the best.

Datek Securities (www.datek.com)
AmeriTrade (www.ameritrade.com)
JB Oxford (www.jboxford.com)
E*Trade (www.etrade.com)
SureTrade.com (www.suretrade.com)
Waterhouse webBroker (www.webbroker.com)

You can find out more about deep-discount brokers online at the Discount Broker Center at The Motley Fool Web site (www.fool.com).

In addition to your name and brokerage account number, there are a couple of important pieces of information you'll need to have under control when you call (or log on) to place a stock order. You'll have to know how many shares you're going to buy or sell of your stock (brokers won't take a dollar-amount order and convert it to shares for you the way mutual fund companies do) and the ticker symbol for the stock (the three-, four-, or five-letter symbol unique to the stock you're trading). But, equally important, you'll also need to instruct the broker what kind of order you wish to enter: **market, limit, stop-loss,** or **stop-limit.**

A **market order** is the most commonly used, and it simply instructs your broker to buy or sell the stock at whatever the prevailing market price is at the time. A market order is generally executed within seconds. No fuss.

A **limit order,** on the other hand, instructs your broker to buy or sell a stock as soon as possible, but it specifies a price above which you're not willing to pay if you're buying, or below which you'll not accept if you're selling. If, for example, you place a limit order to buy 200 shares of Wal-Mart at $22 a share, your broker will fill the order if and when Wal-Mart's ask price drops to that price or lower. If the ask price never gets that low, the order simply doesn't get filled and you haven't bought anything. (When you place such a limit order, you'll have to specify whether you want the order to be good for that day only or until you cancel it. Most brokers allow good-till-canceled orders to remain in effect for thirty to sixty days. Make sure you know the details for your broker before using such an order.)

A **stop-loss order** (commonly called a sell-stop order) is a special kind of order designed to be used as an insurance policy of sorts. Stop-losses instruct your broker to sell a stock you already own if it drops to a certain price (which you determine). In other words, if you've determined that you won't sit still and watch your stock drop below a certain point, you place a sell-stop order at that price (a good-till-canceled order, of course) so that it will be sold automatically should the stock sink to that level or below. There are several dangers with sell-stop orders, though. The first is what we call getting whipsawed. You've been whipsawed when you place a sell-stop order and it is put into effect, kicking you out of the stock at a certain price, and then the stock immediately goes back up in price. You lose two ways when you've been whipsawed. First, you sell the stock at a low price (the bottom of the short correction that triggered your sell-stop order), and then, second, if you decide you really want the stock after all and have to buy it back, you're going to pay a higher price. I've experimented with sell-stops several times and have yet to find a useful method for employing them. In more cases than not, the sell-stops cost me more money in whipsaws than they saved me in protection against a collapse in a stock.

One other thing to be aware of with stop orders is that they do not guarantee you'll get the price you specify when the stock goes down. Assume for a minute you have placed a stop order to sell your 100 shares of Chips 'R Us if it drops to a price of $150, and it closes on Tuesday at $150½. If Tuesday night, while the market is closed, Chips 'R Us announces that a flaw in its next-generation computer chip causes the chip to self-destruct after the millionth calculation, the stock price will plunge. But you're in a jam because when trading opens the next morning, the stock will probably open considerably lower, say at $135 or $140. Your sell-stop order only guarantees that your stock will be sold as soon as it trades at or below your set price. Whether it's 25¢ below or 25 percent below, you're stuck with that price.

That brings us to a variation on the sell-stop—the **stop-limit order.** With this option, when the stock price drops to your preset price, the order is immediately converted into a regular limit order, meaning the next time the stock trades at or above your limit price, it will be sold automatically. The danger with this type of order, of course, is that if the stock drops precipitously and blows right through your limit price, it may not ever get back up to your price and your sale order won't be filled. The idea of protecting yourself against the loss simply hasn't worked.

Despite all these options, I still believe the best course is to stick with simple market orders that you know will be filled right away. The other orders are geared toward the type of investors who try to fine-tune every purchase or sale. For long-term investors who may be holding their stocks for a significant time, an eighth or quarter point here or there isn't crucial. There's much to be said for simplicity in investing, as in life. Play it as smart as you're able, keep your trading simple and use market orders, and profits will probably follow.

One final item about brokers that you should know before we get started picking actual stocks to buy is that most of them prefer to keep possession of your stock certificates in Street Name. That means that you don't actually keep the stock certificates in your possession; the clearing agent for the broker does. If your broker is SIPC insured, though, you don't take on any risk in keeping your stocks in Street Name. In fact, it's safer because you don't have to send the certificates to the broker every time you wish to sell a stock; they're already there. With your stocks in Street Name, you still retain all the rights of ownership, including dividends, voting rights, and any other benefits an individual company might grant you (like the cool giveaways some companies send their shareholders).

• • •

So, the last thing you do before you decide it's time to buy your stock picks is choose your broker. Find the broker that best fits your needs for a balance of low costs and appropriate services. Call or visit the Web sites of several and shop and compare. Then, when you find one that matches your needs, get and complete their new-account application kit (either for a regular account or an IRA account). Submit it with your check to open the account and within a week or two, your brokerage account will be ready for you to make your first stock trades. One final piece of advice—set your account up as both a cash and margin account, even if you never plan to borrow a penny on margin. (Margin is a line of credit from your broker. This doesn't apply to IRA accounts; they are not eligible for margin investing.) It doesn't cost anything to get your account set up as both a cash and margin account, and it may come in handy. With the Securities and Exchange Commission rules requiring you to settle all trades within three working days of their execution, having a margin account can save you the trouble of scrambling. For example, if the price of a stock you buy rises just enough before your order goes through that you actually bought more stock than you had cash in your account for, you have to scramble to get that extra money into your brokerage account within three working days if it's a cash-only account. If you've overspent by ten or twenty bucks and you have a margin account, you can simply let that small balance ride on margin. The interest you'll owe will be pennies and the first dividend you receive in your account will probably pay it off. It's nice to have that safety cushion. I'll discuss margin investing more fully in part 4, "Putting It All Together."

Now you know a little more than you did about what's going on and why and you've picked yourself a broker. It's time to learn about the actual strategies you can use to choose your own investments. You've waded through all the preliminaries, now let's buy some great companies.

PART TWO

Getting Started with Value Stocks

You've dutifully read through *all* the preliminaries. Now you want to know what stocks you should buy and how you can buy them without taking on more stress than you can handle. Well, then, let's pick some stocks.

There are literally thousands of stocks traded publicly from which to choose. We're going to stick with stocks you can find on the major exchanges. In addition to what's available on the New York Stock Exchange, American Stock Exchange, and the web of computers known as the Nasdaq National Market, there is an endless variety of very small stocks that don't show up on the major exchanges. Many of these stocks are listed on the so-called pink sheets and are often penny stocks (issues trading at extremely low prices— often for a very good reason). We will not be talking about these penny stocks, because they represent the single riskiest way to buy stocks. In fact, they're so volatile and easily hyped and manipulated that we believe your odds of making money in these investments are worse than your odds of coming away a winner at the roulette table.

We're also going to pass on foreign stocks, which require even more research than American companies simply because the information is harder to come by and many more variables have to be taken into account. Despite having written off literally thousands of stocks, there are still thousands of legitimate American stocks from which to choose. I have a job, a family, and a life, you say. So how do I choose what to buy and when to buy it and what to sell and when to dump it without spending twelve hours a day poring over financial statements and analyst reports for every company I want to consider?

Don't worry. I promised you a way of picking a winning portfolio that you could manage in under half an hour a year. Was I pulling your leg? Nope.

What we have to do is somehow narrow the field of possible stock choices considerably. Actually, we have to do it in one fell swoop if we're really going to be able to accomplish what I've claimed we can do in the half hour I promised. *All you have to do is find the biggest, best, most reliable and profitable companies around.* But you just said there were thousands upon thousands of companies, Sheard. How'm I supposed to do this?

For the investor who has experience and the time to do individual stock research, ferreting out the great investments from among the thousands of publicly traded American stocks is a rewarding activity, but for most investors, especially those who have been putting their money in mutual funds or letting a broker guide them, such a prospect is too daunting or too time-consuming to consider. What we need, then, is a screen to filter out the vast majority of the prospects and focus on the very few we can manage easily and quickly, yet ones that still afford us the type of long-term gains that put the mutual fund industry to shame.

The Dow Jones Industrial Average

Enter the Dow. The Dow Jones Industrial Average is an index of thirty of America's leading industrial companies. The index is maintained by the editors of Dow Jones & Company, the publishers of *The Wall Street Journal*, *Barron's*, and *Smart Money*, and is intended to represent the overall American industrial sector. It's used as a barometer of how well "the market" is doing, and, in fact, when someone asks, "How did the market do today?" it is usually the performance of the Dow Jones Industrial Average he's referring to.

Charles Dow first created a stock average in 1884 when he totted up a list of eleven companies he believed would stand as a reasonable proxy for the country's economic status. By today's standards, though, it was a very skewed list, including nine railroads and two manufacturing companies. Over the next twelve years, Dow refined his list so that it more accurately reflected the industrial sectors of the American economy. His first list of primarily industrial companies appeared in 1896, and this list is often considered the origin of what we call the Dow Jones Industrial Average today.

By 1928, the list was expanded to include thirty companies, where it has remained ever since. The composition of the list has changed relatively infrequently in the last seven decades, with changes being made only twenty-one times, many of which came as the result of companies merging or splitting up. Partly because of the size of the companies involved, the list tends to be remarkably stable, and, in fact, one company remains from the first industrial version from 1896—General Electric, despite having been dropped from the list for a few years early in the history of the average.

Today, the thirty stocks in the Dow are among the most well-known, the most followed, the most widely owned companies in the world. In terms of sheer magnitude, these are the Olympian giants; the thirty stocks represent about one quarter of the total value of all stocks traded on the New York Stock Exchange.

The Dow Stocks

Here are the thirty stocks that are included in the Dow Jones Industrial Average today, their ticker symbols, and the industry groups they represent:

AlliedSignal	ALD	Manufacturing (diversified)
Aluminum Company of America (Alcoa)	AA	Aluminum
American Express	AXP	Financial (diversified)

AT&T	T	Telecommunications (long-distance)
Boeing	BA	Aerospace/defense
Caterpillar	CAT	Machinery (diversified)
Chevron	CHV	Oil (integrated)
Coca-Cola	KO	Beverages (nonalcoholic)
Disney	DIS	Entertainment
DuPont	DD	Chemicals
Eastman Kodak	EK	Photography/imaging
Exxon	XON	Oil (integrated)
General Electric	GE	Electrical equipment
General Motors	GM	Automobiles
Goodyear Tire	GT	Auto parts and equipment
Hewlett-Packard	HWP	Computers (hardware)
International Business Machines	IBM	Computers (hardware)
International Paper	IP	Paper and forest products
Johnson & Johnson	JNJ	Health care (diversified)
J. P. Morgan	JPM	Banks (money center)
McDonald's	MCD	Restaurant
Merck & Co.	MRK	Health care (drugs)
Minnesota Mining & Manufacturing	MMM	Manufacturing (diversified)
Philip Morris	MO	Tobacco
Procter & Gamble	PG	Household products
Sears	S	Retail (general merchandise)
Travelers Group	TRV	Insurance (multiline)
Union Carbide	UK	Chemicals
United Technologies	UTX	Manufacturing (diversified)
Wal-Mart	WMT	Retail (general merchandise)

Writing about the Dow stocks every day for The Motley Fool, sometimes I begin to question my perspective on these thirty companies. Are they really the global powerhouses we hold them out to be? Are they really ubiquitous? Are they really the bluest of American Blue Chips?

One way to gauge the presence of these stocks in day-to-day American life is to walk through a typical day in a typical American family's existence and see how many of these companies they come into contact with, directly or indirectly. Trying this little experiment, I was astonished to discover that it's completely within the realm of possibility to include all thirty without resorting to any far-fetched scenarios.

Let's follow Miles T. Go, a businessman who travels regularly, through a day in the life and track the number of Dow companies he comes into contact with. After his alarm goes off, Miles rolls over, switches on his nightstand light (bulb courtesy of General Electric) and turns on the television (which he bought at Sears) to catch the news and weather on his local ABC station (Disney).

Still suffering from last night's late meeting, Miles downs a couple of Tylenol (Johnson & Johnson) and his prescription Pepcid (Merck) for his chronic acid reflux condition. Then a quick shower and shave, brushing his teeth with Crest and rinsing with Scope (both from Procter & Gamble). Nothing so far, I think you'll agree, that's at all out of the ordinary.

After breakfast, Miles stops in his home office to check his e-mail and final plans before heading to the airport. He switches on his home computer (an IBM laptop), checks his messages, and prints out the new itinerary for his upcoming meeting (Hewlett-Packard printer and paper from International Paper). He writes himself a note to call his boss from New York on a Post-it note (Minnesota Mining & Manufacturing), packs up his briefcase, kisses his wife and kids, and heads to the airport.

On the way, he notices that his car, a Buick Park Avenue (General Motors with Goodyear Tires), is low on fuel and stops at the corner Chevron station. (Incidentally, one of the components in his antifreeze is manufactured by Union Carbide.) At the airport (which was built using Caterpillar machinery), Miles picks up his ticket, paying with his credit card (from Travelers Group), stops in the newsstand to buy some film for his camera (Eastman Kodak) so he can bring pictures of the project back to his supervisor, and makes a call to his company's main office (using his AT&T calling card).

His flight is on a Boeing jet, powered by an engine manufactured by AlliedSignal. In flight, he drinks a Coca-Cola, served in an aluminum can (courtesy of Alcoa).

When Miles arrives in New York, he picks up his rental car, and heads to corporate headquarters for his meeting. When he arrives, he parks in the building's garage and takes the elevator (United Technologies) up to the ninth floor and into his meeting. After his meeting adjourns, Miles checks into his hotel, grabs a Big Mac (McDonald's), drops off some financial paperwork at his investment adviser (J. P. Morgan), and goes shopping for some gifts for his children, paying for them with American Express traveler's checks.

Later that evening, he plays tennis with a colleague, using a racket made of Kevlar (from DuPont), and then relaxes with his buddy in the lounge, drinking a Miller beer (Philip Morris).

The next morning, after a quick meeting, he gasses up the rental car at an Exxon station before returning to the airport, and then flies home. On his way back to his home, he drops off the film he shot during the meetings to be developed at Wal-Mart. And there you have it. Roughly twenty-four hours, all thirty Dow companies, some more directly than others. And nothing so far-fetched that we'd have to suspend our disbelief.

In other words, the roots of these stocks cover the whole garden. I approached this maze one way, trying to include all thirty companies in a single day, but I challenge you to approach it the other way. Try to imagine a single day in which you could avoid every single one of the thirty companies. I doubt it can be done in America. In other words, these companies really are ubiquitous and a terrific place to begin looking for the backbone of your investment portfolio.

About the Average

Since the Dow Jones Industrial Average had its genesis in the days long before computer sophistication made elaborate mathematical calculations quick and accurate (all jokes about the flaws in the Intel Pentium chip aside), the calculation of the average had to be something Charles Dow could do rapidly by hand in order to get the results published each day. His answer was a simple arithmetical average. He simply added up the prices of the eleven stocks (now thirty stocks) and divided by the number of companies. And this works just fine as a measure of those companies until a special event occurs. Companies sometimes split their shares in half (or other proportions) in order to make the cost of an individual share of stock more affordable for individual investors. When they split their stock, an investor who owns 100 shares worth $80 a share, for example, would own 200 shares at $40 each after the split. It doesn't affect the value of an investor's position in the stock one bit, but the share price is reduced by half (and the number of outstanding shares is doubled). The average for the index of stocks, however, is altered quite a bit, since one of the components is suddenly trading at a price 50 percent lower than the previous day, and yet nothing has really changed.

To account for such events (and for the occasions when companies merge or spin off portions of their businesses, which then go on to trade independently, or when a stock is replaced in the index), Charles Dow instituted the use of a flexible divisor. Any time a distortion in the index would result from one of these unusual events, Dow Jones & Company adjusts this divisor so that the value of the average is consistent. When four stocks were replaced early in 1997, for example, the divisor was adjusted so that the value of the average wasn't distorted. Today, then, to arrive at the value of the Dow Jones Industrial Average, one would add the stock prices for the thirty components and divide by approximately 0.276 (the actual divisor is carried out to many decimal places and for our purposes isn't really important, but if you're curious about it, it's included in each day's *Wall Street Journal*).

For a variety of reasons, critics challenge the usefulness of the Dow Jones Industrial Average, and many of the criticisms are valid. Yet the average nevertheless remains the most popular barometer of the overall stock market, and has, in fact, become a very good measure of American stocks with global reach. Let's look at some of the problems with the average, however. The most consistent criticism of the average is that it focuses only on a small segment of the stock market (and the American economy) and therefore doesn't necessarily do a good job of representing the market as a whole. Until recently, for example, three of the thirty stocks were major American oil companies—Chevron, Exxon, and Texaco. By any measure of fairness, one-tenth of the index devoted to oil seems a bit much. After the last round of revisions, though, Texaco was dropped from the group, leaving Chevron and Exxon as the two remaining oil representatives.

A number of critics (myself among them) have questioned the

logic behind excluding such companies as Microsoft and Intel. These are among the largest companies in the world and are recognized industry giants. Intel, for example, enjoys around 85 percent of the personal computer processor chip market (the brains of the computer), and with the continuing obliteration of Apple Computer as anything other than a minor niche competitor, Microsoft's Windows operating system is the industry standard for personal computers. By any measure, then, these two companies should be included on a rational shortlist of American industrial giants. Yet the editors at Dow Jones & Company do not include them in the Dow Thirty, even after the most recent revision in the spring of 1997. The only possible explanation I can put forth is that they simply will not include a stock that doesn't trade on the New York Stock Exchange, as both Intel and Microsoft trade on the Nasdaq. It's a silly barrier, of course, but it's the only explanation I can offer.

My objections to this glaring oversight aside, the Dow's recent revisions went a long way toward updating the composition of the thirty stocks, eliminating questionable members of the fraternity—Bethlehem Steel, Woolworth, Westinghouse, and Texaco—and adding four more relevant choices for today's industrial economy: Johnson & Johnson, Travelers Group, Hewlett-Packard, and Wal-Mart.

Critics of the Dow, however, claim that focusing solely on the largest industrial stocks doesn't pay credence to the real power and entrepreneurial spirit of the American market, which resides in smaller companies just making their way. A company like Intel or Microsoft, even if added in the most recent revisions to the Dow, wouldn't have been reflected in this index ten or fifteen years ago, precisely the period when these companies were reshaping the landscape of several technology sectors. The Dow favors mature companies, some would say stodgy, and therefore falls short in its efforts to represent the larger American economy. Most institutional investors, while still watching the Dow out of habit, compare themselves to a larger benchmark like the Standard and Poor's 500 Index (the S&P), which as its name implies is an index of 500 leading American stocks. The 30 Dow stocks are also in this larger index, but because the S&P tracks 500 stocks instead of 30, it incorporates a much broader spectrum of companies, both in terms of size and industry sectors. Ironically, the Dow Jones Industrial Average and the S&P 500 Index seem to move virtually in lockstep over long stretches of time. For practical purposes, then, it doesn't matter much which one you choose as your benchmark. If you're beating the Dow Jones Industrial Average consistently, you're probably also beating the S&P 500 Index by roughly the same margin.

Another drawback to the Dow Jones Industrial Average is that it is a price-weighted index. That is, since the method of calculation simply requires the addition of the thirty stock prices (divided by the adjustable factor to account for special events), the stocks with the highest prices have the most influence over the movement of the index. For example, if J. P. Morgan trades at $100 a share and Wal-Mart trades at $33 a share, Wal-Mart's price would have to move three times more than J. P. Morgan's (in percentage terms) to have the same effect on the Dow Jones Industrial Average. Suppose J. P. Morgan stock rises $2 a share. That's a percentage gain for J. P. Morgan shareholders of only 2 percent. But a $2 rise in Wal-Mart (which would have exactly the same effect on the overall movement of the Dow) represents a gain of more than 6 percent for Wal-Mart shareholders. The effect of this method of calculation is to skew the results toward how the highest-priced stocks are performing and minimize the effect of the lowest-priced stocks. The reason for this method, as I mentioned earlier, was that Charles Dow needed a quick manual approach to track the stocks since computers were a distant prospect when the Dow Jones Industrial Average was launched. Today, however, no such impediment exists and a much more representative approach would be to measure the percentage gains in each stock, not the simple price movements. That way, a 5 percent gain in the lowest-priced stock in the index would have the same effect as a 5 percent gain in the highest-priced stock. But history gets in the way, and once an index gets as long in the tooth as the Dow, it's very difficult to change the way things have always been done.

Tied to the problem of using a price-weighted index is the fact that when a stock in the index does split, this simple and financially meaningless event tends to lock in a gain for the index itself. Let me explain.

Companies typically split their stocks after extensive and healthy gains in the price. Many of the mature companies included in the

Dow often allow their stocks to rise to a certain price and then split the stock to bring the price back into a more typical range, one their investors are comfortable with. As we've discussed before, the act of splitting a stock really means nothing in terms of an investor's share of the business, but it's a psychological game companies play. Most investors are more willing to buy 200 shares of a stock at $50 a share than 100 shares of the same stock at $100 a share, despite the fact that the two positions would be identical. So a company splitting its stock is typically a sign that the price has risen of late and these gains in the stock's price, of course, are reflected in the Dow average.

When a company splits the stock, though, the flexible divisor used in calculating the Dow is adjusted so that the index is maintained exactly at the same level. If the Dow is at 7,500, for example, when J. P. Morgan splits two-for-one, the Dow will still be at 7,500 immediately after the split, even though J. P. Morgan's price has been changed, say, from $120 to $60. Because of the price-weighted calculation method, J. P. Morgan's influence over the index itself has now been cut in half. At $120 a share, J. P. Morgan only had to gain 2.5 percent to rise $3 a share. Now at $60 a share, it would have to gain 5 percent to move $3 a share. In effect, then, the gain J. P. Morgan posted before it split is protected inside the value of the index because the act of splitting its stock cuts its influence on the overall index. If the stock were to sink after its recent gains (the reason for the split, remember), the effect of those losses is reduced by half, since the raw share price is now $60 lower than before the split. Again, an average that measures percentage gains or losses in each stock rather than gains or losses in the dollar amounts per share would be much more representative of how these thirty stocks are actually performing.

Despite these drawbacks, the Dow Jones Industrial Average is still the most popular, the most talked about, the most analyzed index of American stocks. This is partly because of its age; Wall Street venerates age (sometimes at the expense of talent), and the thirty stocks comprising the average are genuine top-drawer companies. For those reasons alone, the Dow isn't a bad place to start looking for your first investment selections. These companies also share a significant investment characteristic—they all pay dividends to their shareholders.

As industry leaders, these companies have experienced their extremely rapid growth phase when they were young and climbing toward their present positions as industry leaders. In the typical life cycle of a company, when the extreme rapid growth slows down, the company has to begin looking at new ways to employ its profits. Instead of plowing every penny of profit into expanding the company, mature companies often begin returning the profits not required for research and further development to the owners—the shareholders. One way they do so is through buying their own stock back and retiring the shares. This reduces the number of shares outstanding and therefore increases the shareholder value for those who still own the stock. A more typical way of returning value to the shareholders, though, is through the form of a cash dividend payment. Most large, mature companies (including all thirty of the current Dow stocks) pay a cash dividend (usually once per quarter) to all the common stock shareholders, and it's through these dividends that we'll start to search for our first stock choices.

In fact, dividends are so much associated with the Dow stocks that companies will often boast in their marketing literature and annual reports to shareholders how many successive quarters they've paid a cash dividend, or how many years in a row they've been able to increase the dividend. Within the Dow average, the dividend has almost become a sacred right of shareholders, and if a company were to reduce or eliminate its dividend, it is rightfully taken as a sign that the company is in financial white water without a life vest. Before the recent revisions to the Dow, two of the thirty stocks didn't pay dividends—Bethlehem Steel and Woolworth. Both slashed their cash payments at times when the companies were in financial difficulties and needed to focus on restructuring. When they cut the dividends, both stocks were hammered by investors who read that move as a sign of impending doom. Neither stock has reinstated its dividend and both were replaced in the Dow Jones Industrial Average in the March 1997 revisions. It's as if there is an unwritten commandment for Dow stocks: Thou shalt pay a cash dividend!

High-Yield Investing

Since paying dividends is so firmly entrenched in the Dow, we can take advantage of this almost spiritual attachment to the cash payments and use it to gauge how well companies are faring in relation to each other. Let's look at a simple relationship using the cash dividends—the dividend yield. The dividend yield for any company is a completely objective statistic, calculated by using only two factors, the annual dividend (in dollars per share) paid by the company to its shareholders and the current price per share. If you divide the cash dividend by the current price, you get the dividend yield for that stock. For example, if General Motors pays a quarterly dividend of 50¢ per share, the annual cash dividend is $2. If the stock currently trades at $55 a share, then you calculate the dividend yield this way:

$$\frac{\text{Annual dividend}}{\text{Current price}} = \text{Dividend yield}$$

$$\frac{\$2.00}{\$55.00} = 0.0363 \ (\text{or } 3.63\%)$$

The dividend yield (sometimes simply referred to as yield) for General Motors, then, is 3.63 percent. (Most financial newspapers will publish the dividend yield for each stock in the stock tables, so you won't have to calculate it for yourself, but it's a good thing to know in case you can find only the annual cash dividend figure and the price of the stock.) A dividend yield of 3.63 percent means that if you invest in General Motors at this price and the company pays out the dividend at its current rate over the next year, you will get a return of 3.63 percent on your investment, just through the dividends. This doesn't include any gain or loss you will achieve through the movement in the price of the stock. For many investors, then, the attraction of a relatively high-yielding stock is obvious. Even if the stock's price doesn't increase much, a healthy quarterly dividend check is still going to provide some return on the original investment.

There's much more to the high-yield attraction, though. Since the yield fluctuates based on the daily movement of the stock price and the decision of the board of directors regarding the level of the cash dividend, the yield is a useful tool for comparing how well the stock is doing in relation to the other Dow stocks. Assume that the cash dividend remains constant for a few quarters, as is usually the case. The dividend yield will rise or fall daily as the price moves. As the price of a stock goes up, the yield drops because the stock is more expensive in relation to the cash dividend you'll receive. And, likewise, if the stock price slides, the yield rises because that dividend now represents a larger portion of the stock price. Using our General Motors example, if the company is still paying $2 a share in annual dividends and the price rises from $55 to $75 a share, the dividend yield sinks from 3.63 percent to 2.67 percent. In other words, the cash dividend generates less of a return with the stock price at a higher level. On the other hand, if the price drops from $55 to $35 (and the dividend remains $2 a share), the dividend yield climbs to 5.71 percent.

Within a financial culture that favors high dividends, we can use the yield percentage to compare stocks on a relative basis. This wouldn't work, of course, with all publicly traded companies. A small company just breaking into the market, for instance, is going to use all its available cash to grow. At that stage of its life cycle, it can employ its resources in ways that are more beneficial to future growth than by returning cash to its shareholders. It's simply growing too fast and investing in its plant and product development to pay a cash dividend. Even some giant companies neglect to pay dividends (Microsoft, for example) because they have found ways of using that capital to expand their markets. But for the more mature Dow industrials, a dividend is prized, even expected, and the companies will do everything possible to keep the shareholders happy and continue those quarterly checks. In the meantime, the yield is a great means for us to use in ranking the companies.

Would You Want a Dog?

On a relative basis, then, when one of the Dow stocks has an inordinately high dividend yield, that tells us that it is out of favor compared with the rest of the stocks in the index. (Remember, when the price goes down, as long as the dividend remains unchanged, the yield will rise.) That brings us to one of the most basic—and most abused—clichés about investing: Buy low, sell high. It sounds like the easiest prescription for all investors. To make money long-term, you have to sell your stocks for more than you paid for them. Makes sense, doesn't it?

You'd be surprised just how many investors can't seem to master this obvious requirement. When you get beyond the surface of the truism, the psychology of investing gets very interesting. You see, most people aren't cut out to buy low and sell high. Let's look at what that requires and we'll see why many millions of Americans are flocking to mediocre mutual funds, convinced that even a mediocre return achieved by an Ivy League money manager is better than they can do for themselves.

What does it take to buy low and sell high? Surprisingly enough, it takes the polar opposite of normal human emotions. Let's take some examples from the not-too-distant past. In 1984, a pesticide plant in Bhopal, India, leaked toxic gas that resulted in thousands of deaths and injured many thousands more. The majority owner of the plant was Union Carbide, and the company was sued for damages in excess of $3 billion. Union Carbide's stock plummeted more than 20 percent. With all of the bad press and litigation surrounding the stock, would you have wanted to buy it then?

In 1985, Pennzoil won a mammoth legal judgment against Texaco—$10.3 billion. The devastation to Texaco was so crippling the company had to file for bankruptcy two years later in order to reorganize. The stock dropped nearly 30 percent. Would you have wanted to buy it then?

Four years later, the oil tanker *Exxon Valdez* found the shore rather than the shipping channel as it was trying to negotiate Prince William Sound. The legal claims filed against Exxon immediately sent its stock lower. Would you have faced down the news and bought the stock then?

In fact, all three events proved to be excellent investment opportunities to "buy low." By the time the Union Carbide litigation was settled in 1989, the stock had not only recovered from its low, it was trading near a new all-time high. After reorganization and settling the claim for Pennzoil, Texaco stock climbed from its low of $27 to roughly $60 a share by 1989. And Exxon, which of the three suffered the least after its "event," rebounded relatively soon afterward and has remained a profitable investment for most of the last eight years.

In other words, the time to buy a stock is exactly when no one else wants it. Recall our discussion of supply and demand from part 1. When everyone wants a product and there's a limited supply, the market forces at work will hike the price higher and higher as long as the demand remains in place. But it works in reverse as well. When absolutely everyone is trying to sell a given stock, whoever buys it can usually pick it up for a song—bargain-basement investing, as it were. But the actual act of buying low is terribly hard to do. You have to be somewhat of a contrarian to face down the bad news, look at everyone abandoning a company, and say to yourself, "Now is the time to buy." It simply goes against human nature.

The same is true for selling a stock. Selling high is just as difficult because whenever an investor has enjoyed a nice gain in a stock, the overriding human emotion is greed. "Hold on, it's going to keep rising," you tell yourself. "Sure, it's already doubled in value, but it might go up another fifty percent. Hang on." The problem, of course, is that eventually a stock that has enjoyed a great run isn't a bargain any longer. It's either going to cool off and do nothing for some time, or, worse, it'll start to lose its upward momentum, and like a roller coaster cresting over the highest peak, it may start descending much faster than it climbed.

What most investors do is exactly the opposite of "Buy low, sell high." Let's examine a typical scenario most individual investors will recognize. On a recommendation from his barber, Fearful Freddie buys 200 shares of American Shaving Supplies. The company is supposedly under new management and Freddie's barber assures him that after a quarter or two, the new chief executive officer will have the situation under control. He's turned around four other reorganizing businesses and all four are now thriving. Freddie checks out the company's financial statements and sees that it's not overly burdened with debt and has plenty of cash to keep it on an even keel during the reorganization, so he calls his broker, buys the 200 shares, and starts watching the stock quotes each morning in the paper. The first week, nothing much happens, but Freddie's patient. Not to worry. But then the stock starts to lose ground. It gradually slides from Freddie's purchase price of $50 a share to $49, then $47. A week later, it's lost another point or two. Then, finally, two weeks later, a week before American Shaving Supplies is supposed to announce its quarterly earnings report, the stock is down to $42 a share. Rumors start to fly on Wall Street. Staring a 16 percent loss in the face, Freddie can't take any more and sells out to cut his loss short. The next week, American Shaving Supplies announces a huge new contract with a nationwide hair salon chain as part of its reorganization and releases quarterly earnings that absolutely blow away the estimated earnings from most of the Wall Street analysts. The stock jumps ten points, closing the day at $52 and starting a year-long trend upward. Freddie managed half the equation correctly; he bought the stock of a company that was down on its luck but that had all the promise in the world of making a fine recovery. But he succumbed to one of the two most powerful emotions that ruin investors—individual and institutional alike—fear. Freddie didn't trust the research and the story he believed when he bought the stock, and when it dropped 16 percent, he got nervous and bailed out. Ironically, he sold at precisely the wrong time, the absolute low for the stock, turning the "sell high" part of the equation on its head.

The High-Yield Ten

So what does all of this have to do with dividend yields? By focusing on the Dow stocks, we've pared the universe of thousands of possible investments down to a select group of thirty quality companies. Now, by comparing their dividend yields, we're going to get a ranking of those stocks by a very strong indicator of future value. When the yield is high (because the stock price has slumped—remember the math we did earlier?), the stock has often fallen out of favor (Wall Street has the same trouble with fads and fashion as the rest of us— they're always eager to go with the herd) and is ripe for purchase. On the other hand, when the stock price rises and pushes the yield back down, it's time to look elsewhere for bargains. If, over time, you consistently pick the out-of-fashion stocks—the Dogs of the Dow—you are putting yourself in position not only to outperform the average professional money manager, but also the indices they so often lose to (the S&P 500 Index and the Dow Jones Industrial Average). There's nothing magical about this. There's no stress, no emotion, no intellect involved beyond putting some of your fifth-grade math skills to use. What the high-yield approach to the Dow stocks does is force you to *buy low and sell high*.

In the post–*Jerry Maguire* era, everyone says, "Show me the money," so it's time to look at some historical results to bring to life the actual profits one can make from such a simple approach to investing. The most basic of all the Dow Dividend Approaches is simply to buy the ten stocks in the Dow Jones Industrial Average with the highest dividend yields (in equal-dollar amounts, not equal-share amounts) and then sit on them for a full year. With all of the sources for dividend-yield information available, this procedure will take you less than fifteen minutes to do. You simply write down the yield figures (from a business paper like *The Wall Street Journal* or from an online source like ours at The Motley Fool) and identify the ten paying the highest yields. It's that simple.

This method goes by a number of names, the most popular being the Dogs of the Dow (because the high yield suggests stocks that have had a rough time) and the High-Yield Ten. The strategy has been verified with market-beating results all the way back to the 1920s, but so much has changed in the American stock markets over the course of the last seventy years that numbers from that long ago have little relevance for us in the last years of the twentieth century. Instead, I'll focus on the results beginning in 1971 for a couple of reasons. As Michael O'Higgins points out in his terrific book, *Beating the Dow* (HarperCollins, 1991), securities regulations and the investment industry have undergone remarkable transformations over the years, including such crucial factors as "institutional domination, deregulation of brokerage commissions, derivative instruments like index futures and index options that make possible index investing and give rise to program trading, the domination of OPEC, floating foreign exchange rates—these, and a host of other developments affecting the financial markets in important ways, all happened after 1970" (page 160). For these reasons, the information I'll include here begins with 1971 and extends through the end of 1996, a period of twenty-six years.

There's some debate about what starting date one should use in such historical tests. As O'Higgins argues in *Beating the Dow*, market regulations and the overall culture of the American stock markets changed as we entered the 1970s and comparisons to earlier eras may not be relevant. At The Motley Fool we've tracked the historical returns for these Dow Dividend Approaches as far back as 1961. And while it's true that the 1960s were lousy for investors, the same general patterns of solid performance versus the indices hold true for the high-yield strategies.

The benchmark I'll use is an equally weighted basket of all thirty Dow Jones Industrial components. That is, instead of comparing the strategy returns to the published Dow Jones Industrial Average returns, which as I discussed earlier is a price-weighted index, I'll compare the strategy to the actual returns you would have achieved if you had put an equal-dollar amount into each of the thirty stocks at the beginning of each year. That's a truer reflection of how the Dow Industrials actually performed in any given year.

Let's look at some performance numbers, then. If you had invested $10,000 in an evenly weighted basket of all thirty Dow Industrials at the beginning of 1971, by the end of 1996, your portfolio would have grown to $256,875. That's an annualized return of 13.30 percent. Keep in mind that this is a baseline level of performance the vast majority of mutual funds can't keep pace with. If you had put the same $10,000 into the High-Yield Ten back in 1971, and then updated it once a year to include the current list of ten stocks with the highest yields, your portfolio at the end of 1996 would have been worth $641,897. The annualized return for the High-Yield Ten over the past twenty-six years has been 17.36 percent. (All of the returns in this book, unless otherwise indicated, do not include provisions for taxes or trading costs. Dividends in these models are assumed to sit idle in cash until the portfolio's annual update, at which time they are pooled with the total portfolio for reinvestment in the following year's list of stocks.)

A difference of four percentage points a year between the Dow Thirty and the top-yielding one-third of Dow stocks may not seem like much, but because of the magic of compounded growth, it achieves a tremendous difference over a long period of time. By simply choosing the top ten yielders each year and then going about your business the rest of the time, you would have achieved a total return for the twenty-six years of 6,319 percent. Compare that with the industry benchmark Dow Industrials, which returned a healthy 2,469 percent. In other words, the High-Yield Ten generated a portfolio 150 percent larger than the index that mutual fund managers so often lose to.

If you don't read a page farther in this book, you could stop right now and be a wildly successful individual investor for the rest of your life. By saving money regularly, investing in the top-yielding Dow stocks every year, and living your life without ever giving another thought to stocks, you'd outperform most professional money managers, you'd set up a healthy college fund for your child, and you'd prepare well for a terrific retirement. I know it sounds too easy, but it really is that easy. Too many investors, especially professional ones, make the mistake of believing that simplicity equals a lack of sophistication and success, but as with many things in life, simplicity carries its own rewards. Besides the psychological relief of not having to become a slave to your investments, the Dow Approach avoids all of the traps that ruin returns for most investors: it avoids the kind of frequent trading that pushes up costs (activity does not equate to excellence), it avoids market timing, it avoids short-term taxation on gains (for a review of the recently revised tax laws, see the end of part 2). By keeping the discipline of a simple but sound investment approach—one based on a contrarian view of the market that buys blue chip stocks when no one else wants them and then rotates out of them after they've enjoyed the expected recoveries—you can generate consistent returns without becoming a Wall Street analyst or a mutual fund investor. In fact, you're likely to be better off without such "advantages."

The remarkable aspect of this strategy is its amazing consistency. The following table lists the year-by-year returns from 1971 to 1996 for the basket of all thirty Dow Industrial stocks as well as the High-Yield Ten. The dollar amounts represent the growth of an original $10,000 portfolio after each year's returns.

In the last twenty-six years, the High-Yield Ten group has lost money only twice, with the worst loss giving up 10 percent during the brief recession in 1990. The Dow Industrials lost just over 9 percent in that year. The other loss was a very small one in 1977, a 3 percent drop in a year when the Dow lost more than 13 percent. The entire group of thirty Dow Industrials, however, has suffered losses in five of the last twenty-six years. And of the five losing years, three of them represented individual losses of 10 percent or more.

Year	Dow 30 Return	Portfolio Value	High-Yield 10 Return	Portfolio Value
		$ 10,000		$ 10,000
1971	9.06%	$ 10,906	6.38%	$ 10,638
1972	16.70%	$ 12,727	23.90%	$ 13,180
1973	-10.86%	$ 11,345	3.89%	$ 13,693
1974	-16.91%	$ 9,427	0.99%	$ 13,829
1975	44.24%	$ 13,597	50.99%	$ 20,880
1976	31.28%	$ 17,850	39.43%	$ 29,113
1977	-13.44%	$ 15,451	-3.15%	$ 28,196
1978	2.52%	$ 15,840	2.55%	$ 28,915
1979	11.34%	$ 17,637	8.24%	$ 31,298
1980	25.31%	$ 22,101	31.23%	$ 41,072
1981	-3.26%	$ 21,380	4.25%	$ 42,817
1982	19.59%	$ 25,569	20.85%	$ 51,745
1983	35.63%	$ 34,679	39.22%	$ 72,039
1984	0.51%	$ 34,855	6.36%	$ 76,621
1985	29.77%	$ 45,232	30.50%	$ 99,990
1986	21.69%	$ 55,043	26.20%	$126,188
1987	11.96%	$ 61,626	9.09%	$137,658
1988	14.64%	$ 70,648	17.96%	$162,381
1989	31.97%	$ 93,234	29.68%	$210,576
1990	-9.17%	$ 84,684	-10.01%	$189,498
1991	31.48%	$111,343	43.95%	$272,782
1992	10.96%	$123,546	6.24%	$289,803
1993	17.96%	$145,735	23.68%	$358,429
1994	3.73%	$151,171	2.43%	$367,138
1995	36.66%	$206,590	37.16%	$503,567
1996	24.34%	$256,875	27.47%	$641,897

The real telling example for how well this approach soars in strong markets and holds up well in weak markets is the last major bear market we've suffered—1973 and 1974.

During the bear market of 1973 and 1974, the average stock was hammered, with the Dow Industrials losing 26 percent and many other stocks losing as much as half their value. Yet during this same "awful market," the High-Yield Ten group actually made a profit— ever so slight, but still a profit—in both years. By investing in companies that are out of favor and beaten down, when a bear market comes along, the height from which your stocks will fall is already much lower than for most other stocks, so the sting is taken out of a weak stretch. And when the market recovers, your bargain holdings are ripe to soar. Look, for example, at the gains in the two recovery years after the 1973–74 bear market (a two-year total return of 111 percent for the High-Yield Ten in 1975 and 1976), and again in the year after the 1990 recession (a 44 percent gain in 1991).

The patient and disciplined investor—one who removes emotion completely from the equation and buys stocks based on long-term sound investment principles—survives the weak market years and then sparkles during the strong ones. By focusing exclusively on the Dow Thirty and their dividend yields, we have a simple method (thirty minutes a year tops) that has a proven record for decades (remember, this has worked since the 1920s) and is entirely objective and unemotional. There's no guesswork involved, no intuition, no self-doubt or fear that you've made a mistake. You simply follow the few easy steps and buy a portfolio of top-flight-but-out-of-favor American companies and wait for them to spring back.

A Sample

Let's walk through the mechanics of implementing the strategy now, and identify a High-Yield Ten portfolio using sample numbers. The following table lists the thirty Dow stocks, their stock prices (converted from fractions into decimals for easier use), their annual cash dividends, and their dividend yields (the cash dividend divided by the current price). Many papers will list the yield for you, already calculated. If your paper does that, half your work is done. If you have to calculate the yield yourself, it might take you ten minutes a year longer to manage your portfolio. Can you spare it?

Once you have pulled out (or calculated) the thirty dividend yields for the Dow stocks, the next step is to rank them in descending order and identify the ten stocks with the highest yields.

Most newspapers round off the yield figures to one place beyond the decimal point (e.g., 3.2 percent). I prefer to carry it an extra place because doing so results in very few ties, but if your paper only

Stock	Symbol	Price	Dividend	Yield
Alcoa	AA	$ 78.00	$1.00	1.28%
AlliedSignal	ALD	$ 86.00	$1.04	1.21%
American Express	AXP	$ 78.25	$0.90	1.15%
AT&T	T	$ 36.63	$1.32	3.60%
Boeing	BA	$ 55.56	$0.56	1.01%
Caterpillar	CAT	$108.25	$2.00	1.85%
Chevron	CHV	$ 75.50	$2.32	3.07%
Coca-Cola	KO	$ 69.88	$0.56	0.80%
Disney	DIS	$ 76.00	$0.53	0.70%
DuPont	DD	$ 62.50	$1.26	2.02%
Exxon	XON	$ 63.31	$1.64	2.59%
General Electric	GE	$ 69.88	$1.04	1.49%
General Motors	GM	$ 56.56	$2.00	3.54%
Goodyear	GT	$ 63.00	$1.12	1.78%
Hewlett-Packard	HWP	$ 56.88	$0.56	0.98%
IBM	IBM	$ 94.50	$0.80	0.85%
International Paper	IP	$ 51.19	$1.00	1.95%
Johnson & Johnson	JNJ	$ 64.75	$0.88	1.36%
J. P. Morgan	JPM	$109.25	$3.52	3.22%
Kodak	EK	$ 79.31	$1.76	2.22%
McDonald's	MCD	$ 48.56	$0.33	0.68%
Merck	MRK	$103.31	$1.68	1.63%
Minnesota Mining & Manufacturing	MMM	$101.31	$2.12	2.09%
Philip Morris	MO	$ 44.75	$1.60	3.58%
Procter & Gamble	PG	$144.13	$1.80	1.25%
Sears	S	$ 55.81	$0.92	1.65%
Travelers Group	TRV	$ 67.56	$0.60	0.89%
Union Carbide	UK	$ 48.75	$0.75	1.54%
United Technologies	UTX	$ 86.13	$1.24	1.44%
Wal-Mart	WMT	$ 35.06	$0.27	0.77%

carries the yield to tenths, there's nothing wrong with using their figures. If, however, you have a tie for the final spot, turn to the stock price as your tiebreaker. Take as your tenth stock the one with the lower stock price of the two tied companies. (When I discuss some variations on this approach later, I'll explain why we break the tie this way.) Using the sample data I have included here, the ten highest-yielding Dow stocks would be:

AT&T	3.60%
Philip Morris	3.58%
General Motors	3.54%
J. P. Morgan	3.22%
Chevron	3.07%
Exxon	2.59%
Kodak	2.22%
Minnesota Mining & Manufacturing	2.09%
DuPont	2.02%
International Paper	1.95%

Once you've identified the ten high yielders, you calculate how much money you'll invest in each stock (your total dollar investment divided by ten), and then calculate how many shares of each stock you can purchase with that amount. For example, let's assume you're planning to invest $20,000 in the High-Yield Ten. That means you have $2,000 to invest in each stock. To calculate how many shares you can buy of each stock, the first thing you have to consider is the cost of your commissions. If you pay $15 per trade, reduce the investment amount by the cost of the commission before you make your calculation.

Using the prices from the table on page 78, you would take the $2,000 you have for each stock, reduce that by the commission per trade ($15), and then divide that result ($1,985) by the cost per share of each stock. You'd be able to buy 54 shares of AT&T, for example ($1,985 divided by $36.63 per share equals 54.2 shares). Since you can't buy fractional shares, you must round the number down to the next whole number. Do this for each of the ten stocks using current prices (if you can get the ask prices from your broker rather than the last trade price, your calculations will be even more accurate in determining how many shares you can afford).

The necessity for rounding down the potential shares you would buy for each stock is not only because you have to buy shares in whole numbers (unlike mutual funds, where fractional purchases are accepted); it's also necessary because the stock market doesn't stand idle while you're making your investments. The prices fluctuate constantly, so it helps to have a little cushion of extra cash in case the price of one or more of your stocks moves slightly between the time you make your calculation and place your order and the time your order is executed by your broker. Normally, with these very large and liquid stocks, such movement isn't very volatile and your orders are often filled virtually instantly, but nothing is more frustrating than placing your orders in the hope of getting as fully invested as possible and then finding out when you get your confirmation notices that you actually invested $8.41 (or some such piddling amount) more than you actually have cash for in your account. Now you have to wire enough to cover the amount (which usually costs you more than the amount itself) or sell something you just bought

Stock	Available	Stock Price	Shares to Buy
AT&T	$1,985	36.63	54
Philip Morris	$1,985	44.75	44
General Motors	$1,985	56.56	35
J. P. Morgan	$1,985	109.25	18
Chevron	$1,985	75.50	26
Exxon	$1,985	63.31	31
Kodak	$1,985	79.31	25
Minnesota Mining & Manufacturing	$1,985	101.31	19
DuPont	$1,985	62.50	31
International Paper	$1,985	51.19	38

to cover the gap. If for no other reason, this is why I recommend you open your account as both a cash and margin account. If you overspend by ten bucks and you have a margin account, forget it. Your broker lends you the ten bucks automatically and your first dividend check or two will pay it back automatically. You don't have to try desperately to get the money there within the SEC's three-day settlement window. (Be extra careful with your calculations if you're buying stocks in an IRA account. Margin investing is not allowed in IRAs, and if you've already invested your annual limit of $2,000, you can't just send them the extra $10 to cover the difference. You must be extra careful not to overspend such an account. It's best just to leave a 1 percent or 2 percent cushion of cash sitting in your account rather than risk such a situation.)

One Year Later

Once you've placed your purchase orders for the ten stocks, there's nothing to do for the next twelve months. Depending on how closely you want to monitor your portfolio, you can watch the prices daily or completely ignore your stocks until a year later; it's entirely up to you because nothing else is required. Most investors, especially the first time they use this approach, like to follow along a little more closely because they're understandably nervous about being "in the market." But if watching the daily price swings makes you nervous, the best thing you can do is go spend time with your children, pick up those dusty woodworking tools, or start writing the next Great American Novel. Your stocks will take care of themselves and this strategy calls for you to ignore anything that happens during the course of the year. If one or more of your stocks starts to go down, don't let it scare you into an emotional decision to sell. And, likewise, if one starts soaring, don't let it cloud your judgment either.

A year later, you'll reevaluate your portfolio and start over for the next twelve months. Because of the new tax laws regarding capital gains, you should make your annual adjustments (or adjustments every eighteen months) to your portfolio at least one day after your anniversary date if you're invested in a regular taxable account. (In an IRA, the holding period isn't important to the IRS.) The IRS currently has a tax limit on long-term capital gains (those held at least eighteen months) of 20 percent, and on stocks held at least a year of 28 percent, so getting that long-term distinction saves a bundle in taxes if you happen to be in a marginal tax bracket above 28 percent. Short-term capital gains on stocks held less than twelve months are taxed at your ordinary income tax rate, which can go as high as 39.6 percent at the federal level. The Dow Approach takes advantage of that break on long-term holdings. (See the end of part 2 for more on the differences between twelve- and eighteen-month holding periods.)

When it's time to reevaluate, then, here's the process. You want to start each new cycle essentially as if you were beginning from scratch. That is, the ideal is to begin each cycle with evenly weighted dollar values in each of the ten stocks. Since you already own ten stocks, though, this will require a little adjusting, but nothing dramatic.

Step One

The first step is simply getting the list of thirty Dow stocks together, as you did at the beginning of your first investments, and identifying which ten are the current highest yielders.

Step Two

Compare that new list from step one against the list of ten stocks you currently own. In most cases, about half of the list will have changed over the course of the preceding twelve months. Any stocks you already own from the first year that are no longer on the current list of high yielders need to be sold.

Step Three

The next step is simply calculating what your individual positions should be worth for the new period. So find your total portfolio value and divide it by the number of stocks you intend to hold (ten). Your total portfolio value is the sum of the individual stock values you still own, plus your cash. The cash will be from the stocks you sold in step two, plus any dividends you received during the year. This is also the best time to add new cash to your portfolio that you've saved throughout the year. Since you're updating anyway, you'll save a few dollars on commissions if you make all your trades at one time each year.

Step Four

Now compare the values of the stocks you're still holding from last year's portfolio that you're carrying over into the new year. Ideally, you want to adjust them to equal the value per position you just calculated in step three (by buying more shares if the value is too low or selling a few shares if what you already own is more than the value from step three). A word of caution here, though. There's no good reason to buy or sell a very small number of shares just in the name of making your positions perfectly equal. If a stock you already own is close to the "ideal" value for the coming year, go ahead and live with a small discrepancy. That makes more sense than paying the trading cost for a tiny transaction. In this case, close enough is good enough.

Step Five

With the cash you still have on hand, you should have just enough left to buy the new stocks you're adding to the portfolio for the next cycle, in the amounts you calculated in step three. Then you sit tight for another year or eighteen months. The whole process can be done in less than a half hour once you've run through it a time or two, and half of that will be the phone call or log-in time on the Internet to your broker to place the new orders.

Example

Run through an example with me. (Get some paper and a pencil out, Fool. There will be a quiz after third period!) Let's say you've just finished your first year with the High-Yield Ten. You started with $20,000 and the year has been a pretty good one, returning 21 percent so that your new total value is $24,200.

Here are the ten stocks you had for the first year and their current values:

Chevron	$ 2,360
J. P. Morgan	$ 2,500
Caterpillar	$ 2,200
American Express	$ 2,600
DuPont	$ 2,150
Exxon	$ 2,275
Merck	$ 2,400
General Electric	$ 2,600
Philip Morris	$ 2,500
Eastman Kodak	$ 2,015
Cash on hand	$ 600
Total value	$24,200

The new list of ten stocks for year two includes:

Chevron
Eastman Kodak
DuPont
Caterpillar
Philip Morris
Exxon
Johnson & Johnson
AlliedSignal
Minnesota Mining
General Motors

The six italicized stocks are on both the first year's list and the current list, so you will continue holding them for another year. The other four names are new additions to your portfolio for year two.

The next task is to sell the four stocks from your old group of holdings that are no longer on the new list for the next year. That means selling J. P. Morgan (worth $2,500), American Express (worth $2,600), Merck & Co. (worth $2,400), and General Electric (worth $2,600).

You now hold six stocks from your previous group, with a total value of $13,500. And your cash on hand equals $10,700 (the proceeds from the sale of the four stocks plus the $600 in cash you already had). Your total portfolio value is still $24,200. In reality, of course, you would have had to pay commissions on each of the four sales you just made, so your cash value would be reduced by the total of those commission costs as well, but for this example, we'll skip the commissions to make the rebalancing principle clearer.

Now calculate the value each position should be to start the coming year. Your grand total value is $24,200 and you will own ten stocks, so each position should equal $2,420. It's time to look at the six stocks you are still holding and adjust them to equal $2,420.

Your position in Chevron is worth $2,360, so you need to buy $60 more to bring it in line with the new value of $2,420. Your position in Eastman Kodak is worth $2,015, so you need to buy another $405 worth. Your position in DuPont is valued at $2,150, so you need to buy $270 more. Your position in Caterpillar is worth

$2,200, so buy another $220 worth. Your position in Philip Morris is worth $2,500, so in this case you would need to sell $80 worth. And finally, your position in Exxon is worth $2,275, so you would buy another $145 worth. This brings all six positions to the new ideal level of $2,420. The five purchases and one sale reduce your cash balance by $1,020, leaving you $9,680.

With that cash balance on hand, you have exactly enough to buy the four new stocks (Johnson & Johnson, AlliedSignal, Minnesota Mining & Manufacturing, and General Motors) at $2,420 each. Again, let me remind you that you should account for commissions in these calculations at whatever your broker's rate is, and as I've already discussed, the purchases and sales never come out exactly to the dollar. You'll have to round down to whole share numbers when you place actual orders. Finally, remember that this example is the *ideal* updating and rebalancing method. Some of the adjustment transactions here (buying $60 more of Chevron or selling $80 of Philip Morris, for example) are small enough that you'd probably simply skip them and live with a slight discrepancy in the positions. Make this commonsense decision based on how much it's going to cost you in commissions to make such a small transaction.

Summary

Satisfied? There are no anxious moments here. No ambiguous data. No one churning your account or hitting you with a hard sell. You simply look at stocks from thirty of the biggest companies in America and let the numbers choose ten stocks for you. Here's all there is to it:

Choosing the High-Yield Ten and Updating a Year Later

- Collect the dividend yield data for all thirty Dow Jones Industrial stocks and rank them in descending order.
- Select the ten stocks with the highest yields. If there's a tie for the final spot in the ten, select the tied stock with the lower stock price.

- Buy all ten stocks in equal-dollar amounts (not equal-share amounts) and hold them for a full year and a day (or for eighteen months and a day).
- When you update a year later, get the new list of high-yielders from the Dow Thirty.
- Sell any of your current holdings that are not still on the new list of top-ten stocks.
- Calculate your new ideal position value (your total portfolio value divided by the number of stocks you'll hold—ten, in this case).
- Adjust the stocks you still own, if necessary, to bring them in line with the new ideal position value.
- Buy the new stocks for the coming year with the remaining cash.

If you want an easy entry into the stock market, one that costs relatively little to administer (from $100 to $250 in total commissions each year, depending on your broker's rate), and one that has consistently beaten the industry benchmark S&P 500 Index for decades (17.4 percent a year versus 13.3 percent since 1971), you could stop with this page of the book and proceed merrily with your life, confident that your investment approach has beaten the vast majority of mutual fund managers' returns over the past decade. But I suspect you'll keep reading, won't you? We've just gotten started and what I have to tell you in upcoming sections is the story of further research into the Dow Dividend Approach, research that has yielded a strategy offering even better returns while reducing the cost of trading and without increasing the amount of time you must spend researching and maintaining your portfolio. Enter Michael O'Higgins and Beating the Dow!

Beating the Dow

Michael O'Higgins is an Albany, New York, money manager and author. In The Motley Fool area, he's become something of a hero because his research into the Dow Dividend Approach has spurred so many of us into high-yield investing of our own, as well as further research into the strategy. In 1991, O'Higgins popularized the Dow Dividend Approach in a best-selling book called *Beating the Dow*. It was the first book I read on stock investing and I can trace my interest in stocks to two very specific events—my finding The Motley Fool by chance one day on America Online and my reading of O'Higgins's book, which was recommended by the Fools. It was exactly the kind of book I needed to read because, like all of our Dow Approaches, it laid out a logical strategy that could be used even by someone like me in a completely objective and unemotional way.

I've since gone on to read scores of other investment books that are now considered classics in the field, those by Peter Lynch, those about Warren Buffett, various books on financial analysis and technical analysis, personal finance books galore, but I keep returning to *Beating the Dow* for one very simple reason: I know I can do what O'Higgins teaches. I admire a lot of the other books and have learned quite a bit from them, but I never felt I could put them to use directly. After all, while Peter Lynch talks about investing in what you know, I was a lecturer in literature and composition. That doesn't open a lot of doors to knowledge about stocks that trade publicly. Also, Lynch is a little disingenuous claiming we have the same advantage as he does in picking up useful information. When he was managing Fidelity's massive Magellan Fund, company representatives came to his office to pitch their stories to him. The only companies that ever came by my house were representatives for Avon cosmetics and the *Encyclopaedia Britannica*.

Beating the Dow, though, *is* something anyone can follow easily, and the method is so simple that it requires nothing that a decently educated junior high school student can't comprehend. As you saw in the section on the High-Yield Ten approach, the Dow Dividend models don't require any hi-tech tools. They don't require any special financial analysis (other than the ability to look up or calculate the dividend yield for each stock). They don't even require much time, with the right resources, perhaps as little as fifteen or twenty minutes a year.

What Michael O'Higgins brings to the model, though, is a slight modification requiring a single extra step, but the difference in historical returns is amazing. As *The Hitchhiker's Guide to the Galaxy* enjoins, though, *Don't panic*. The extra step O'Higgins includes is as simple as you can imagine, using data you've already collected for each stock.

O'Higgins builds on the basic high-yield investing philosophy with a discovery about the correlation between stock price and the volatility of a stock's price swings. To put it bluntly, stocks with lower prices are more volatile. This should come as no surprise if you think of changes in stock prices in percentage terms and then relate that to the way the market does business. Stock prices generally are quoted in eighths of a dollar (or increments of 12½¢). While it's true that trades can be executed in even smaller fractions (sixteenths, thirty-seconds, even, on rare occasions, sixty-fourths, but you might as well be quoting the stock in pesos at that point), the very liquid stocks like those in the Dow Industrials typically trade in increments of one-eighth. Compare, then, the difference in percentage terms of a stock movement of the same dollar value for two issues trading at very different prices. If a $20 stock moves an eighth, it represents a change of 0.625 percent. The same move of one-eighth in a $120 stock, though, is only a change of 0.104 percent. That's a significant difference for the smallest typical movement in a stock.

Imagine now a market moving rapidly, carrying most stocks along with it. What you'll see mimics closely the action of white water. If a river is raging along and you drop two objects into the current—one a cork, the other a massive log—which will move faster in the current? The cork floats lightly along the surface, getting swept along at a dramatic pace. The log, however, because of its size and weight, will ride somewhat lower in the water. It'll still move along, of course, but at a somewhat slower pace than the cork that is being hurtled along the surface. Such is the case with low-priced and high-priced stocks in a rapidly moving market. The low-priced stocks can be swept along at faster percentage gains because of the relative difference between an equal-dollar movement and the stock's price. In other words, that $20 stock is likely to be more volatile than the $120 stock when the market perks up or drops down, all other things being roughly equal.

Don't take that as a sign that you should simply go out and buy very low-priced stocks. In fact, as I mentioned when I defined penny stocks, that may be the quickest way to go broke in the stock market.

But if you've identified a group of top-quality stocks that you believe are undervalued and out of favor, likely to recover in the next year or two, then focusing on volatility can actually help your returns. After all, the assumption is that these high-yielding Dow Industrials are going to rebound, so looking for a way to determine which ones might rebound the most dramatically can boost your gains over the straight high-yield approach.

This is exactly what Michael O'Higgins's research concluded. In *Beating the Dow*, O'Higgins presents the results of a number of experiments in which he sought the best series of variables for the Dow stocks. He tested traditional fundamental criteria like price-to-book-value ratios, price-to-sales ratios, and price-to-earnings ratios. He tested market-timing techniques in which one stayed invested part of the year and out of the market for the rest of the time. He tested methods based on earnings estimates generated by professional analysts. He tested more complex combinations of multiple variables. Each time, though, he came back to the same conclusion: A combination of high yield and low price for the Dow Jones Industrials is a simple and amazingly effective strategy.

While recognizing the merits of a high-yield approach, many investors nevertheless balk at the low-price element. Isn't price fairly arbitrary? For example, if a company splits its stock two-for-one, how are the company's business prospects any different from the day preceding the split? All they've done, the theory goes, is changed an arbitrary pair of numbers (the price per share and the number of shares outstanding). And, for most purposes, this is exactly true. A split is virtually meaningless in that it changes the company and its business prospects not one bit. But keep in mind that the high yield for the stock is what sparked our interest in it initially. Without that high yield, a stock's low price doesn't appeal to us. It's the combination of high yield and low price that appeals to Beating the Dow followers. (Note: A stock split does not affect a stock's dividend yield. When the price is split, say two-for-one, the dollar dividend is reduced by the same percentage, leaving the yield precisely the same. A split, then, cannot artificially boost a stock into our high-yield rankings.)

O'Higgins's theory about the link between low price and volatility has been confirmed by other research as well. Norm Fosback also tackled this question in his book *Stock Market Logic*. Fosback's research indicated that price is a good indicator of a stock's future beta. (Beta is a measure of volatility, giving a comparison between the individual stock and the overall market. For example, a stock with a beta of 1.0 should move roughly the same percentage amount as the overall market. A stock with a higher beta will move more than the market in percentage terms, and a stock with a beta lower than 1.0 would be less volatile than the market.) In fact, price turns out to be an even better indicator of future beta than past beta is.

I can see your eyebrows starting to lift. ("I thought he said this stuff was going to be simple?") Let's bring the discussion back to practical matters. If you have a group of stocks that you've been able to identify as prime candidates for growth over the next year or so, and you know that low price has been identified as a good indicator of future volatility, which stocks do you choose out of the group? (Now let's not always see the same hands.) Exactly. The Dow high-yielders with the lowest stock prices. Simple as that. That is precisely what Michael O'Higgins's modification to the high-yield approach entails. You simply pare the field of ten high-yield Dow stocks down to a group of five, based on stock price. (I told you it would be easy, but I wanted you to know *why* it works, not just *how* it works.)

Let's review the steps involved, then, in the Beating the Dow variation.

- Identify the ten stocks with the highest dividend yields from among the thirty Dow Jones Industrials (just as with the High-Yield Ten strategy).
- Rerank the list of ten stocks in ascending order based on stock price per share. (That is, the stock with the lowest price per share is number 1, the stock with the highest price number 10.)
- Select the five stocks with the lowest stock prices. These are the Beating the Dow stocks.
- Buy them in equal-dollar amounts (not equal-share amounts) and hold them for a year and a day.
- After the year is up, follow the same updating and rebalancing procedure I outlined for use with the High-Yield Ten approach. The only difference is you're working with a five-stock portfolio rather than one with ten positions.

The process, then, only includes one additional step beyond what is required for the High-Yield Ten strategy, that of choosing the five stocks with the lowest stock prices out of the ten highest-yielding Dow Industrials.

What kind of difference does this variation make in the overall returns? Let's use the same assumptions we used for the High-Yield Ten model. We'll begin in 1971 with a portfolio of $10,000, reinvesting the whole portfolio (plus any dividends earned in the previous year) at the beginning of each new year in equal-dollar amounts in each of the five Beating the Dow stocks. The returns do not include any provision for trading costs or taxes. (Keep in mind, though, that trading costs are reduced with this variation because you would only buy five stocks instead of ten.)

If you recall, a $10,000 investment in all thirty Dow stocks at the beginning of 1971 would have grown to $256,875 by the end of 1996, an annualized return of 13.30 percent. The same $10,000 in the High-Yield Ten stocks would have grown at an annualized rate over the twenty-six years of 17.36 percent, bringing the portfolio total to $641,897. Using the five-stock Beating the Dow method, however, an identical $10,000 investment in 1971 would have grown to—ready for this?—more than a million dollars ($1,064,576, to be precise). That represents a compound annual growth rate of 19.67 percent. Compared to the High-Yield Ten, that's only an annual difference of just over two percentage points per year, but when you compound that 2.3 percent every year for twenty-six years, you add nearly 66 percent to your total portfolio value compared with the High-Yield Ten.

That's right! An investment of $10,000 and a whopping half hour a year since 1971 would have generated a portfolio in a tax-deferred account of more than a million dollars. This isn't the stuff of infomercials where you hear stories about your neighbors who have supposedly turned "no money down" into $8.6 gajillion in thirty days. It takes time, discipline, courage, and patience for this kind of investment approach to work, but as you can see, with real numbers that anyone could have achieved, it really does work, and it really is as easy as I've suggested. No complex analysis, no guesswork, no emotion.

As you can see from the next table, the advantages of the Beating the Dow five-stock approach are plain. Over the last twenty-six

Year	Dow 30 Return	Portfolio Value	High-Yield 10 Return
		$ 10,000	
1971	9.06%	$ 10,906	6.38%
1972	16.70%	$ 12,727	23.90%
1973	−10.86%	$ 11,345	3.89%
1974	−16.91%	$ 9,427	0.99%
1975	44.24%	$ 13,597	50.99%
1976	31.28%	$ 17,850	39.43%
1977	−13.44%	$ 15,451	−3.15%
1978	2.52%	$ 15,840	2.55%
1979	11.34%	$ 17,637	8.24%
1980	25.31%	$ 22,101	31.23%
1981	−3.26%	$ 21,380	4.25%
1982	19.59%	$ 25,569	20.85%
1983	35.63%	$ 34,679	39.22%
1984	0.51%	$ 34,855	6.36%
1985	29.77%	$ 45,232	30.50%
1986	21.69%	$ 55,043	26.20%
1987	11.96%	$ 61,626	9.09%
1988	14.64%	$ 70,648	17.96%
1989	31.97%	$ 93,234	29.68%
1990	−9.17%	$ 84,684	−10.01%
1991	31.48%	$111,343	43.95%
1992	10.96%	$123,546	6.24%
1993	17.96%	$145,735	23.68%
1994	3.73%	$151,171	2.43%
1995	36.66%	$206,590	37.16%
1996	24.34%	$256,875	27.47%

years, it has produced annual returns of roughly two and one-third percentage points better than the High-Yield Ten approach. And it has achieved returns of more than six percentage points a year better than the thirty Dow Industrials. (Don't forget that the vast majority of stock mutual funds don't even keep pace with the Dow Thirty, let alone the Dow Dividend Approach models.) In addition, by purchasing only five stocks instead of ten, the total trading costs are cut in half. Above all else, though, the strategy retains the advantage of perfect simplicity. You have a set of concrete rules to follow that takes emotion completely out of the equation and allows you to

Portfolio Value	Beating the Dow 5	Portfolio Value
$ 10,000		$ 10,000
$ 10,638	11.77%	$ 11,177
$ 13,180	22.18%	$ 13,656
$ 13,693	18.98%	$ 16,248
$ 13,829	−3.46%	$ 15,080
$ 20,880	63.09%	$ 25,582
$ 29,113	50.91%	$ 38,606
$ 28,196	2.21%	$ 39,459
$ 28,915	4.35%	$ 41,175
$ 31,298	2.81%	$ 42,332
$ 41,072	45.39%	$ 61,547
$ 42,817	−1.26%	$ 60,772
$ 51,745	27.31%	$ 77,368
$ 72,039	36.77%	$ 105,817
$ 76,621	11.23%	$ 117,700
$ 99,990	39.71%	$ 164,439
$126,188	24.06%	$ 204,002
$137,658	12.14%	$ 228,768
$162,381	14.80%	$ 262,626
$210,576	12.33%	$ 295,008
$189,498	−17.34%	$ 243,854
$272,782	59.14%	$ 388,068
$289,803	19.95%	$ 465,488
$358,429	30.49%	$ 607,415
$367,138	6.27%	$ 645,500
$503,567	30.25%	$ 840,764
$641,897	26.62%	$1,064,576

focus on the rest of your life, all the while generating returns that mutual fund managers would give their partners' left arms for. Remember, by sheer dint of size, traditional mutual funds can't just follow this approach and meet these returns. To qualify as diversified funds, they cannot invest more than 5 percent of their capital in any one stock, so they're required to hold a minimum of twenty positions. You're not laboring under any such restriction and can quite easily hold five or ten stocks as your overall investment portfolio.

A final advantage is that even while achieving these stellar returns, the strategy has still remained reasonably stable in weak markets and has suffered only three losing years since 1971. During the bear market of 1973 and 1974, the approach gained nearly 19 percent in 1973 and then suffered a minor loss of 3.5 percent in 1974. So while the overall "market" was getting thrashed, the Beating the Dow approach posted a two-year total profit of nearly 15 percent. Now that's what I call holding up under pressure! The two other losses included a 1 percent slip in 1981 and a weak showing in the recession of 1990—a loss of over 17 percent. Nevertheless, look at the recovery years following these losses and your patience would certainly have been rewarded. After the bear market of the early 1970s, the five-stock Beating the Dow model had successive annual gains of 63 percent and 51 percent. After the minute loss in 1981, the model had annual gains of 27 percent and 37 percent. And after the worst loss of the twenty-six-year period in 1990, the model bounced back with a scorcher in 1991 of 59 percent. Patience, discipline, and a complete absence of emotion wins the day again.

High rewards, you should know, also generally carry with them a degree of higher risk, and such is the case when switching from a ten-stock portfolio like the High-Yield Ten to a strategy with only half as many holdings. In a five-stock Beating the Dow portfolio, each position represents 20 percent of your entire portfolio, whereas only 10 percent was at risk in any single stock in the High-Yield Ten. If a stock were to completely fall apart during the year you hold it, whether because of a calamity (legal or physical) or an unforeseen change in the market atmosphere, the difference to your total portfolio is exaggerated if you are only holding five stocks.

Let's assume Diversified Integrated Possibilities is a Dow Industrial stock and it showed up in your portfolio one year. Diversified Integrated Possibilities makes three extremely successful cosmetic products (hence the "Diversified"). The company claims that including them in one's daily hygiene regimen (hence the "Integrated") all but guarantees one an appearance on next month's cover of *Cosmopolitan* or *GQ* (hence the "Possibilities"). The Food and Drug Administration, however, has determined that if one uses all three products together, dire consequences can result, including the loss of one's hair, extreme swelling of the ears, and a general blotching of one's face that brings to mind a severe case of chicken pox.

Apparently, the chemists at Diversified Integrated Possibilities tested the products only in isolation but never considered the possibilities of their use in combination. When the FDA announces the results of its study, imagine what happens to the stock. That's right; it traded at $50 yesterday and today the fear of lawsuits and competition from products that don't make you look like a cartoon character have dropped the price all the way to $25 a share. Your investment in Diversified Integrated Possibilities has been given a 50 percent facial overnight.

If your portfolio is worth $20,000 and you're holding ten stocks in equal proportion, the loss in Diversified Integrated Possibilities is only going to be $1,000, or 5 percent of your portfolio. There's no doubt that it is still painful to watch your portfolio drop 5 percent overnight, but it's hardly fatal. (And the scenario is, of course, extreme. Even the real disasters that befell Exxon and Union Carbide didn't result in 50 percent losses.) If Diversified Integrated Possibilities were only one of five stocks, though, as in a Beating the Dow portfolio, the loss doubles, since your money is concentrated in half as many stocks.

The advantage of volatility, which over time boosts the returns of the Beating the Dow approach, then, can be a double-edged sword. With a concentrated portfolio, a superstar performance can make your portfolio soar. But when a stock breaks up on the rocks, it threatens the whole ship's stability. Any losses you suffer with a more concentrated portfolio will test your resolve and patience even more than with the High-Yield Ten. To make the approach work for you consistently, you'll have to fight the ever-present threat of emotional decisions. The natural reaction in a situation like the one I described for Diversified Integrated Possibilities would be to sell out to protect against further losses. Typically, though, that would be the worst decision. Often such reactions to news turn out to be overreactions, and with the stock's yield already relatively high (given that it's in your portfolio), such a time would be a great long-term buying opportunity, not the time to look for the lifeboats. Remember, these Dow giants are almost unsinkable and will generally recover with a vengeance once they're thoroughly out of favor with Wall Street. That's, of course, when Dow Dividend investors want to buy them.

To see the volatility at work in the more concentrated portfolio, look again at the table comparing the returns since 1971 for the Dow Industrials (thirty stocks), the High-Yield Ten, and the Beating the Dow five-stock model. On the downside, when the more concentrated model struggles (as it did in 1990), the losses can be greater than with the more stable index of thirty stocks. While the Dow Thirty lost 9 percent in the recession of 1990, the five Beating the Dow stocks dropped more than 17 percent. On the upside, however, that extra volatility generally works very much in your favor. Look specifically at the returns in the next year, 1991. The overall index recovered from the recession the previous year by posting a handsome 31 percent gain, yet the five Beating the Dow stocks raced along at a faster clip, gaining 59 percent. The same phenomenon is evident in the fast-paced markets of 1975 and 1976 (following the last major bear market in 1973 and 1974). While the Dow Industrials picked up 44 percent and 31 percent gains in the two recovery years, the five Beating the Dow stocks soared to gains of 63 percent and 51 percent.

The direct correlation between fewer stocks and higher volatility doesn't always come to pass, of course, but over the long run, the relationship often plays out that way. One notable example is during the bear market years themselves. While the Dow Thirty were losing a cumulative 26 percent in 1973 and 1974, focusing on the lowest-priced stocks of the ten highest yielders (the Beating the Dow group), you would have recorded a net gain for the two years of nearly 15 percent.

If you're interested, then, in the higher returns the Beating the Dow approach has recorded compared to the High-Yield Ten, you have a couple of options to consider. The first is to accept a greater risk associated with a more concentrated portfolio. Where you had only 10 percent of your portfolio at risk in any one stock with the High-Yield Ten, you're placing 20 percent of your total value in each stock with the Beating the Dow approach. The second option is to consider the Beating the Dow approach as a core for your overall portfolio and add to it a second strategy to complement the high-yield Dow stocks. I'll discuss several possibilities for such a complementary strategy in part 3.

The Best of the Best—the PPP

If one carries the logic of Michael O'Higgins's research to its inevitable conclusion, one would expect to find that the historical returns for each of the positions in the High-Yield Ten should decrease as the price increases. That is, of the ten stocks each year, the cheapest one should be the best performer and the highest-priced stocks should trail the field. This is, of course, not really the case. The long-term average returns include a range of performances for each of the positions on the list of ten and it would be wrong to assume that the lineup would follow the averages precisely in any given year. Nevertheless, the historical returns for the ten positions do follow the general trend that led to the development of the Beating the Dow strategy of paring the field of ten stocks in half by their stock prices.

O'Higgins discovered an anomaly in this pattern, though, and it has led to a range of further research by members of The Motley Fool community. As I said, common sense and logic would suggest that the cheapest of the ten highest-yielding Dow stocks should be the star of the portfolio, but, in fact, this is anything but the case. Ann Coleman, one of a cadre of number-crunching Fools, went through the history of the Beating the Dow results and separated each year's results into components based on the stock position on the Beating the Dow list. That is, she pinned down how the lowest-priced stock did each year, the second-lowest-priced, the third-, and so on. And sure enough, her research showed that there was a general trend (not perfect, but general) in performance down from the lowest-priced stocks to the higher-priced stocks. There was one noticeable exception, though. Over a long period, the lowest-priced stock lagged the entire field of ten. The cheapest stock actually produced the worst long-term returns of the entire group.

"Doesn't that destroy the whole theory?" I hear you groan. Not at all. In fact, O'Higgins mentions just such an anomaly in *Beating the Dow*. On occasion, one of the Dow stocks will get so beaten down, it's not just out of favor as we typically see in this group. It's so far out of favor, it's in real financial trouble and may significantly lag behind the rest of the high-yield group for months or years. We find a recent example in Woolworth. As the dime store business segment of Woolworth was dying off and the company was trying to manage the transition to specialty retail stores (Foot Locker stores, for example), the company hit more than just hard times. Its restructuring resulted in management shake-ups and eventually the complete elimination of its cash dividend. In the Dow culture, remember, eliminating a cash dividend is tantamount to signing your own death warrant. Right before Woolworth slashed its dividend, it was the lowest-priced of the Dow high-yielders. And as you might expect, the stock was hammered when the company announced the suspension of its cash dividend. Not too long afterward, both Woolworth and the other stock that no longer paid a cash dividend —Bethlehem Steel—were replaced as Dow components.

In some cases, then, the stock we might assume to be in the best position to soar (the lowest-priced of the High-Yield Ten) is actually a stock you'd like to avoid. It doesn't happen every year, naturally; in many years, that cheapest stock is a spectacular holding. But that cheapest stock happens to be in trouble often enough and dramatically enough that over many years, it ruins the average return for that place in the standings. What O'Higgins claimed and what Ann Coleman's research confirmed is that the second stock on the Beating the Dow list (the second-lowest-priced stock of the High-Yield Ten) was the single-best-average performer over the long run.

The position performs so well, in fact, that it blows away the returns of the other Dow Approach strategies I've discussed, but investing your entire portfolio in a single stock is as close to gambling as you can come without entering the penny stock racket. I would never recommend it, but examining the numbers does help to explain how the combination of high yield and low price can be effective.

Using the same starting point of $10,000 in 1971 as I outlined for the other models, let's look at how this one-stock approach performed (what Michael O'Higgins calls the Penultimate Profit Prospect, or PPP). From 1971 through 1996, the PPP strategy returned a compound growth rate of 24.64 percent a year. That's nearly double the 13.30 percent achieved by the total index of thirty Dow Industrials. That 24.64 percent annualized return would have turned the original $10,000 into more than $3 million by the end of 1996. But, of course, those impressive numbers come with enormous volatility

Year	PPP Return	Portfolio Value
		$ 10,000
1971	35.33%	$ 13,533
1972	35.29%	$ 18,309
1973	43.94%	$ 26,354
1974	- 7.84%	$ 24,288
1975	136.20%	$ 57,367
1976	49.67%	$ 85,861
1977	7.27%	$ 92,104
1978	1.01%	$ 93,034
1979	- 12.77%	$ 81,153
1980	51.25%	$ 122,745
1981	16.12%	$ 142,531
1982	81.39%	$ 258,537
1983	36.98%	$ 354,144
1984	- 3.96%	$ 340,120
1985	26.60%	$ 430,592
1986	29.27%	$ 556,626
1987	5.46%	$ 587,018
1988	16.65%	$ 684,756
1989	11.39%	$ 762,750
1990	- 15.76%	$ 642,541
1991	182.37%	$1,814,342
1992	24.10%	$2,251,598
1993	38.52%	$3,118,913
1994	- 37.78%	$1,940,588
1995	23.15%	$2,389,834
1996	28.52%	$3,071,415

and risk compared to the other Dow Dividend Approaches. In 1994, for example, Woolworth was in this favored position before sinking even further into the lowest-priced position. During the year, when it announced its dividend cut, the stock compiled a 38 percent loss, which would have resulted in a dollar loss for our hypothetical portfolio of nearly $1.2 million. Ouch! (Of course, it had reached more than $3 million in twenty-three years, but losing a million dollars in a year would upset even the most stoic among us.) In fact, the one-stock model had still not recovered to its 1993 value by the end of 1996.

On the other hand, look at the performance of the one-stock approach after the bear market of 1973–74 and again after the recession in 1990. In the recovery year in 1975, Woolworth carried the PPP mantle and recorded a gain of 136 percent. In 1991, Goodyear Tire was the PPP stock, recording the best gain of the twenty-six-year model history, a monumental rise of 182 percent.

Enter The Motley Fool

The amazing historical returns for the Penultimate Profit Prospect confirm O'Higgins's theory that the increased volatility associated with lower-priced stocks would boost the already impressive returns of the Dow High-Yield strategy. The lowest-priced stock, however, was so out of line occasionally that it actually hurt the returns of the Beating the Dow five-stock approach over the long run.

With O'Higgins's research in hand, Ann Coleman and other Fools began experimenting with the historical data to see just how well the approach would have done since 1971 if we simply ignored the cheapest stock of the ten and used a four-stock Beating the Dow approach (BTD4). As you might expect, dropping the cheapest stock, with its long-term mediocre history because of the occasional dog with fleas, improved the historical returns for the portfolio. Where the five-stock Beating the Dow strategy earned an average 19.67 percent per year from 1971 through 1996, the four-stock approach earned 21.93 percent per year, simply by eliminating the cheapest stock on the Beating the Dow list and investing equal-dollar amounts in the second, third, fourth, and fifth stocks on the list.

A seemingly modest increase of 2.26 percentage points a year makes a huge difference to a long-term investment, however. Going back to our original hypothetical investment of $10,000 in 1971, the growth of the Beating the Dow Four would have generated a portfolio worth $1,731,555 by the end of 1996. The value for the same investment in the Beating the Dow Five grew only to $1,064,576. By wearing a flea collar of sorts to eliminate that unreliable cheapest stock, the historical returns for the last twenty-six years would have created an additional $666,979 for our hypothetical investor. That's an increase of 63 percent over a model (Beating the Dow Five) that

Year	BTD4 Returns	Portfolio Value
		$ 10,000
1971	19.89%	$ 11,989
1972	13.15%	$ 13,566
1973	26.16%	$ 17,114
1974	5.30%	$ 18,021
1975	68.71%	$ 30,404
1976	54.11%	$ 46,855
1977	0.66%	$ 47,165
1978	9.89%	$ 51,829
1979	9.99%	$ 57,007
1980	45.47%	$ 82,928
1981	−5.98%	$ 77,969
1982	39.50%	$ 108,767
1983	34.75%	$ 146,563
1984	10.24%	$ 161,571
1985	41.10%	$ 227,977
1986	28.22%	$ 292,312
1987	1.48%	$ 296,638
1988	13.91%	$ 337,900
1989	8.45%	$ 366,453
1990	−14.88%	$ 311,925
1991	66.08%	$ 518,044
1992	29.94%	$ 673,147
1993	37.62%	$ 926,385
1994	1.06%	$ 936,204
1995	41.23%	$1,322,202
1996	30.96%	$1,731,555

is already so far ahead of the market indices that it puts most mutual fund managers to shame. (Remember that the same investment in an equally weighted basket of the Dow Thirty stocks returned a total portfolio worth only $256,875 since 1971.)

In terms of portfolio volatility, there were still just two losing years since 1971 using the Beating the Dow Four variation. In 1981, the approach dropped 6 percent, but that was sandwiched in between gains of 45 percent in 1980, 40 percent in 1982, and 35 percent in 1983. The second losing year was, as with the other variations of the Dow Dividend Approach, during the recession in 1990—a loss of 15 percent. Again, however, the recovery year following the worst loss was terrific, a 66 percent profit in 1991. That's still an annualized return of nearly 19 percent for the pair of years that includes the strategy's worst performance in over two decades. Perhaps even more remarkable was the 33 percent total gain for the model in 1973 and 1974, the bear market that wiped away 26 percent of the value of the overall Dow Thirty.

The Foolish Four

The development of the original Foolish Four approach takes the Beating the Dow Four variation one step farther. Given that the lowest-priced stock of the High-Yield Ten has weakened the performance of the Beating the Dow Five and we know that the single-strongest stock of the group is the Penultimate Profit Prospect, the Foolish Four was developed as The Motley Fool's Dow portfolio of choice in order to take advantage of both of those statistical trends.

The Foolish Four, like the Beating the Dow Four strategy, automatically bypasses the lowest-priced stock of the High-Yield Ten and includes the next four lowest-priced stocks (positions two through five on the Beating the Dow list). To capitalize on the historical strength of the Penultimate Profit Prospect, though, the Foolish Four strategy calls for a doubling of the weight of the PPP stock. Think of this method in terms of buying five positions, but two of the positions are in the same stock—the PPP. In terms of percentage weightings, then, your Foolish Four portfolio would look like this:

Stock #2 40% of the portfolio
Stock #3 20% of the portfolio
Stock #4 20% of the portfolio
Stock #5 20% of the portfolio

By increasing the concentration in a single stock, of course, the same warnings need to be raised regarding volatility. As with the single-stock PPP variation, the fortunes of a single stock dictate to a large degree your success or failure for the year. Historically, taking on the extra volatility and concentration has been rewarded with higher annual returns, but the level of risk you're willing to accept is a personal decision only you can make. There's nothing wrong with opting for a slightly lower risk and a more conservative approach if it lets you sleep at night. Investing isn't just about making the most money possible, it is about making the best return possible within your personal tolerance for risk and volatility. Investors who piled into Woolworth in 1994, expecting the PPP stock to carry them to record highs, know the pain associated with a heavily concentrated investment gone sour.

Updating a Foolish Four portfolio looks a bit more complicated than a regular Beating the Dow portfolio, since one of the stocks is weighted more heavily than the others, but in reality, you follow the same steps involved in updating any Dow Dividend Approach portfolio. Follow along as I run through a brief example. Assume that last year, your Foolish Four stocks were purchased in the following amounts:

Chevron	$4,000
Caterpillar	$2,000
Kodak	$2,000
DuPont	$2,000

When the year ended, the values were:

Chevron	$4,600
Caterpillar	$2,100
Kodak	$2,500
DuPont	$3,000
Cash	$ 300

The new Foolish Four rankings for your second year are:

Caterpillar
Chevron
Exxon
American Express

Following the same procedures we use for the other approaches, we would sell the stocks we hold now that are no longer on the list for next year (Kodak and DuPont). That raises $5,500 in cash. The total value of our portfolio is now $12,500. To calculate the value of the new positions, divide the total value by the number of positions. In this case, remember to count the PPP stock as two positions, for a total of five. The new average position should be worth $2,500 going into year two ($12,500 ÷ 5 = $2,500).

Chevron is still on the new year's list, but it's no longer the PPP stock, so it should be weighted as a single position. We have to sell $2,100 of Chevron stock, then, to make it equal to our new position value of $2,500. Caterpillar is the new PPP stock, so it should be worth two positions, or $5,000 to begin the year. The current value of the holding in Caterpillar is only $2,100, so we need to purchase an additional $2,900 to bring it up to speed. Our cash now equals $5,000 ($300 from cash on hand, plus $5,500 from the sale of Kodak and DuPont, plus $2,100 from the partial sale of Chevron, less $2,900 for the additional purchase of Caterpillar). That leaves exactly enough cash to make the two new purchases (Exxon and American Express) at $2,500 apiece. All in all, six trades were made: two outright sales of stocks no longer on the list (Kodak and Du-Pont), two adjustments to the stocks being carried over from the previous year (a partial sale of Chevron and an additional purchase of Caterpillar), and two new purchases (Exxon and American Express). The procedure for the Foolish Four, then, is just as simple as with any of the other Dow Dividend variations; the only difference is that you're loading up on the position that has been the best performer historically in buying a double position in the PPP stock. It still requires no more than half an hour a year, very few trades (six in this example), and the returns have been nothing short of market thrashing for the last two and one-half decades. It's time to take a peek at the numbers and see just how much of an improvement the Foolish Four is over other variations.

By way of review, let's look at the model returns we've seen so far. An equal investment in the thirty Dow Industrials each year from 1971 through 1996 would have grown at an annual rate of 13.30 percent. Narrowing that field to the High-Yield Ten improved the returns significantly, to 17.36 percent a year. Narrowing the field

Year	Foolish 4 Returns	Portfolio Value
		$ 10,000
1971	22.98%	$ 12,298
1972	17.58%	$ 14,460
1973	32.09%	$ 19,100
1974	2.67%	$ 19,610
1975	82.20%	$ 35,730
1976	53.23%	$ 54,749
1977	1.98%	$ 55,833
1978	8.12%	$ 60,366
1979	5.43%	$ 63,644
1980	46.63%	$ 93,321
1981	−1.56%	$ 91,866
1982	47.88%	$ 135,851
1983	35.20%	$ 183,671
1984	7.40%	$ 197,262
1985	38.20%	$ 272,616
1986	28.43%	$ 350,121
1987	2.28%	$ 358,104
1988	14.46%	$ 409,886
1989	9.04%	$ 446,939
1990	−15.06%	$ 379,630
1991	89.34%	$ 718,792
1992	28.77%	$ 925,588
1993	37.80%	$1,275,461
1994	−6.70%	$1,190,005
1995	37.61%	$1,637,566
1996	30.47%	$2,136,532

further, choosing the five stocks with the lowest prices out of the High-Yield Ten (the Beating the Dow approach), the returns climb to 19.67 percent. By throwing out the lowest-priced stock of the Beating the Dow approach, the remaining four stocks (the Beating the Dow Four) grew at a 21.93 percent clip over the twenty-six years. (The PPP stock gained 24.64 percent a year, but it's hard to consider that a realistic option. Too risky, too much like gambling.) The Foolish Four took advantage of that historical performance of the PPP and raised the bar again, to 22.91 percent a year from 1971 through 1996. That's only a single percentage point over the Beating the Dow Four, but one percentage point compounded over twenty-six years will pay for a lot of Maxflis for your retirement practice rounds.

Returning to our initial hypothetical investment of $10,000 in 1971, the Beating the Dow Four (BTD4) strategy increased the value of the portfolio to $1,731,555. Using the Foolish Four approach, though, which buys the same four stocks each year, the only difference being an overweighting in the PPP stock, our hypothetical investor would have generated a portfolio worth $2,136,532. The difference is more than $400,000 for his retirement fund, close to 25 percent more than with the straight four-stock Beating the Dow strategy.

The same patterns of volatility that we saw with the Beating the Dow variations are present in the Foolish Four method as well. This shouldn't be a surprise, since the same core of stocks is included in each of the variations. The difference lies in fine-tuning which ones to include and in what proportion. This fine-tuning, though, makes a significant difference over a period of several decades, as you can see in the $400,000 difference between the Beating the Dow Four and Foolish Four models from 1971 through 1996.

The Unemotional Value Approach

For quite some time, I marveled at the Foolish Four returns but could never quite escape a nagging doubt that we were missing something. I was uncomfortable with the idea that we automatically skipped that cheapest stock because of the fact that it fell apart in some years. What about the other years? Were we overlooking some terrific opportunities in the number-one slot? If so, is there a way to predict with any consistency when we were likely to see the cheapest stock on the list do a nosedive? These questions gnawed at me quietly for several months while I was involved in other Foolish projects, but eventually I sat down with our Dow database from 1961 through 1995 (all that I had available at the time), to see what I could see, if you will. If a pattern were evident, I hoped to find it. If not, that was fine, too; at least I'd looked.

The first thing I noticed is that the cheapest stock turned out often to be a very strong stock, as the theoretical logic of high yield and low price might suggest it should be. With the Foolish Four approach, while we were avoiding those years when it was a lousy performer by avoiding the position altogether, we were also losing out on some amazing opportunities the rest of the time. For example, in 1972, the slot was filled by United Aircraft, which gained 58 percent that year. In 1975, it was Chrysler with a gain of 41 percent. In 1980, Goodyear Tire & Rubber held the cheapest spot and recorded a gain of 45 percent. And again in 1983 and 1987, the cheapest stock was a winner, a 45 percent gain for Woolworth and a 55 percent gain for USX, Inc., respectively. It seemed apparent, then, that the cheapest stock might represent a real opportunity if there were a way to avoid the big losers that sometimes fall into that slot.

My next task was to look at those losers in the hope of finding something obvious to indicate which ones might fall apart in our hands. I got very lucky.

After looking at several of the worst offenders, I noticed a pattern emerge right away. In the vast majority of cases where the cheapest stock suffered a meltdown, it also happened to be the stock with the highest dividend yield. Not only was it the highest yielder but also the cheapest stock of the high-yielders. This brings us to the obvious conclusion known as the Chocolate Theory (or beer or . . . well, whatever you fantasize about). The Chocolate Theory stated simply: Too much of a good thing, whether you admit it or not, will jump up and bite you.

Stocks that sport a high yield are undervalued in our fundamental view of the Dow universe, and, as a rule, choosing the lower-priced stocks in the group places volatility on our side. But, apparently, if you carry those good things to extremes, you end up with a stock leaving the Undervalued Meadow and sinking into the Slough of Financial Despond. You want examples? Here we go.

In 1971, Anaconda was both the highest yielder and the cheapest of the High-Yield Ten. While it dropped 21 percent, the rest of the Beating the Dow Four stocks (the BTD4) posted a gain of 20 percent. In 1974, it was Chrysler's turn, dropping 39 percent while the Beating the Dow Four eked out a 5 percent profit. In both 1978 and 1979, Chrysler was again in the meltdown position, sporting the highest yield and lowest price of the High-Yield Ten. In 1978, Chrysler lost 18 percent versus a gain of 10 percent for the Beating the Dow Four, and in 1979, Chrysler lost another 26 percent from the same position versus a gain of 10 percent again for the remaining Beating the Dow stocks. In 1982, Manville entered the hot seat, dropping 22 percent while the Beating the Dow Four posted a 40 percent gain. A decade later (1992), Westinghouse followed suit, losing 20 percent while its peers gained 30 percent.

There have been two notable exceptions to this pattern since 1971, however. In 1975, Chrysler redeemed itself briefly before plunging again. From the number-one yield and number-one price position, however, Chrysler generated a 41 percent gain. Nevertheless, the rest of the Beating the Dow stocks in 1975 posted a much stronger performance, a gain of 69 percent. Skipping Chrysler that year would still have proven a fortunate decision. And in 1980, Goodyear Tire & Rubber was in the dual number-one slot and posted a gain of 45 percent. This also didn't detract from the pattern, however, as the remaining Beating the Dow stocks also posted gains of 45 percent.

Over a twenty-six-year period, then, there were eight occasions when a stock with the highest yield and the lowest price of the High-Yield Ten made dramatic moves. Six of those moves were sizable losses while the remaining Beating the Dow stocks posted gains. Including the number-one stock in those years would have been a great drag on one's portfolio. In the remaining two years, the dual number-one stock posted solid gains, but in neither case did those gains surpass what the rest of the Beating the Dow portfolio would have achieved without the stock. In one of the two cases, it posted a gain significantly below the group's return. It appears, then, that Dow stocks with extremely high dividend yields (relative to the remaining twenty-nine Dow components) and extremely low share prices (the lowest of the High-Yield Ten) should be thrown out of our approach unmercifully. Get the hook!

But the rest of the time, it's a good idea not to throw out that cheapest stock. It's often a fine performer and follows the basic logic behind the approach: high yield and low price are a good combination. It's when those good things get taken to extremes that you need to worry.

How does this pattern change the Dow model? Very little, in fact, but the minor variation included in the Unemotional Value approach has proven consistently to be beneficial. Here is the process, then, that you would follow to identify the Unemotional Value stocks:

- Identify the ten highest-yielding Dow stocks (as with all the other Dow Dividend Approaches).
- Rank the ten stocks in ascending order by stock price.
- If the stock with the highest yield is also the lowest-priced stock (out of the group of ten), eliminate it from the list. If it's not both the highest-yielder and the lowest-priced, keep it on the list.
- Buy the four lowest-priced stocks remaining on your list in equal-dollar amounts and hold for a year.

Unemotional Value is basically a compromise between the original Beating the Dow model, which automatically buys the five lowest-priced of the ten high-yielders, and the Foolish Four, which automatically skips the cheapest of those high-yielders in favor of a double position in the Penultimate Profit Prospect (the second-lowest-priced stock). If the cheapest of the High-Yield Ten isn't sitting in the danger seat (highest yield *and* lowest price), then the Unemotional Value model includes it just as Beating the Dow would as a matter of course. If the cheapest stock does show signs of being a potential loser (that dangerous combination again), Unemotional Value follows the lead of the Foolish Four approach and skips that number-one stock.

Incidentally, beginning in 1998, Tom and David Gardner have revised the original Foolish Four method to adopt my four-stock Unemotional Value approach. With its better returns and lower risk, it's a better core approach for new investors. If you're coming to our online forum after having read *The Motley Fool Investment Guide*, don't let their explanation of the original Foolish Four approach throw you. The "new" Foolish Four and the Unemotional Value approach are identical now. Foolish research inevitably leads to revisions.

It may appear at first that the method is much more complicated than the variations I've already discussed, but the additional test you apply to the questionable stock takes less than five seconds. You've already collected the yield data and price data. All you have to do is eyeball that top-ranked Beating the Dow stock to see if it is also topping the high-yield list. If it is, then red flags should fly and alarm bells should sound. Skip it because you don't need to take the risk.

Let's look at an example from recent months. Imagine that the following list represents the top ten Dow stocks, sorted by dividend yield.

The list is in order for the High-Yield Ten (descending order by divided yield). If the stocks are reranked for the Beating the Dow order (in ascending order by share price), the list changes thus:

Stock	Symbol	Price	Dividend	Yield
AT&T	T	$ 33.00	1.32	4.00%
Philip Morris	MO	$ 42.56	1.60	3.76%
General Motors	GM	$ 57.75	2.00	3.46%
J. P. Morgan	JPM	$107.94	3.52	3.26%
Chevron	CHV	$ 77.63	2.32	2.99%
Exxon	XON	$ 62.88	1.64	2.61%
Kodak	EK	$ 68.81	1.76	2.56%
Minnesota Mining & Manufacturing	MMM	$100.31	2.12	2.11%
DuPont	DD	$ 66.19	1.26	1.90%
Caterpillar	CAT	$ 56.38	1.00	1.77%

To test for the Unemotional Value rankings, simply compare the top stock in the two lists. If it is identical, as it is in this example with AT&T, that stock is eliminated and you buy the next stocks in order from the second list (the list sorted by stock price). If the top stocks were not the same for both lists, no stock is eliminated and you begin your purchases with the top stock from the second list. That's the only difference between the Unemotional Value variation and the other Dow Dividend strategies I've already discussed.

If we compare the returns for a four-stock Unemotional Value approach to the Beating the Dow Four, we find very little difference over the last twenty-six years. Where the Beating the Dow Four gained an annualized 21.93 percent, the Unemotional Value Four

Stock	Symbol	Price	Dividend	Yield
AT&T	T	$ 33.00	1.32	4.00%
Philip Morris	MO	$ 42.56	1.60	3.76%
Caterpillar	CAT	$ 56.38	1.00	1.77%
General Motors	GM	$ 57.75	2.00	3.46%
Exxon	XON	$ 62.88	1.64	2.61%
DuPont	DD	$ 66.19	1.26	1.90%
Kodak	EK	$ 68.81	1.76	2.56%
Chevron	CHV	$ 77.63	2.32	2.99%
Minnesota Mining & Manufacturing	MMM	$100.31	2.12	2.11%
J. P. Morgan	JPM	$107.94	3.52	3.26%

returned 21.96 percent. The difference on an original investment of $10,000 in 1971 is only $14,561. (The Beating the Dow Four was worth $1,731,555 after 1996 versus $1,746,116 for the Unemotional Value Four.) That difference alone isn't all that impressive, but if we extend the history farther into the past to include the 1960s (a decade that was not a terrific one for stocks overall), the advantage of the Unemotional Value strategy becomes a bit more marked. Over the thirty-six years from 1961 to 1996, the Beating the Dow Four variation returned an annualized 16.93 percent. A $10,000 stake in 1961 would have grown to nearly $2.8 million. The Unemotional Value Four, on the other hand, fared better in the weak decade of the 1960s, returning 18.11 percent for the entire thirty-six-year stretch. The same $10,000 in 1961 would have grown to just over $4 million with the Unemotional Value Four. While there's little difference since 1971 using this approach, the longer period shows it to have performed much better in the weak 1960s.

The completely unexpected bonus of this research into the Unemotional Value model was that it provided an alternative to the seemingly insurmountable returns generated by Michael O'Higgins's one-stock Penultimate Profit Prospect. Using the Unemotional Value approach (dropping the cheapest of the high-yielders only when it was also the highest-yielder) and generating a two-stock portfolio each year actually outperformed the much-lauded Penultimate Profit Prospect single-stock approach. Of course, including a second

Year	Unemotional Value 4 Returns	Portfolio Value
		$ 10,000
1971	19.89%	$ 11,989
1972	24.91%	$ 14,975
1973	25.74%	$ 18,830
1974	5.30%	$ 19,828
1975	68.71%	$ 33,452
1976	36.92%	$ 45,803
1977	5.32%	$ 48,239
1978	9.89%	$ 53,010
1979	9.99%	$ 58,306
1980	45.47%	$ 84,817
1981	−4.63%	$ 80,890
1982	39.50%	$ 112,842
1983	41.74%	$ 159,942
1984	6.38%	$ 170,147
1985	22.85%	$ 209,025
1986	27.30%	$ 266,089
1987	20.07%	$ 319,493
1988	13.62%	$ 363,008
1989	15.28%	$ 418,476
1990	−17.61%	$ 344,782
1991	81.61%	$ 626,159
1992	29.94%	$ 813,631
1993	26.22%	$1,026,966
1994	4.72%	$1,075,438
1995	30.58%	$1,404,307
1996	24.34%	$1,746,116

stock also cuts the potential disaster possible if your single stock plummets. No one will suggest to you that a two-stock portfolio is diversified either, but a comparison of the Unemotional Value Two with the Penultimate Profit Prospect supports my contention that, in many cases, we can identify a financially troubled stock in our group before it caves in and thus improve our chances over the long run of outperforming the market benchmark indices.

"Show me the numbers," I know. Here we go.

Year	Unemotional Value 2 Returns	Portfolio Value
		$ 10,000
1971	32.27%	$ 13,227
1972	46.79%	$ 19,416
1973	43.94%	$ 27,947
1974	9.09%	$ 30,488
1975	88.95%	$ 57,606
1976	43.89%	$ 82,890
1977	7.84%	$ 89,389
1978	6.65%	$ 95,333
1979	6.69%	$ 101,711
1980	42.73%	$ 145,172
1981	16.88%	$ 169,676
1982	66.18%	$ 281,968
1983	40.92%	$ 397,350
1984	5.63%	$ 419,721
1985	30.38%	$ 547,232
1986	18.34%	$ 647,594
1987	30.13%	$ 842,714
1988	17.50%	$ 990,189
1989	19.62%	$1,184,464
1990	−21.47%	$ 930,160
1991	106.86%	$1,924,129
1992	43.60%	$2,763,049
1993	20.25%	$3,322,566
1994	−5.35%	$3,144,809
1995	4.74%	$3,293,873
1996	18.89%	$3,916,085

If you recall, the PPP one-stock approach returned an astounding 24.64 percent a year from 1971 through 1996. That rate of growth would have turned $10,000 in 1971 into $3,071,415 by the end of 1996. Using, however, the Unemotional Value approach to choose two stocks each year actually returned an annualized gain of 25.81 percent over the same twenty-six years. The original $10,000 would have grown into a phenomenal $3,916,085. Spreading your money over two stocks instead of piling it all into the PPP stock generated an additional $844,670 in total value during the twenty-six years. That's nearly 28 percent better than the PPP approach generated after two and one-half decades of compounding. Amazing what that extra percentage point a year will create, isn't it?

While 1990 still represented a painful decline of more than 21 percent, the number of losses with the Unemotional Value Two decline when compared with the Penultimate Profit Prospect, and so do their severity. During the twenty-six years, the Unemotional Value Two suffered only two losses, 1990 and 1994 (a drop of just over 5 percent). O'Higgins's one-stock approach lost ground in five years, with the most severe coming in 1994 (a wipeout of 38 percent). While it's true that the PPP approach's best years are untouchable (136 percent in 1975 and 182 percent in 1991), the overall long-term return is still higher with the two-stock Unemotional Value approach. Sacrificing a little in the glory years has been compensated for in the remaining years, cutting the volatility without giving up long-term performance.

Let me repeat that I'm not suggesting you invest your life savings in two stocks—far from it. I'm presenting these numbers in support of a theoretical model that can be incorporated into your own investing, not necessarily as an approach you should emulate directly. A more realistic way to use the performance of the two-stock Unemotional Value approach is to create a blended approach. Just as the Foolish Four compromised between the four-stock Beating the Dow approach and the Penultimate Profit Prospect, we can develop a four-stock version of the Unemotional Value with increased weight placed on the top two stocks. For lack of an obvious and memorable name for such an approach, we've fallen into calling it the Unemotional Value Four Plus, or Juiced (UV4+) in The Motley Fool forum. Once an approach acquires a name online, it's hard for it to recover, so we may well be stuck with the ugliest acronym in financial history. So be it. I'll take ugly and effective over a cute disaster any day.

Here's the process involved in setting up a juiced Unemotional Value Four Plus (UV4+) portfolio:

- Identify the ten highest-yielding Dow Industrial stocks.
- Rank the ten stocks in ascending order by stock price.

- If the highest-yielding stock is also the cheapest stock on the list of ten, eliminate it from your list. If the highest-yielder is not also the cheapest of the ten, leave it on your list.
- From the remaining stocks (either nine or ten of them, depending on whether you eliminated one in the previous step), select the four stocks with the lowest prices. They are the Unemotional Value Four.
- Weight them with the two cheapest stocks getting twice as much investment capital as the third and fourth stocks. That is, the two cheapest stocks would each get one-third of your total portfolio value and the remaining two stocks would each get one-sixth of the total.
- Hold for one year.

If you were investing $20,000, for example, and wish to use the juiced Unemotional Value Four Plus approach, the investment would be broken down this way:

Stock #1	$6,667
Stock #2	$6,667
Stock #3	$3,333
Stock #4	$3,333

When the year ends, you would rebalance your holdings in the same fashion as you would if using the Foolish Four approach, or any other Dow strategy: sell the stocks no longer in the current rankings positions, calculate the new position values for the coming year, adjust any stocks you're carrying over from one year to the next to equal the value calculated in the previous step, and then buy the new stocks for the following year.

As you've undoubtedly predicted by now—you're way ahead of me—the returns for this approach fall somewhere between the straight four-stock Unemotional Value approach (with all four positions weighted equally) and the pinnacle of Dow Approach returns, the two-stock Unemotional Value approach.

And you'd be right!

Where the four-stock Unemotional Value approach recorded an annualized gain of 21.96 percent from 1971 through 1996, and the two-stock approach returned an annualized 25.81 percent, the juiced four-stock variation generated compounded gains of 23.37 percent annually for the twenty-six-year period. Keep in mind that the closest comparison for this approach is probably the original Foolish Four variation, which blends a four-stock selection process with an overweighting of the favored stock. The Foolish Four return, by way of comparison, was 22.91 percent.

As I mentioned previously, the gap between the two approaches is only modest from 1971 through 1996, but widens even farther if you include the poor-performing 1960s. The Foolish Four returned an annualized gain of 17.44 percent from 1961 through 1996, compared with 19.35 percent for the Unemotional Value Four Plus. That gap represents the difference between $3.26 million and $5.83 million on a $10,000 investment compounded over the entire thirty-six years. Since 1971, a $10,000 investment in the Unemotional Value Four Plus would have grown to $2,351,731, an increase of more than $200,000 (or 10 percent) over the total achieved by the Foolish Four. In addition, the volatility and worst-case years are minimized with the approach. From 1971 through 1996, there has only been a single losing year for the Unemotional Value Four Plus variation, a loss of 19 percent in 1990, which was followed immediately by a 90 percent gain in 1991. All that and we're still working with a completely unemotional model that a child can follow easily, one that only takes a half hour to complete each year, that requires fewer than ten trades each year, and that generates only long-term capital gains. What better way to launch your investment career in the stock market?

If you adopt the Dow Approaches as your own, you'll be the envy of the investment community, which flounders year after year chasing the next "hot" stock and "sure thing." Give us those boring, out-of-favor, contrarian blue chips, and while the Wise are walking around with QuoTrek machines taped to their foreheads and daily calls to adjust their holdings, we'll enjoy life and still outperform the Wall Street crowd. Just call us Fools.

Summary

You now have the details for one of the most powerful and consistent strategies for individual investors who want a low-maintenance and completely objective approach to equity investing. By taking all of the guesswork out of the equation, the individual investor can remain disciplined and focused on long-term results, not the daily fluctuations that ultimately do in Wall Street money managers and short-term traders.

Here now is a summary of all the Dow Dividend Approach variations I've covered, and a table comparing the annualized returns from 1971 through 1996, as well as the result of a mythical $10,000 portfolio compounded throughout the entire twenty-six years.

- Dow Thirty—all thirty Dow Jones Industrial Average stocks, weighted in equal-dollar amounts.
- High-Yield Ten—the High-Yield Ten (HY10) are the ten Dow Jones Industrials with the highest dividend yields (annual dollar dividend per share divided by current stock price per share), weighted in equal-dollar amounts.
- Beating the Dow—the High-Yield Ten, re-sorted in ascending order by share price. The standard five-stock Beating the Dow (BTD5) approach includes the five stocks in the High-Yield Ten with the lowest stock prices. The four-stock Beating the Dow (BTD4) approach automatically excludes the cheapest stock from the Beating the Dow Five and includes the remaining four stocks. Both models weight each position in equal-dollar amounts.
- Penultimate Profit Prospect—the Penultimate Profit Prospect (PPP) stock is the second-lowest-priced stock of the High-Yield Ten.
- Foolish Four—the Foolish Four (FF) stocks are identical to the four-stock Beating the Dow approach. Instead of all four stocks being weighted equally, however, the PPP stock is weighted to equal 40 percent of the total portfolio and the remaining three stocks are weighted at 20 percent each.
- Unemotional Value—as with the Beating the Dow approach,

the Unemotional Value variations take the High-Yield Ten and reorder them in ascending order by stock price. If the stock with the highest yield is also the stock with the lowest price among the High-Yield Ten, Unemotional Value portfolios exclude it. Otherwise, none of the High-Yield Ten is excluded. The Unemotional Value approach can either be used with equally weighted positions or in a *juiced* variation in which the first two stocks (UV2) are weighted twice as heavily as the others in the portfolio. A *juiced* Unemotional Value portfolio is designated with a plus sign after the number indicating how many stocks are included. For example, a four-stock portfolio in which the two lowest-priced stocks are overweighted is referred to as a UV4+ variation (Unemotional Value Four Plus). As with other Dow Dividend Approaches, any number of stocks can be included in an Unemotional Value portfolio (from two to ten), although the most common variations are four or five stocks.

Approach	1971–1996 Annualized Growth Rate	Growth of $10,000 from 1971 to 1996
Unemotional Value Two	25.81%	$3,916,085
Penultimate Profit Prospect	24.64%	$3,071,415
Unemotional Value Four Plus	23.37%	$2,351,731
Foolish Four	22.91%	$2,136,532
Unemotional Value Four	21.96%	$1,746,116
Beating the Dow Four	21.93%	$1,731,555
Beating the Dow Five	19.67%	$1,064,576
High-Yield Ten	17.36%	$ 641,897
Dow Thirty	13.30%	$ 256,875

The returns from any one of these variations are remarkable considering that more than 80 percent of professional stock mutual fund managers don't even keep pace with the returns of the Dow Thirty, let alone the various Dow Dividend strategies.

Once before, I told you that you could stop reading and be a very successful long-term investor (after my discussion on index funds). And I'm going to tell you so again now. You can stop right here and use just the Dow Approaches for the rest of your investing career and you'll be the envy of the vast majority of investors, professional or amateur. As you can tell, though, by the number of pages still under your right thumb, there's more to the story.

If all this has only whetted your appetite for a more aggressive strategy, move on to "Diversifying with Growth Stocks," where I'll outline my research into mechanical screens you can use to implement a more aggressive investing strategy. But you must always understand that when you adopt a more aggressive approach to investing, you have to be willing to accept the volatility that goes with it. Happily, the increased returns that come with such volatility often will repay you for that risk. Nevertheless, there are some screens as objective and unemotional as the Dow Approaches for you to experiment with as a way of supplementing your core of Dow stocks.

A Few Foolish Words About Taxes

Recently, new federal tax laws were enacted that have a potential impact on the Dow Approach models. So let me outline the major aspects of the new tax laws that pertain to us as long-term investors and then discuss specifically how the new laws might affect investors using the variations of the Dow Dividend Approach, including Unemotional Value.

Despite all the talk about tax reform and simplification, the new tax law has done everything possible to complicate the tax picture for most individuals. Nevertheless, there are some tax reductions in the new law that help investors, and it is these that I'll focus on. Suffice it to say, the changes to the investment rules are just a fraction of all the changes to the tax code. Your accountant's workload is safe, indeed.

I'll begin with individual retirement accounts, since one of the best ways for your stock portfolio to compound at maximum warp speed is to avoid paying out a chunk in taxes each time you update your holdings. In an individual retirement account, you can do just that by investing the way you like (in the Dow stocks or another set of well-chosen stocks) and still avoid the tax man to a degree.

Under the old tax rules, anyone with earned income could contribute to an individual retirement account (IRA) up to a maximum of $2,000 per year. And for some taxpayers, such contributions were tax-deductible, meaning the amount you saved wasn't included in your taxable income that year. In other words, you contributed pretax money, a bonus because more of your salary went to work in your portfolio and avoided taxation for a number of years.

The problem with this system, however, is that if the taxpayer is also a participant in an employer-sponsored retirement plan—a 401(k) or 403(b) plan—the rules eliminate the tax deduction for IRA contributions for most taxpayers. A big incentive to use the IRAs was eliminated, so many people didn't bother any longer. Sure, you were still entitled to contribute $2,000 a year, and it would grow tax-deferred until you began withdrawing after age fifty-nine and one-half, but losing the tax deduction took the starch out of the program.

With the old IRAs, when you begin withdrawing money, after age fifty-nine and one-half, the withdrawals (both pretax contributions and gains over the years) are then taxed as ordinary income, presumably at a lower tax rate than when you were actively in the workforce. (Any after-tax contributions are only taxed on the gains, since the contributions are funds that had already been taxed when they were earned as part of your salary.)

The new tax law has liberalized the limits on deductible contributions somewhat. But, more important, it has created a new class of individual retirement account—the Roth IRA. The Roth IRA eliminates any question of deductibility. Contributions simply are not tax-deductible. Shucks! But here's the incentive. As long as the taxpayer's Roth IRA account is open for a minimum of five years and the withdrawals don't come before age fifty-nine and one-half (or upon the taxpayer's death or disability, or for the purchase of a first home), the entire account is tax-free. That's right, no deferred taxes to pay when you withdraw the money, no cartoon anvil hovering in midair over your head, waiting to crash down when you look up. For most taxpayers, since participation in a company retirement plan kills the deductibility component of a regular IRA anyway, the Roth IRA is a wonderful addition to retirement planning. One other bonus is that contributions to a Roth IRA can be made even after one reaches age seventy and one-half, which is not the case in a regular IRA.

Roth IRAs are available to taxpayers whose annual adjusted gross income is less than $110,000 (single) or $160,000 (joint). Allowable contributions start to phase out at $95,000 (single) and $150,000 (joint).

The contribution limits are the same as before, a maximum of $2,000 per year. This doesn't mean you can contribute $2,000 each to a regular IRA and a Roth IRA; it's a maximum of $2,000 per year per taxpayer, regardless of which IRA plan you choose. One other advantage of the new Roth IRA is that you can convert an existing regular IRA to a Roth IRA by paying the accrued tax liability in the regular plan and then transferring the money to the new Roth IRA. For younger taxpayers who aren't in the highest ordinary income tax brackets, or for any taxpayer whose regular IRA is relatively small, this might be a good option to take advantage of the future tax-free growth offered by the Roth IRA.

The other relevant aspect of the new tax laws for stock investors is the change to the capital gains tax rates and holding-period requirements. Under the old law, gains on stocks held one year or less were taxed as ordinary income at whatever the taxpayer's individual marginal tax rate was. Gains on stocks held for more than one year (a year and a day) were taxed at either the taxpayer's ordinary income tax rate or 28 percent, whichever was lower. So investors in the higher tax brackets (31 percent and 39.6 percent) had a reduced cap on their investment taxes as long as they held everything for at least one year. Obviously, the gap between 28 percent and 39.6 percent is significant enough that investors had to identify the after-tax growth rates of different investment strategies before deciding which was more appropriate for their tax situation.

As with the IRA rules, the new capital gains rules, while advantageous to investors, are much more complicated. Let's start with what's the same. Gains on stocks held a year or less will still be taxed at one's ordinary income tax rate. So if you're in the 15 percent bracket and hold a stock nine months, any gain will be taxed at 15 percent. If you're in the highest bracket, any gain on a similar holding will be taxed at 39.6 percent (ouch).

If you hold a stock at least a year but not more than eighteen months, the old maximum rate of 28 percent still applies. (If you're in the 15 percent bracket, of course, you'd still just pay 15 percent. The 28 percent rate is the *maximum* rate on stocks held over a year but less than eighteen months.)

Where the big change comes in is when you hold a stock at least eighteen months. A new capital gains tax rate has been established in which the maximum rate on these "medium-long-term" holdings is now 20 percent, a nearly 30 percent reduction from the old maximum rate of 28 percent. For taxpayers in the 15 percent tax bracket, there's also a break for holding stocks at least eighteen months, a 10 percent tax rate. Under the new rules, then, there's a significant advantage in holding stocks eighteen months rather than only a year, a 20 percent tax rate for most investors and a 10 percent rate for those in the 15 percent ordinary income bracket.

This obviously has ramifications for our Dow Dividend Approach models, which have always been based on a one-year holding cycle in order to qualify for long-term holding status under the old rules. Keep in mind first that if an investor continues with the one-year holding cycle we've followed for many years, nothing changes in terms of taxes under the new rules. The maximum tax rate is still 28 percent for such holdings. But now that there's a carrot dangling in front of us for holding stocks an extra six months, should we change the Dow Dividend Approach model?

As I write this, our own Motley Fool staff of researchers is re-creating a history for the Dow Approaches on an eighteen-month cycle to see what effect the longer holding period would have had on returns over the last several decades. In the meantime, though, there is some research to suggest that for this approach, anyway, holding for eighteen months instead of twelve may even improve the returns, not to mention grab us a tax reduction.

Lawrence S. Pratt presented a study titled "Toward an Optimal Stock Selection Strategy," in the June 1995 issue of the *Economic Education Bulletin* (vol. 35, no. 6), which is published by the American Institute for Economic Research in Great Barrington, Massachu-setts. Pratt's study tested holding periods from one to thirty-six months for the Dow stocks in combinations from one to a group of all thirty stocks (ranked by dividend yield). The study covered the twenty years from December 1974 to December 1994.

What Pratt found is that the optimal holding period for the Dow stocks ranged from sixteen to nineteen months, depending on how many of the thirty stocks one includes. For the ten stocks we're concerned with—the top ten yielders—the optimal holding period was eighteen or nineteen months, with an annualized return of 18.05 percent for both periods. Contrast that with the twelve-month hold-ing period return of 17.25 percent for the top ten yielders. For differ-ent numbers of stocks up to ten, the optimal holding period ranged consistently from seventeen to nineteen months.

Given these data, then, the new eighteen-month holding period required for the lower capital gains tax rate (20 percent) should not hurt the Dow Approaches at all. In fact, it should boost the returns because it extends our traditional annual holding period right to the point where Pratt found that the optimal holding period rests (eighteen or nineteen months). Plus, it reduces trading costs and qualifies all gains for a much lower tax rate.

If our own historical study of an eighteen-month holding period confirms Pratt's research, the tax law changes will have proven to be a multiple bonus: better returns, lower trading costs, and much lower taxes. And if our own research specifically on the Dow Dividend Approaches doesn't confirm Pratt's study, the very worst scenario is that we are right where we were before the tax law changed—not a bad alternative as we've already seen. Join us online at The Motley Fool (www.fool.com) as we continue our research into these and many other Dow-related issues.

Diversifying with Growth Stocks

By now, you've read the many reasons why you should consider investing in the stock market in the first place, and learned about a set of completely unemotional strategies that you can use to select a portfolio of high-yielding, large-capitalization stocks. Human nature being what it is, though, many of us may find it difficult to sit idle for a year or two while we hear of so many terrific companies advancing at the speed of light. What about the next Microsoft or Intel? Isn't there something we're missing by limiting ourselves to thirty Dow stocks, and only searching the higher-yielding ones to boot?

Of course we are, to some degree. Keep in mind, though, you don't have to own every terrific stock to do exceptionally well. If the thought of missing out on the next superstar drives you nuts, there's a padded room with your name on it somewhere. No one can follow every stock trading publicly, and no one anywhere can manage to invest in *every one* of the great stocks that appear each year. It's impossible, but fortunately for our mental and financial health, it's also not necessary. Nevertheless, there's much to be said in looking beyond the Dow stocks for terrific investments. In fact, what many investors do is start with a Dow strategy to get comfortable with investing in individual stocks rather than mutual funds. Then, as they get acclimated to "the market," they begin to branch out into the world of so-called growth stocks. (It can be argued convincingly that Coca-Cola and McDonald's—both Dow stocks—are classic growth stocks, so the distinction can sometimes be less than useful. For our purposes, we won't define value and growth stocks so much by company as by the characteristics of the stocks' situations we use to identify good investments. A single stock might well be both a growth and a value stock at the same time, so we're not going to get bogged down in philosophical or theoretical distinctions.)

As much as I am a fan of the Dow Approaches, as I became a more experienced investor, I felt that it made sense to explore the possibilities outside of the Dow universe for expansion of my portfolio. My primary objective, though, was to discover a strategy as simple and entirely objective as the Dow Approach. That means the method to select the stocks must be easy to follow for everyone, eliminating all subjectivity, all emotional decision making, all second-guessing, yet it must perform even better than the Dow Approach. If I couldn't beat the returns available with a simple high-yield Dow Approach, I didn't see much point in complicating my investment strategy *and* weakening my returns. So I did what any former graduate student would do; I camped out in the library and my local bookseller and began reading all I could get my hands on to see if I could beat Beating the Dow at its own game: a straightforward mechanical approach that shattered the performance of the market indices, and along with them, the overwhelming majority of mutual funds and Wall Street hotshots.

One of the first lessons I learned in academics is not to reinvent the wheel. The goal of research is not to experiment within an intellectual vacuum, but to take what has been done before and advance it in a new direction—one hopes in a more profitable one, but even dead ends teach the researcher something. Such was the case with all of the Foolish experimentation with the Dow Approaches. Michael O'Higgins took the straightforward high-yield strategy and improved it by reordering the stocks by price (Beating the Dow). The Fools improved on O'Higgins's model by eliminating the sometimes-weak cheapest stock and overweighting the expected star (the Foolish Four approach). And then I carried the Foolish Four one step farther by discovering a pattern that suggests when we should skip the cheapest stock and when we should include it (the Unemotional Value approach), improving the model one step farther while preserving the simplicity and the unemotional quality of a mechanical strategy. My research into growth stocks, then, began with the idea of using what I could from work done before mine and then fashioning a model to fit my own needs: it must be completely mechanical; the information required to use it must be readily available and inexpensive (better yet, free); it must be easy enough to use that virtually anyone could follow it without my help once they learn the steps; and, most importantly, it must perform even better than the Dow Approaches. Starting out, I was just naïve enough that I didn't realize what a hurdle I had placed in front of myself.

Fortunately, I got fairly lucky early in my research journey. Given my love of lists, statistics, rankings, and other objective ways of ordering my universe (some might call it anal retentive), I was naturally drawn to any stories or claims of unifying systems that have reportedly performed exceptionally well. One problem with most such claims, though, is that the systems include so many variables and so much subjectivity that ten different people trying to use them might well come up with ten different interpretations of the approach. To me, that was no help. Some of the other systems that reported stellar numbers included such seemingly illogical correlations that I couldn't make sense of them. If the method, for example, required me to examine the astrological sign of the company's CEO and the official tree of the state in which the company's home office resides, and then compare the P/E ratio with the number of corporate officers holding advanced degrees from a university west of the Mississippi River, and then . . . Well, you get the picture. I'm too married to logical simplicity to trust patterns that far-fetched. Unlike William Blake, I see neither angels nor fiends in trees.

I quickly discovered, however, one source of information and rankings that fit my criteria extremely well. After seeing several newspaper and television ads for the *Value Line Investment Survey* and its simple ranking system (see? marketing does work), I went to my local library and pored over *Value Line* to see if I could use it to help build my own model. The survey presents a wealth of objective historical data and analytical tools (ratios, averages, and the like) that traditionally has been used by investors to perform serious investment analysis. But I went into my examination of *Value Line* somewhat jaded, both because of the other so-called systems I had already examined and because I had heard such disparaging comments made about *Value Line*. "They're always slow to change their rankings." "All of their analysts are rookies who couldn't get hired by real Wall Street firms." "No *real* analyst respects their survey." But I tried to reserve judgment and decided to look into the details for myself.

The element that attracted me most about *Value Line* right from the beginning was that they publish a "grade" for each stock, ranking it in relation to all of the other stocks included in their survey (some 1,500 American issues, nearly 1,700 in all) in terms of its "timeliness" as an investment over the next six to twelve months. As a teacher at the time, I could understand grades; "A" is better than "B" (or, in this case, "1" is better than "2"). All of the ambiguity is removed if you can attach a tangible score or grade to the stock. You can look at two stocks and immediately have a handle on which one is supposed to be a better investment over the coming year. The important question to me, of course, was whether *Value Line*'s ranking system was any good. Did it really work?

Value Line has been using its timeliness ranking system since April of 1965. So we now have more than thirty-two years of results to consider. (At the time I began experimenting with *Value Line*— early in 1995—I had just over thirty years' worth of data to consider.) And despite all of the carping I had heard about *Value Line*, the ranking results had been remarkable, significantly outperforming the market averages for over three decades. Simply buying all of the stocks that carried a timeliness ranking of 1 on the first of the year and holding them throughout the whole year would have produced an annualized return of 15.98 percent from April 16, 1965, through June 30, 1997. That's a cumulative return of 11,939 percent. To put that in monetary terms, imagine investing $20,000 in these stocks back in April of 1965. Today, the value of the portfolio would be more than $2.4 million (excluding taxes and trading costs).

That record by itself would have outdone the vast majority of mutual funds. But by "unfreezing" the system—that is, allowing for the weekly changes in the ranking system and updating the group of top-ranked stocks—the performance record soars from 15.98 percent to 20.94 percent. As we know from the earlier parts of this book, a difference of five percentage points a year is enormous if you compound the gains over several decades. The same $20,000 in the "frozen" record that grew to $2.4 million would have grown to $9.3 million using the "unfrozen" record. I find it astonishing that anyone could denigrate a thirty-year performance like this one. Any Wall Street money manager with such a track record would be placed among the brightest gods of the financial Mount Olympus!

What the track record told me was that here is a fundamental research system that has worked wonderfully for virtually my entire lifetime and I can use it as a starting point for my own investment research into growth stocks, and all for the cost of a trip to the library or a personal subscription. (It's not cheap, however. At just under $600 a year for the standard subscription, it's a cost of investing that has to be accounted for. But most public libraries subscribe to it, so there's a terrific alternative for the cost-conscious investor.) I was also enthralled, of course, with the objective nature of the ranking system, exactly the kind of objective data I was hoping to discover and make use of. And one final arrow in this database quiver is that the performance of the ranking system is a real-time track record. With fairly complex ranking systems, back-testing the results can always be a problem because the tendency is to make the research fit the results you already have, and the more complex the model is, the more suspect the results. But the *Value Line* ranking system was carried out in real time. They publish a new edition each Friday and the results are tabulated as they go. In other words, there's no gimmick in their results. The ranking system they've devised simply works.

There is one drawback, however, and it serves as the launching pad for all of my research into growth-stock screens. In *Value Line's* system, there are always 100 stocks that carry the top ranking (a "1" on their timeliness scale). For the average investor, trying to buy 100 stocks and then keep the portfolio updated with a handful of rankings changes each week would be a nightmare proposition in terms of trading costs. Between commissions and spreads, a modest portfolio, even a generous one, would give away far too much money in trading costs to make holding such a widely diversified portfolio feasible. Holding that many stocks is something a mutual fund can do, but not an individual investor. (And given that *Value Line* also manages several mutual funds, one has to wonder why they don't have a better track record. A big part of their funds' mediocre performance is that the managers keep too much of the portfolio in cash, trying to play futile market-timing games. If they simply followed their own rankings and stayed fully invested, they'd have a dynamite historical record.)

After researching *Value Line*'s long history, I knew that I had a database I could work from, but I needed to discover a reasonable way of whittling down the field of 100 top-ranked stocks to a size that would be manageable for an individual portfolio. There had to be *some* way to identify which of the 100 stocks might fare better than the overall group over the coming year.

Because *Value Line* includes so much fundamental financial data for each stock, I began my quest by testing out a few of these statistics to see if I could find a key to narrowing the possibilities. But nothing remarkable jumped out right away, so I turned my search away from the data on the individual stock pages.

In the "Summary and Index" section of *Value Line*, you'll find a weekly overview of all the stocks in their universe, with important data points for each stock in one simple table. In the back of "Summary and Index," though, *Value Line* prints a sequence of screens that filters out groups of stocks based on various financial criteria. For example, you'll find high-yielding stocks, biggest "free-flow" cash generators, lowest P/Es, widest discounts from book value, and several more.

Investing for Growth

My first growth-stock model grew out of one of the screens included in the "Summary and Index" section each week. On the inside back cover of the weekly insert (page 39), you'll find a screen called "High Growth Stocks." When I first saw this page, I didn't know that it would launch a two-year investigation into modeling with the *Value Line* rankings, but I should have foreseen it. The high-growth screen narrows all of the stocks in the *Value Line* universe down to approximately 100 companies that have demonstrated the most consistent earnings growth over the previous decade and are expected to continue such growth for the next five years. Since my goal was to develop a model based on growth stocks, it was a logical connection to make, and *Value Line* made it so easy by sorting these stocks out for its readers.

The stocks making this list have outgrown 90 percent to 95 percent of their peers over the last decade *and* are expected to keep doing so for at least the next five years. To me, this was a logical place to start building my model. As with the timely stocks list, though, we're faced with a choice of 100 companies. How to whittle the field down? Combine the high-growth screen from page 39 with the timeliness ranking, of course.

Let's look at the timeliness ranking in more detail. What exactly does it measure? While the exact formula *Value Line* uses to rank the stocks is proprietary, they have published the basic elements of the model: short- and long-term earnings growth momentum, short- and long-term price momentum, and earnings surprises. Both the timeliness ranking system, then, and the high-growth screen are concerned with the fundamental element that drives stock prices—earnings growth. The timeliness ranking also gives a nod to more current factors, such as how well the stock has been performing recently and whether or not recent earnings have been accelerating or decelerating more than the analysts suspected. For a high-growth model such as the one I had in mind when I began my research, this combination of rankings seemed promising. And, fortunately, making a stock pass both tests (the highest timeliness ranking *and* inclusion on the high-growth stocks page) limits the number of potential stocks to roughly twenty at any given time. That's still more stocks than most individual investors would purchase, but not unreasonably so. Nevertheless, I wanted to pare the field down to a consistent and affordable number, and I chose the somewhat arbitrary number ten.

Okay, we've narrowed down the field considerably for this model, one that has come to be known on The Motley Fool as Investing for Growth—or IFG. Starting with the 1,700 stocks in the *Value Line* universe, we filter out all but the 100 or so with the best historical and projected growth rates (or, rather, we let *Value Line* do it for us on page 39 of the "Summary and Index" each week). Of those 100 or so stocks, we eliminate all but the stocks with the top timeliness rating for the next six to twelve months. That generally leaves us with about twenty stocks to consider. And we haven't even picked up a pencil yet. All you have to do is run down the list of stocks on page 39 and tick off each of the ones that have a "1" ranking. (Okay, I overestimated how long it would take. Maybe forty-five seconds!)

Now, the work begins. We have to cut this list down to ten stocks. To narrow the list to our final ten candidates, once again, I turned to the *Value Line* rankings to find a determining factor that would be consistent with my goals of growth and simplicity. One seemingly logical choice was *Value Line*'s own system of industry rankings.

Each of the 1,700 stocks is categorized into one of ninety-seven separate industry groups and many of the analytical reports in the *Value Line Investment Survey* are tied to these industry groups. Each group's analysis is updated quarterly (although the timeliness and industry rankings are updated weekly). The industry ranking is derived using a composite of the timeliness rankings of all the stocks in that industry group. So if several companies within, say, the semiconductor group are ranked high on the timeliness scale, the group's industry ranking is also likely to be high. Each group is ranked relative to the other ninety-six groups and assigned a score from 1 to 97, with 1 being the best. Since stocks in the same industry group will often move as a pack, it makes sense to give some heed to these industry rankings as well as the individual stocks' timeliness rankings.

So Investing for Growth uses the industry ranking as the final ordering test for the remaining stocks in our pool of candidates. Taking those stocks that are both high-growth stocks and carry a timeliness ranking of 1 (approximately twenty stocks), you would list them by industry ranking and then simply include the top ten in your Investing for Growth portfolio. Every quarter, you update the portfolio, just as one does when updating a Dow portfolio: sell any stocks no longer on the list, rebalance any positions being carried over that are significantly out of balance with the other stocks, and then purchase the newcomers to the Investing for Growth rankings to flesh out a ten-stock portfolio.

Let's look at an example to show how this process works. Again, all of the data you'll need to identify the ten Investing for Growth stocks appear on page 39 of *Value Line*'s weekly "Summary and Index." In this sample, the following seventeen stocks appearing on the high-growth stocks page all carried a number 1 timeliness ranking. They're presented with their industry groups and rankings:

Stock	Industry	Ranking
ADC Telecom (ADCT)	Telecommunications equipment	1
Air Express International (AEIC)	Air transport	49
CDI Corp. (CDI)	Industrial services	37
Casey's General Stores (CASY)	Grocery	17
Computer Associates (CA)	Computer software and services	5
Disney (Walt) (DIS)	Recreation	44
Green Tree (GNT)	Financial services	22
Hewlett-Packard (HWP)	Computer and peripherals	11
Intel Corp. (INTC)	Semiconductor	2
KLA Instruments (KLAC)	Precision instrument	42
Medtronic, Inc. (MDT)	Medical supplies	9
Micron Technology (MU)	Semiconductor	2
Mylan Labs. (MYL)	Drug	20
Stryker Corp. (STRY)	Medical supplies	9
Sysco Corp. (SYY)	Food wholesalers	30
Tellabs, Inc. (TLAB)	Telecommunications equipment	1
Vishay Intertechnology (VSH)	Electronics	7

If we reorder the stocks by industry ranking, our top ten would include:

Tellabs, Inc.	1
ADC Telecom	1
Micron Technology	2

Intel Corp.   2
Computer Associates   5
Vishay Intertechnology   7
Stryker Corp.   9
Medtronic, Inc.   9
Hewlett-Packard   11
Casey's General Stores   17

If we were going to begin an Investing for Growth portfolio on that date, then, we would buy these ten stocks (in equal-dollar amounts, not equal-share amounts). Or if we were *updating* an existing portfolio on that date, we would adjust our current holdings to match this list.

One thing you'll notice from the list above is that there are several stocks from a single industry represented in the Investing for Growth rankings. This is typical of the Investing for Growth rankings, and it represents both a blessing and a curse that ultimately led me to direct my research to other growth models (but I'm getting ahead of myself). For the moment, ignore the fact that as many as four or five stocks may come from the same industry group. More immediately, it can present a pedestrian problem if several stocks from the same industry group end up tied for the tenth and final spot in the portfolio. If that happens, you must either stretch your portfolio to include all the tied stocks or use some easy tie-breaking system to determine which stock is actually the tenth one.

The first tiebreaker is simply to compare the "Estimated Growth 3–5 Years" figures included on the high-growth stocks page. Since we're hoping for continued high growth from these companies, I use the higher projected growth rate as the first factor in breaking a tie. If by chance the two stocks have the same estimated growth rate, I compare the "Growth Past 10 Years" figures and choose the one with the best historical rate of growth. In the final analysis, the previous decade may or may not be indicative of future growth, but with all else being equal, it provides an easy and objective way to break the tie.

And if the stocks are still tied? In the model's history, this has never happened to my knowledge, but if and when it does, you could choose from a number of other criteria—the safety ranking, the dividend yield, a coin toss. (Flipping a coin is probably as sound a technique as many I've heard propounded by managers with millions of dollars under management!) Don't get too caught up in tie-breaking trivia, however. The process isn't that scientific and keeping it simple is half the goal.

In short, look at page 39 of the weekly "Summary and Index," put a check mark next to the ones with number 1 timeliness rankings, and then select the ten of those with the highest industry rankings. Start to finish, it might take you three or four minutes (if you stop to answer the phone while you're doing it, that is), and requires no math skills or financial analysis experience other than the ability to look at two numbers and determine which one is higher. As with the Dow Approaches, it's completely mechanical, taking all the guesswork and emotions out of the equation.

After you place your orders with your broker and your stocks have been purchased, *wait thirteen weeks.* That's right, you have a full quarter-year break before you have to do anything else. Rock back with a cocktail (colorful umbrella recommended) and take a three-month vacation from your investment concerns; get back to your everyday life, or, heck, watch the stocks in your portfolio daily if you like. It doesn't really matter. For the next thirteen weeks, you *won't* do anything to your portfolio. Mark down on your calendar a date thirteen weeks from your purchases.

In the meantime, have your broker simply deposit any dividends you receive into your cash account; make sure the companies do not reinvest the dividends in more shares of stock. Since you may be selling the stock in three months, the added paperwork of setting up dividend reinvestment plans (or DRiPs) would be a nightmare for stocks you're potentially holding only a few months. Just take whatever interest rate your broker is paying on your cash account and let the money sit there until you renew your portfolio at the end of the quarter.

Just make sure you've circled that next date on your calendar and are ready to go when it shows up. Okay . . . flip-flip-flip-flip! (Picture the old movie shot with a magical wind tearing pages off a calendar.) Thirteen weeks just went by. You've fallen in love with the outrageously good stocks that Investing for Growth has bequeathed you, and can you believe it? Parting is such sweet sorrow; but that's what is in store. Some of them must go.

The first step is to identify the new list of ten Investing for Growth stocks, just as you did thirteen weeks earlier. Turn to page 39 in the "Summary and Index" and tick the stocks ranked number 1 for timeliness; then identify the ten with the best industry rankings. Since 1980 (the first year *Value Line* published the high-growth stocks screen), the average quarterly update would have seen approximately half of the stocks on the old list of ten needing replacement. (This will be important to remember when we discuss trading costs.) Then go through the update procedure I've laid out already for both the Dow Approaches and this model (sell the stocks no longer on the list, adjust the retained stocks if necessary, and buy the new additions to the list).

When I originally announced the Investing for Growth model in our online forum, I recommended that investors *should not* rebalance the weighting of stocks they were holding from one quarter to the next. My reasoning was that if a stock was scorching ahead, why cap its growth by selling a few shares each quarter to bring it back in line with the other positions? "Let your winners run," as another Wall Street cliché would have it. And, to some degree, it's a good idea. But when left unchecked, such rapid growth in a single stock can ultimately lead to devastating results. If a stock has such a phenomenal run that it grows to an inordinately large percentage of the portfolio, when it finally tumbles—and all such superstars eventually take tumbles—it is so overweighted that it often brings down the entire portfolio.

For example, the brief *Investing for Growth* primer we published online in The Motley Fool came out in 1995, almost at the peak of the technology surge that year. I reasoned in that publication that one should let the winners alone, chiefly because doing so for most of 1994 and 1995 had led to phenomenal results on the back of Micron Technology and other semiconductor companies. The Investing for Growth model had included Micron Technology early in its fabled rise, at a split-adjusted price near $16 a share. In a little over a year, Micron Technology was trading as high as $95 a share— a breathtaking gain of nearly 500 percent in just over one year. During that run, of course, the model's position in Micron Technology grew and grew as a percentage of the total portfolio until, at its peak, it was well over a quarter of the entire portfolio. When Micron Technology finally collapsed, its descent was just about as steep as its ascent had been. And along with the stock, the model portfolio plunged into the Slough of Despond, and stayed there for many months, trying to recover from the motion sickness from the roller-coaster ride of 1995.

Had the model been rebalancing the portfolio's weightings periodically, such a devastating loss would have been mitigated. It is true, by taking a little money out of a superstar performer on its way up, you may sacrifice a small share of the profits you might have achieved by staying fully invested in it the entire way, but when the virtually inevitable downturn comes, you will have spread enough of the profits from that superstar around to the other stocks in the portfolio that the loss in the single position won't crush the overall portfolio. My thinking on this strategy, then, has changed over the last several years. I now believe one *should* periodically rebalance a portfolio so that no single position grows to be too large a percentage of the overall value. It's a risk-control measure that simply plays the averages. If a single stock is 40 percent of one's portfolio and it loses 50 percent of its value, the entire portfolio takes a 20 percent loss just from that one stock. If the same stock gets cut in half but only represents 10 percent of your portfolio, the overall loss is only 5 percent—a much more palatable loss to the overall portfolio.

Now you know how to identify the ten stocks to purchase. And you also now know when and how to make the necessary switches. So for those of you whose interest is piqued, it's time to look at just exactly why the simple Investing for Growth model works.

As the long-term returns suggest (over 25 percent a year from 1980 through 1996), the approach *does* work. That, in the end, is what really counts. However, since the Fool in me can't help but ask, "Why?," I want to spend a little time exploring this question.

This strategy is really a blend of two investing approaches: fundamental analysis combined with momentum investing. Since the market prizes a company's ability to make money above all else (something easily quantified every quarter in earnings per share), the companies that *make* the most money typically see their stocks rise the most in price. The fundamental investor will try to identify those companies that consistently outperform their competitors in this vital area—earnings growth. Earnings growth also happens to be one of the two principal components of the *Value Line* ranking system. To be ranked among the top 100 stocks means precisely that a company is increasing its earnings at a faster pace than its competition. That's the fundamental part of the equation.

But Investing for Growth also takes price momentum into consideration, and the model's success proves that momentum really works. It's simply true that the stock market tends greatly to favor certain industries at certain times. It might be computer technology stocks this year, and energy stocks the next, whatever. But when a whole industry is performing better than the overall market, investors pay attention and want a part of it. This will often boost the prices of all the stocks in the hot industry even higher—which can be a dangerous thing when the momentum tide suddenly turns.

Ah . . . but by *combining* momentum investing with fundamental investing, Investing for Growth attempts to include the best of both approaches. It only selects stocks in industries that are performing better than the majority, but within those industries, it roots out the best individual companies. That is partly a function of their earnings growth, but also partly a function of *Value Line*'s selectivity.

Investing for Growth is essentially a series of screens that identify only the best of the best in terms of long-term growth and price momentum. So long as the stock market continues to reward those companies that generate the best earnings over time, and so long as investors continue to want to have a share in "hot" stocks, Investing for Growth should continue to select winners.

The Results

When we first published the *Investing for Growth* primer in 1995, the model had posted gains of 28 percent a year since 1980—*after commission costs!* But as I mentioned earlier, 1995 and 1996 pointed out a flaw in the Investing for Growth approach, one that cost the model two years of painful underperformance relative to the stock market. That flaw, as I hinted previously, is a tendency to be too concentrated in a single industry. When the model holds three to five stocks in a single industry group, and that group falls on hard times before the model can rotate out of those stocks, it's like a balloon that comes untied. It sounds ugly and disappears quickly. Such is the case with the late 1995 and early 1996 performance for the Investing for Growth model portfolio. While the S&P 500 gained 34 percent in 1995, Investing for Growth gave back much of its phenomenal early-year profits to close with a disappointing 25 percent gain. And in 1996, another terrific year for stocks in general, the Investing for Growth model didn't recover well. Stacked against a 20 percent gain for the S&P 500, the model bested the market by only 5 percent. These two years, then, have dragged the historical returns since 1980 down to 25 percent a year (including the cost of commissions). The S&P 500 recorded an annual gain of 12 percent over the same seventeen-year stretch (not including dividends).

Granted, that performance is nothing to be sneezed at, more than doubling the market for seventeen years, but there are a few drawbacks to the approach I need to make clear. First, as I mentioned, it tends to get too heavily weighted in one or two sectors at a time. When that overweighted sector soars, as semiconductor stocks did in early 1995, there's nothing but dancing in the streets. But when the party ends, the hangover can be enormous (going on eighteen months now).

Another drawback is that this approach requires both more and more-frequent trading than any of the Dow Approaches, even though the model's returns have outperformed the Dow Approaches since 1980. For example, if five of the ten stocks need to be replaced each quarter, that equates to ten trades every three months (five sales and five purchases). That's not including any trades one would make to adjust a position that has grown out of balance with the others. Since the model updates quarterly, we're really looking at forty to fifty trades per year, considerably more than with the Dow Approaches, obviously. Even at the low end of the deep-discount broker commission range, that is $400 to $500 in trading costs per year. So to make this approach financially feasible, it would have to be implemented using a considerable amount of money.

How much money? A good benchmark we recommend in The Motley Fool discussions is to keep annual commission costs under 2.5 percent of your total portfolio value. For example, if your portfolio is worth $30,000, your goal is to keep commissions under $750 a year at a maximum. Ideally, 1.5 percent is a better goal, since 1.5 percent is the average expense ratio for the mutual fund industry. (We like to perform better than they do on all fronts, performance as well as associated costs.) So for Investing for Growth, with commissions of, let's say, $450 a year, the minimum threshold investment would be $18,000. That keeps trading costs at 2.5 percent of the total. A better target would be the 1.5 percent level, which would require a minimum investment of $30,000. Obviously, then, this approach is not for very small portfolios or for investors who still pay much higher commissions per trade than the deep-discount brokers charge. The extra few percentage points of theoretical return over the Dow Approach can disappear in brokerage fees if one tries this approach with too little money or pays too much per trade.

A final disadvantage of this approach, and the one that, for me anyway, provided the impetus to do further research into growth-stock models, was the added burden of taxation. This is even more relevant today with the passage of the 1997 tax reforms, which extended the holding period to get the most favorable capital gains tax treatment. The vast majority of the stocks that show up in the Investing for Growth rankings do not remain there a full year. They are typically sold six to nine months after they have been purchased. So almost all gains, then, are considered as short-term holdings by Internal Revenue Service rules and are taxable as ordinary income. Depending on what tax bracket you fall into, this may be a substantial drawback to the approach. With the highest federal tax bracket at 39.6 percent, these gains could be taxed fairly heavily. In comparison, stocks held at least one year are taxed at a maximum capital gains tax rate of 28 percent, and those held for at least eighteen months are taxed at 20 percent (or 10 percent for taxpayers in the lowest tax bracket).

The recently reduced long-term rate of 20 percent means that a short-term approach has to perform that much better than it might have a year ago to provide the same after-tax return. With the Dow Approaches performing over 20 percent a year and only being taxed at 20 percent (if held for eighteen months), that sets a pretty high standard for any short-term strategy to clear when faced with higher ordinary income tax rates. For example, if a Dow Approach portfolio earns 23 percent before taxes, its after-tax return (at a 20 percent tax rate) is 18.4 percent. Meanwhile, at the highest ordinary income tax rate of 39.6 percent, it would take a pretax return of 30.5 percent to achieve the same result after Uncle Sam takes his cut. And as impressive as the Investing for Growth returns have been, they haven't been that high.

What good is the model then? Excellent question. What many Foolish readers have been doing is using the Investing for Growth rankings, not so much as a model to be followed blindly, but as a starting point for further research. Of the list of ten stocks (or even from the larger list of all stocks meeting both the high-growth and timeliness rankings criteria), a reader may find one or more stocks that fit into a longer-term strategy or portfolio mix that he can hold on to for long-term capital gains. Some of the best-performing Investing for Growth stocks over the years performed wonderfully well for long periods of time. Taking the rankings as a launching point for more Foolish research (using some of the evaluation tools presented in David and Tom Gardner's *The Motley Fool Investment Guide*) is a useful strategy as well. Use the rankings as a way of narrowing the list of possibilities down to a manageable number that you can then examine individually in your own stock evaluations. It's no longer completely unemotional and mechanical if you follow that route, but for investors who want help in identifying some promising candidates, it's a good start. And if you really want a completely mechanical, unemotional, market-thrashing growth strategy, keep reading. (I told you Investing for Growth was just the beginning step in my growth-stock research, didn't I?)

Summary of Investing for Growth

- Start with page 39 of the *Value Line Investment Survey*'s weekly "Summary and Index"—the high-growth stocks page. Everything you need for Investing for Growth is included on that single page.
- Identify the stocks from that page with timeliness rankings of 1.
- Rank those stocks by the *Value Line* industry rankings, from lowest to highest.
- Select the top ten stocks from the list. Buy in equal-dollar

amounts (not equal-share amounts) and hold for thirteen weeks. At the end of the quarterly holding period, reevaluate your holdings. Retain anything still in the current Investing for Growth rankings and sell anything no longer on the current list. Replace what you've sold with the new top-ranked stocks. Periodically rebalance the weightings of all ten holdings so that no single stock grows to be too large a proportion of the portfolio.

• In the case of a tie for the final spot in the Investing for Growth top ten, the first tiebreaker is *Value Line's* estimated growth rate for the next three to five years. If that estimate doesn't settle the tie, the second tiebreaker is the historical growth rate over the previous ten years (also listed on the same page 39 from the "Summary and Index").

From Investing for Growth to Unemotional Growth

After the Micron Technology debacle of 1995 and 1996, when the Investing for Growth model was suitably smacked in the head for having such an overweighting in one sector (and one stock), I decided to continue researching ways of using the *Value Line* ranking system profitably on a smaller scale. Undoubtedly, there are many ways to narrow the field of 100 top-ranked stocks down to a manageable handful. And while I was fortunate that Investing for Growth, a very early attempt at such a feat, was successful, it definitely had flaws I hoped to iron out with further research.

By using the industry rankings as my final ordering screen (after narrowing the field by selecting from the high-growth stock list), I was almost by definition putting myself in a position of overweighting at least one industry sector. The industry rankings being composite scores of the individual stocks' timeliness rankings, it makes sense that if three or four quality growth companies carry top timeliness rankings, that industry is almost guaranteed a good industry ranking. The Investing for Growth series of screens, then, was in some regards counting the good timeliness rankings twice and loading up on a single sector. When the sector soared, life with Investing for Growth was sweet. When it dropped . . . well, choose your own favorite painful metaphor (root canal, head into a brick wall, etc.). So I had reservations about the efficacy of using the industry rankings as the final ordering screen.

I also noticed that a number of stocks that carried number 1 rankings for timeliness weren't making the high-growth stocks page, simply because they hadn't been growing at phenomenal levels for long enough. Lacking a ten-year track record of such consistent high growth, a stock wasn't eligible for the list on page 39. Many terrific opportunities were slipping by because they simply hadn't been around long enough to pass the ten-year test. That meant it was time to go back to square one with my research—back to the list of 100 timely stocks in the *Value Line* ranking system.

In 1996, I began to experiment with factors like earnings momentum and relative strength (a stock's price performance in relation to all other stocks in the market). Building on the work of William O'Neil, the publisher of *Investor's Business Daily* and author of *How to Make Money in Stocks* (2nd ed., McGraw-Hill, 1995), and Connecticut money manager and author James P. O'Shaughnessy's first book, *Invest Like the Best* (McGraw-Hill, 1994), I started to combine my *Value Line* starting point with other criteria to see if I could generate even better returns and eliminate some of the nagging items from the Investing for Growth model.

I started to compare the performance of the *Value Line* top 100 stocks each week against the best stocks in the earnings per share and relative strength rankings listed each day in *Investor's Business Daily*.

Each day, *Investor's Business Daily* updates a massive database of stocks traded on the New York and American Stock Exchanges, as well as the Nasdaq National Market. The paper uses proprietary computer models to achieve its rankings for earnings per share (EPS) and relative strength (RS) rankings, but, essentially, the rankings time-weight the earnings growth and price performance respectively of every company and then rank each stock relative to all other stocks in percentiles based on these two factors, up to a 99 rating.

Here is the summary *Investor's Business Daily* provides for the criteria involved in its ranking system: "EPS Rank measures a company's earnings per share growth in the last five years and the stability of that growth. The % change in the last two quarters' earnings vs. same quarters a year earlier is combined and averaged with the five-year record. Result is compared to all companies in the tables and ranked on a scale of 1 to 99, with 99 the highest." And for relative strength: "Rel Str (Relative Price Strength) measures daily each stock's relative price change over the last 12 months compared to all other stocks in the tables. Results are ranked 1 to 99."

A 99 rating for relative strength, for example, means that the stock's price performance has been better than 99 percent of all other stocks in the database. Likewise with the earnings per share ranking. Obviously, having such objective and easily comparable rankings played right into the kind of models I was hoping to build. If a stock carries a 99 ranking for EPS growth, that's better than one with a 75 ranking. Easy. But does it really work that easily?

After several months of relatively informal watching and tracking, it became fairly clear that the stocks sporting the best relative strength rankings from *Investor's Business Daily* were outperforming the rest of the stocks in the *Value Line* top-ranked group. But I've been tricked by short-term performance many times in the past and didn't get too excited without any long-term results on which to judge the performance of such an approach. Logically, this performance makes sense to a degree. Stocks that are performing very well tend to keep doing so for some time. As with other moving objects, momentum tends to keep going in the same direction until some significant force pushes it into a different one. That required force for a stock could be something like an unexpectedly weak earnings report or a major production snafu or a legal debacle that wipes out potential future revenue. But it usually requires something significant to stop a good stock suddenly. Momentum, then, is something worth looking into in addition to the fundamental strength that goes into the timeliness rankings from *Value Line*.

In David and Tom Gardner's *The Motley Fool Investment Guide*, I had already received one lesson in relative strength investing (it was one of the Foolish screens outlined for growth stocks) and had Jim O'Shaughnessy's second book, *What Works on Wall Street* (McGraw-Hill, 1997), been out at the time, I would have had yet another powerful endorsement for the power of relative strength. After months of following my informal test, then, I was ready to commit to another mammoth research test. (Testing these models requires several hundred hours because the data are not available readily or in electronic form for many of the resources. I was fortunate in testing Investing for Growth that my local university library had an extensive archive of past issues of *Value Line*. But adding *Investor's Business Daily* to the mix wasn't as easy. Simply gathering ten years of data required trips to three separate libraries across the country. My thanks go to the staff of the Minneapolis Public Library, which, much to my surprise at the time, had the most extensive and complete archive of past issues of *Investor's Business Daily* I ran across. I have no doubt they were glad to see me leave so that they could rebuild their archives after all my rooting around.)

My first theory was that adding a second screen using the relative strength rankings from *Investor's Business Daily* to the original screen based on *Value Line*'s timeliness rankings would make for a powerful combination of fundamental strength and momentum. My one concern was that it seemed to work best in my short-term observations when updated as frequently as every month. That could mean quite a bit of trading if the results proved worth pursuing. But one lesson I learned in my early studies is not to rule anything in or out too quickly and to gather as much data as possible in order to check alternatives if the original theory doesn't hold up. So, off to libraries around the land I went, using old *Value Line*s for each month to generate the list of 100 stocks (ranked number 1 for timeliness), and then gathering and compiling the earnings per share and relative strength rankings for those stocks on the same dates from *Investor's Business Daily*. Because of the relatively brief publishing history of *Investor's Business Daily* and the limitations of the archives I was able to use, the first full year of data I was able to compile is for 1987. Ideally, of course, I would have liked to gather data for many years before 1987, all the way back to the 1970s in order to include the last really ugly bear market, but I had to make do with what I could actually get. Despite the limited nature of the history (just over a decade), I take some solace in the fact that *Value Line*'s ranking system extends all the way back to 1965, even though the overlay I use on top of their ranking system only goes back to 1987. In addition, the decade's worth of data does include the market crash year of 1987 itself, as well as a slight recession in 1990. Even though the decade includes a number of fabulous years for the market overall, they haven't skewed the compound return for the decade compared with a much longer history. Since the beginning of 1987, when the S&P 500 Index stood at 242, the overall market barometer has grown at an annual pace of 13.3 percent to its current level just over 900. While that's perhaps one or two percentage points above its rate of growth in previous decades, I think critics who go on and on about an unprecedented market explosion are confusing point growth with percentage growth. A gain of 100 points on the S&P 500 when it was back around 300 was a major event, a gain of 33 percent. Today, however, a 100-point gain or loss for the index only represents 11 percent. It pays to keep the percentage gains in perspective rather than focusing solely on point gains. So, then, the last decade has had some wild swings but on the whole has seen the markets grow at an ever-so-slightly-better-than-average rate. Between that typical performance and the much longer-term record of the *Value Line* ranking system, I went into my tests with as much confidence as is possible in a mere decade's worth of data.

After gathering the data from *Value Line* and *Investor's Business Daily* back as far as I could (to the beginning of 1987), I began to test whether my initial theory of choosing the *Value Line* top-ranked stocks (using the 100 with number 1 timeliness rankings) that also carried the highest relative strength rankings would be an improvement over the original Investing for Growth screens. After examining about five years of the data, though, I was disappointed to discover that the approach was not really an improvement at all. The returns were averaging in the 20 percent to 25 percent a year range, very much the same range as Investing for Growth, but the relative strength screen required far more trading and carried as much if not more volatility.

To my amazement, however, a close cousin to the relative strength theory worked phenomenally well. Since I had already gathered all of the data for the earnings per share rankings as well, I began to test a similar screening routine, starting with the 100 top-ranked stocks from *Value Line* and then choosing the top ten (or five) of those 100 based on *Investor's Business Daily*'s earnings per share (EPS) percentile rankings. Here, then, is the method I used in screening for these stocks, what we now call in The Motley Fool the Unemotional Growth approach:

- Begin with the 100 timely stocks from the *Value Line Investment Survey* (located on page 27 of the weekly "Summary and Index").
- Look up each of these 100 stocks in the latest issue of *Investor's Business Daily* and record both the earnings per share (EPS) and relative strength (RS) rankings for every stock. You'll find these rankings just to the left of the company's name in the daily stock tables. (A timesaving hint: Don't bother recording anything for stocks that have an EPS ranking under 90; they won't end up in your elite group at the end.)
- Sort the stocks in descending order by the earnings per share ranking. You're likely to have many stocks on your list with EPS rankings of 99 or 98, so use the relative strength (RS) ranking to break ties where needed.
- Select the top five (or ten) and purchase in equal-dollar amounts (not equal-share amounts).
- One month later, evaluate the stock list again and adjust your portfolio as necessary, selling any stocks no longer on the Unemotional Growth list, adjusting any positions if necessary to maintain a reasonable position balance, and buying the new stocks on the list.

To remain consistent in all of my testing, I chose the first Friday of each month as my update weekend, simply because *Value Line* is published each Friday. Any starting point would be fine as long as you get into a regular update cycle. And to make sure I was using the most recent rankings from *Investor's Business Daily*, I used Monday's newspaper (which, in fact, is published on Saturday morning). For example, if the first Friday of January falls on the third, I use that day's new *Value Line* rankings and the *Investor's Business Daily* rankings from the Monday, January 6 newspaper (available on the morning of the fourth). Confused yet? Don't be. Just grab the most recent issue of both *Value Line* and *Investor's Business Daily* and have at it. The whole screening process can be done in about thirty minutes once you get comfortable with it. It doesn't require anything but page 27 from *Value Line*, a current *Investor's Business Daily*, a pencil, and a piece of paper on which to write down the best stocks, and the ability to distinguish which of two numbers is larger. No computers, no advanced mathematics skills, no detailed financial analysis, no guesswork, no emotions, no problems. Let the numbers tell you what to do.

When I did the updates to the model I tested, I did not break ties for the final position on the Unemotional Growth list. If the fifth and sixth stocks on the list (or the tenth and eleventh in the ten-stock version) carried identical earnings per share and relative strength rankings, I included them both rather than complicate the procedure. My goal was to test whether this simple screening process worked in the aggregate, not to try to make as fine a distinction between two individual stocks as possible. So in months when there were six stocks, the weighting for all six stocks was assumed to be perfectly even; I didn't try to carry half positions in two stocks for the final spot on the list—too confusing for someone who lives for simplicity.

Each month, then, I generated a list of the top five (and ties) and top ten (and ties) Unemotional Growth stocks and compiled their price changes from the closing bell on the Friday they were "added" to the model to the closing bell on the first Friday of the following month. I did not make any allowance for taxes, trading costs (which I'll discuss later), or dividends. This is a simple test to see if choosing stocks this way selects stocks that tend to go up. And does it?!

The results from 1987 to the present have been eye-popping, to say the least. Let's get the numbers out of the way so we can talk about why this screening process seems to be so strong. (Results begin and end each year on the first Friday of January. Dividends are not accounted for in the results for both the Unemotional Growth models and the S&P 500 Index.)

Let's talk about these returns in dollar amounts for a moment to see just how phenomenal they've been. Had you invested $50,000 into the S&P 500 Index on the first Friday of 1987 and simply left it there, it would have grown to approximately $152,000 by the first Friday of 1997—one decade later. (Actually, it would have grown a little more since this figure does not include dividends, but for the sake of focusing on capital appreciation, I've only calculated the changes in price for these models.)

Year	UG5	UG10	S&P 500
1987	21.32%	25.21%	0.26%
1988	6.25%	9.42%	13.59%
1989	86.53%	51.79%	25.49%
1990	−3.06%	−7.68%	−8.86%
1991	150.23%	119.79%	30.64%
1992	38.44%	41.15%	3.90%
1993	35.52%	37.76%	7.85%
1994	4.14%	−4.77%	−1.96%
1995	53.43%	36.07%	33.88%
1996	87.95%	46.87%	21.29%
Total	3,186%	1,462%	204%
Annual	41.80%	31.63%	11.74%

Putting that same $50,000 into a ten-stock Unemotional Growth portfolio and updating it each month would have increased your nest egg to $781,000 over the same decade (again, no taxes, dividends, or trading costs are included).

By focusing solely on the top five Unemotional Growth stocks, however, the overall return increases exponentially. Instead of the $152,000 one would have accumulated with the S&P 500 Index, or the $781,000 achieved in the Unemotional Growth Ten, a $50,000 stake in the Unemotional Growth Five would have soared to a total of more than $1.6 million—in just ten years! That's 110 percent better than the return for the ten-stock model and 981 percent better than the return for the industry standard S&P 500 Index. (You remember that index, don't you? The one 82 percent of all mutual funds failed to keep pace with over the same decade?)

I can hear you now: "No way! Over forty percent a year for ten years? What's the catch? There's gotta be a catch!" Well, there's no real catch, but there are a couple of potential warnings that I want to make very clear. First, this is only a ten-year history, much shorter than I would like to have. But the *Value Line* ranking system—the bedrock of the Unemotional Growth screen—has been pasting the market since 1965.

Second, it can be extremely volatile and requires nerves of steel and extreme discipline to follow to the letter. Could you sit still while your Unemotional Growth portfolio drops 26 percent over a three-month stretch, or would you panic and get out? That's what happened in the first three months of 1997, when the model had successive monthly losses of 8.55 percent, 9.44 percent, and 10.81 percent. If that kind of volatility will frighten you out of the approach, it's not for you. You'd have sold out at the bottom and missed the next four months of solid recovery, gains of 18.35 percent, 9.27 percent, 11.32 percent, and 8.21 percent. (Through the first seven months of 1997, the Unemotional Growth Five has rebounded from the early losses to post a gain of 15.07 percent.) During the October crash of 1987, the model lost a mammoth 37.48 percent in a single month, yet for an investor willing to ride the roller coaster, the entire year still ended in a gain of 21.32 percent (while the S&P 500 Index was essentially even). On the positive side of the ledger, the model has posted monthly gains of better than 20 percent on six different occasions since the beginning of 1987. (For a complete breakdown of the month-by-month returns, see the chart at the end of part 3.) In the ten-year history, the five-stock model has only underperformed the S&P 500 Index one time, in 1988, where it lagged the market by a fraction more than seven percentage points.

Third, the monthly updates require quite a bit of trading, which can lead to a number of concerns. Obviously, every time you place a trade you're forking over a commission to your broker and losing a percentage on the spread between the bid and the ask price, so the trading costs on an aggressively updated model like this one will lower the model's hypothetical returns a few percentage points per year, depending on the size of your portfolio and the broker you use. If one or two of the five stocks need to be replaced each update, that's two to four trades each month, or twenty-four to forty-eight a year. Add another twelve trades a year or so to accomplish any adjustments to positions that are out of line and you could be looking at sixty trades a year for the five-stock model. Obviously, then, it means you're best served using this approach through a very low-priced broker. Even at $10 a trade, annual trading costs could run as high as $600. Keeping our 2.5 percent absolute limit on trading costs in mind, that would require a portfolio of at least $24,000 to make the trading costs feasible.

Also, by updating frequently, you're almost sure to be generating short-term gains (stocks held less than one year), which will be taxed at your ordinary income tax rate. Currently, the highest federal tax bracket is 39.6 percent. If the model returns 41.8 percent a year, let's reduce that to 37 percent to allow for the costs of trading. That represents an after-tax return of 22.3 percent—quite a hit going to Uncle Sam. Nevertheless, on an after-tax basis, that's still a better return than any of the other models I've included in this book. If you're in a lower tax bracket, of course, the bite from that ordinary income tax rate won't be as large. Even better, consider using this approach in a tax-deferred account, such as an IRA or a 401(k) if your employer has set one up that permits you to buy stocks directly. In a tax-deferred account, the only drawback is the trading costs; the long-term versus short-term holding distinction is eliminated altogether and your gains are preserved.

The Unemotional Growth approach doesn't come without its share of attendant concerns, but it's an approach that you may find useful in the right circumstances. It's aggressive investing, indeed, it's volatile, and it generates short-term holdings and as many as fifty to sixty trades per year (although I'll discuss ways to reduce that number dramatically). If those factors can be managed, though, through deep-discount brokers and tax-deferred accounts, it can be a powerful growth tool. Let's talk now about why it works.

Quite simply, Unemotional Growth is a momentum strategy. But when most investors think of momentum strategies, the image evoked is one of a stock going straight up and more and more investors piling in simply because the price is going up. And there are endless examples of stocks following this pattern, soaring higher and higher as more and more "momentum" investors throw money at the stock, regardless of whether the company's making any money or not. In fact, most such bandwagon investors are probably not even aware of what the fundamental outlook for the company is. They've looked at a chart of the stock price, saw the stock was going up, and could tell by the daily trading volume that the market's "players" were interested in this stock; that was enough to get them to commit their investment dollars.

The problem with this scenario, as you might suspect, is that if the stock is only going up because of price momentum, fueled by short-term speculators, sooner or later someone will realize the stock's fundamental value doesn't justify the excessive rise in price and the money will flow out of the stock just as quickly as it flowed in. The sickening plunge that inevitably results will wipe out any paper profits you had in the stock unless you were lucky enough, or genius enough (but I'd assume it was the former), to get out at the top of the crest. This is the most dangerous of all timing games. If you're wrong about when to get in or when to get out, you'll get slaughtered. And the whole sequence can occur over a few days or weeks. To be nimble enough to play such a game is virtually impossible for the typical investor. And, in fact, Fools don't even consider it investing. It's akin to betting on football games. In a few hours, you'll know the outcome, and it's no surprise that most gamblers are long-term losers, both on Sunday's National Football League game and on short-term trading in the stock market.

Fools like to stack the odds in their favor whenever possible. As I discussed in part 1, we're not risk-averse. You have to be willing to put money at risk in the market in order to achieve the kind of growth that will stay ahead of inflation and build wealth over many years. But there's a huge difference between calculated risk and silly tosses of the dice.

So how are the odds in our favor with Unemotional Growth? The first champion we have fighting for us is the *Value Line* ranking system itself. Since the 1960s, this simple objective system, which incorporates long- and short-term earnings histories, as well as long- and short-term price histories and earnings surprises, has been beating the stock market indices soundly. We've all heard that "past performance is no guarantee of future returns," but I'd rather have a three-decade history in my corner than facing me across the ring. How about you? Using the timeliness ranking as our first screen gives us a quality check that has been proven through all types of markets (bear and bull and everything in between). If we went no farther, we know that we'd be working from a winning approach right there.

But we have another champion working for us, and this is where a slightly different definition of momentum investing comes into effect. I wrote in the first part of this book, when discussing the basics of stock market investing, that the single most powerful force in determining the price of a stock is the company's bottom line— its earnings per share. If a company is spending money on plant and equipment, salaries, research, advertising, product development, and the entire range of potential business costs, yet can't turn a profit, all its hard work isn't going to save the stock price. The company that balances costs and revenues the best, providing a product or service that the consumer wants at a price he's willing to pay, is the company that will generate good earnings. And good earnings, in the long run, will determine the stock price. Sure, there are seemingly innumerable complications in this simple formula in real life. But the entire labyrinthine scheme ultimately comes down to how much the company is able to generate in profits and how well the profits continue to grow.

So what's the logical place for us to turn for Unemotional Growth once we've narrowed the field to the best 100 stocks in the *Value Line* universe? (I'm still seeing the same hands every time.) That's right—earnings per share. (If you got it right, you can stay after class and help clean the chalkboard.)

Being the efficient and economizing investors that we are (my mother would say "lazy," but since she's not writing this book, I get to color it the way I want), we want an easy and objective way to compare the earnings numbers for a range of companies. Have to keep things unemotional and straightforward. This is where the EPS (earnings per share) ranking from *Investor's Business Daily* comes in. With a quick glance at the EPS rankings for the 100 top-ranked stocks in *Value Line*'s weekly publication, you can determine which stocks have generated the best earnings recently. (Okay, the glance actually takes about half an hour, but what else were you going to do Saturday morning, watch fishing on TV? And people tell me televised *golf* is boring!?)

The beauty of knowing how stocks are performing relative to all other stocks in recent quarters (remember that each company reports its earnings performance publicly every quarter in statements that must be filed with the Securities and Exchange Commission) is that we get a clearer sense of the momentum in *earnings*, not just the momentum in price. The same laws of physics seem to apply to earnings as to price movements. Companies (or bodies) moving in one direction tend to keep moving in that direction until something powerful comes along to divert them from their path. In other words, companies doing well often continue to perform well for some time before they cool off or the competition catches up. (The same is true of companies performing poorly, of course. If you discover a company going the wrong direction for a few quarters on its earnings reports, the odds are that it's going to continue to struggle for some time.)

Earnings growth—the arteries of the Unemotional Growth approach if the *Value Line* ranking system is the heart—is, of course, nothing new to investors who use fundamental analysis (that is, looking at the company's business and financial strength to determine if the stock is a good value rather than focusing on the price chart, which is the basis of technical analysis). And some research has even demonstrated that for longer holding periods (say, a year or more), earnings growth isn't the best factor to focus on. James O'Shaughnessy, for example, in his best-selling book *What Works on Wall Street*, discovered that factors such as low price-to-sales ratios and relative price strength worked extremely well in combination and that earnings growth wasn't a useful screen. His reasoning, with which I agree entirely, is that the stock market is ultimately fairly efficient given enough time. In other words, the news of a company's good (or ill) fortunes regarding earnings will be taken into account in the stock's price and the news doesn't give individual investors an advantage. And on a one-year cycle, as O'Shaughnessy was working with in his book, that is indeed the case.

But the market's "efficient" nature isn't as timely as one might suspect, despite this age of instant information via electronic networks, twenty-four-hour cable TV news, and round-the-clock trading for institutional investors. When a company begins posting terrific earnings numbers, it can be quite some time before "the market" picks up on it and the news works its way into the current stock price. The lag time between the company's earnings perking up and the market catching on to the news is where Unemotional Growth makes hay.

By focusing on a limited number of prospects to begin with (the 100 *Value Line* choices for growth over the next year), and then concentrating on a single variable (the EPS ranking from *Investor's Business Daily*, which is updated every day and incorporates each earnings report virtually immediately), we have a very simple, very timely screen that points to stocks that are potential winners in the coming months. By reevaluating monthly, we're always incorporating the latest earnings rankings into our model, picking up stocks much more quickly than "the market" typically does. And buying a stock before it becomes Wall Street's darling, of course, is how one makes huge gains. If you're able to identify a stock that looks good fundamentally (a key component in the *Value Line* timeliness rankings) at a time when it begins to post earnings that are better than the vast majority of all other stocks (evidenced by a high EPS ranking from *Investor's Business Daily*), you stand a good chance of buying it at a reasonable price before the price-momentum investors start noticing it. Once the story is no longer exactly news, though, and those price-momentum investors have started feeding on the stock like sharks around chum, you've made a tidy little fortune by having identified the winner early.

What about selling? How does the model identify which stocks to sell? As most veteran investors will tell you, buying a stock is easy. You've done your analysis of the company, you're confident that you're buying the stock at a fair price, and you expect it to go the way you've planned. You wouldn't buy the stock otherwise, of course. But selling a stock is much more difficult, simply because so many more emotions are involved in the decision for most investors. If the stock's been a huge success, investors are often torn between wanting to enjoy the great fun and profits a little longer (everyone hates to sell a winner only to see it double again) and fearing that they'll give back everything they've gained. If the stock's done nothing, however, there's always doubt that perhaps one is just being impatient. A little more time and my original analysis will be borne out, they tell themselves. And perhaps the hardest emotional crisis is when you're faced with a big loser. Again, a range of emotional responses comes into play. Should I get out now and cut my losses? Should I hang on and hope for a rebound that will at least get me back to even? Should I hope that my original analysis is valid and buy more (often called doubling down), since if I'm right the stock is now an even bigger bargain at this price?

Any one of these questions—these emotional dilemmas—can paralyze or panic an investor into making a poor decision. Using a periodic evaluation like the mechanical screens in Unemotional Growth (or even Unemotional Value from part 2), however, eliminates all of these emotional questions and removes any chance of second-guessing yourself. With Unemotional Growth, you will without doubt see both winners and losers and a lot of stocks in between. But you'll never have to agonize over a sell decision because the rankings make them clear-cut for you. If you're updating your Unemotional Growth stocks monthly (as I did in my hypothetical testing), you'll simply generate the current rankings and then follow the discipline ruthlessly. If a stock is no longer in the current rankings, the screen is telling you there's a stock somewhere else that's a better place for your money to be. Put it there. End of discussion. If the stock you already hold is still the best place for your money, it will still be in the rankings when you reevaluate. You can continue to hold it with confidence.

Is the system perfect? Of course not. There's no such thing in investing. If it were perfect, the model portfolio wouldn't have gotten slaughtered along with the rest of the market in the "crash" of October 1987. If it were perfect, it would never pick a loser, or even a stock that goes nowhere. If it were perfect, it would never tell you to sell a stock one month, only to tell you to buy it back a month or two later. (This does happen periodically around the edges of the ranking system. If you're following the rankings precisely, a stock moving from number six to number five one month, and then back to number six the next month, would generate some unnecessary trading. Use common sense here in determining whether to make such a minuscule adjustment to your portfolio.)

But the screen doesn't have to be perfect to be successful. All it has to be is better than average over long stretches of time and the investor using it will generate returns that would be the envy of professional money managers coast to coast. And in using the mechanical nature of the rankings, you never have to wonder whether or not it's the right time to invest in the market. You're always as fully invested as possible, knowing that in the long run, the stock market is the best place to be, and that bull markets tend to run much longer than bear markets. Taking the pain in market downturns is no fun, but it beats sitting on the sidelines trying to guess when to jump back in the market while the market climbs and climbs. Just ask anyone who got out of the market in early 1995 because, with the market at all-time highs, they were fearful of a huge correction. Over the next two years, the Dow Jones Industrial Average went from 4,000 to 8,000. If you're going to talk about risk, make sure you include the risk of missing a great opportunity as well. In addition to keeping you fully invested at all times, of course, the Unemotional screens eliminate the agonizing decisions about what to sell and when to sell. The rankings provide you with all of that information automatically. All you have to do is be disciplined enough and have faith enough to do what the rankings tell you. That's the best way to invest unemotionally.

Let me digress for a few minutes to bring in an analogy from my favorite pastime outside of investing—golf. In golf, each hole and each course has a benchmark against which the golfer can compare his or her score. This score—par—is the theoretical score one would record if the hole is played correctly. A hole with a par of three assumes one shot to reach the green from the tee area and two putts on the green to hole out. A par four assumes two shots to reach the green and two putts, and a par five assumes three shots to reach the green and two putts. On each hole, then, a golfer gets an immediate sense of how well or poorly he is playing. If it takes three shots to get on the green on a par three hole, something went haywire. If a golfer reaches a par four in two shots, but only needs a single putt to finish the hole, he played the hole "under par."

In investing, the major market indices (the Dow Jones Industrial Average and the S&P 500 Index) serve as par, the benchmark against which we can always measure individual stock and portfolio performance. And in golf as well as investing, to beat par is an impressive feat. Par on most golf courses is 72 strokes, and yet the average golfer can't shoot better than 100 if he plays by the rules, counting penalty strokes and not taking "mulligans" (the adult version of those "do-overs" we used to call on the playground). And as I pointed out when I discussed mutual funds, 82 percent of all stock funds over the last ten years couldn't break par either (beat the S&P 500 Index).

The fans, of course, love to see a golfer shoot really low scores. When a superstar beats par by five or six shots on a tough course, all we mere mortals can do is marvel at the effort and dream about playing such a round ourselves. But one doesn't have to be a superstar, posting scores in the low 60s (even the occasional phenomenal score in the 50s), to be remarkably successful as a professional. A golfer with the ability to shoot even par consistently on fine golf courses would rank as one of the best professionals on the PGA Tour. It sounds boring, but it's true. As proof, Golf.com, one of the many Web sites available for the fans to follow the sport, features an area called "Mr. Par." Each week of the regular PGA Tour season, the site tracks the performance of a mythical golfer who shoots even par in every single round of golf in the year. After the first two rounds, if even par is good enough to make the cut (where the tournaments trim the field to the best players that week at the halfway mark of the tournament), Mr. Par gets credit for the amount of money a golfer shooting even par that week would have won. If even par misses the cut, Mr. Par doesn't make a penny that week. Obviously, on tougher golf courses, where the scores aren't as good for the whole field of golfers, Mr. Par's record is much better. On easier courses, Mr. Par is likely to be making early flight reservations after Friday's second round. He won't be playing on the weekend.

Just how well would our boringly consistent par-shooter do over the course of a season? In 1996, Mr. Par would have ranked fifty-fifth on the money list for the PGA Tour, earning a healthy $365,008. To put that in perspective among professionals, the top 125 golfers on the money list earn full exemptions to play the tour the following year, a coveted distinction. The top thirty gain entry into the prestigious Tour Championship that concludes the regular season. So while not quite in the elite among professionals, Mr. Par did quite well for himself without shooting a single spectacular score. Through thirty-four events in the 1997 season, he's doing even better, earning $452,426, good enough for forty-second place on the money list. Amazingly, Mr. Par, Sr., the Senior Tour equivalent to Mr. Par, has done even better in 1997. Earning $605,431 through twenty-eight events, Mr. Par, Sr., is ranked thirteenth on the money list for the Senior PGA Tour.

The point, of course, is that as an investor, you can mark out a similarly impressive record just by keeping pace with the S&P 500 Index over many years. The vast majority of stock mutual funds haven't done it, but you can do that without a second thought, simply by investing in an index fund that mirrors the benchmark. By investing in well-selected individual stocks, however, you should be able to shoot under par and put yourself in the elite group. We've already seen how the Unemotional Value approach has beaten the market indices for several decades, and how the Unemotional Growth approach has shattered the indices' performance over the past decade. So perhaps level par in the investing world isn't really a tough-enough benchmark, but as the professionals have such a hard time beating it, I guess we'll have to leave it in place and concentrate our efforts on consistent outperformance.

Now if you learn best, as I do, by seeing a task accomplished rather than hearing about the process, let's walk through the Unemotional Growth approach for a few months so the process for updating the monthly holdings is clear. (Just ask my golf teacher about the blank looks on my face when he talks about pronation and swing plane. "Oh, it should feel like that? Now I get it!" is more my speed.) And since I've often been accused of being an eternal optimist (how else can I advocate staying fully invested always?), I'll choose a three-month period from the decade's best year, 1991, just to keep the best face on everything. (Keep in mind, though, whether it's been a good month or a bad one, the process is exactly the same.)

The first Friday of 1991 fell on January 4. The first step, then, is to get the list of 100 top-ranked stocks from the January 4 issue of the *Value Line Investment Survey* (you'll find it on page 27 of the section called "Summary and Index"). Then, with the Monday, January 7, issue of *Investor's Business Daily*, which is actually published on Saturday morning, look up each of the 100 stocks, searching for any stock with an EPS ranking of at least 95. When you find one, record both the EPS and RS rankings (listed side by side in *Investor Business Daily*'s stock tables) on a separate sheet of paper. Do this for each stock with a high EPS ranking. On this particular date, eleven of the 100 stocks actually had EPS rankings of 99—the best possible ranking. With so many stocks tied for the top slot, obviously, there's no way to distinguish among them strictly based on EPS rankings, so we have to turn to the relative strength ranking to break the ties.

Here is the list of eleven stocks, sorted by relative strength rankings (the tiebreaker when EPS rankings are identical) for the January 4, 1991, update:

Stock (Symbol)	EPS	RS
American Power Conversion (APCC)	99	98
Intelligent Electronics (INEL)	99	97
Novell (NOVL)	99	97
Blockbuster Entertainment (BV)	99	96
Cordis Corp. (CORD)	99	96
Costco Wholesale (COST)	99	96
Conner Peripherals (CNR)	99	95
Microsoft (MSFT)	99	95
Varian Associates (VAR)	99	91
General Housewares (GHW)	99	88
Wendy's International (WEN)	99	88

To narrow the field down to our top five choices, then, you begin pulling from the top of the list, including American Power Conversion, Intelligent Electronics, and Novell. But three stocks are tied for the fourth and fifth spots in our model with identical rankings of 99 for EPS and 96 for RS. Again, in my hypothetical modeling, I did not try to break such a tie, but included the extra stock, holding six stocks that month instead of five, and weighting all six stocks equally. In reality, you'd be forced to make a decision if you're trying to minimize your trading costs by not completely rebalancing your stock positions each month. But I wanted to keep the test simple and objective, so stocks with identical scores were included even at the risk of including an additional holding in some months.

So for January we have our list of stocks (six of them); let's see how we fared. American Power Conversion returned 9.09 percent, Intelligent Electronics returned 41.46 percent, Novell returned 36.36 percent, Blockbuster Entertainment returned 1.01 percent, Cordis returned 25.58 percent, and Costco Wholesale returned 19.17 percent. Since we assumed an equal-dollar investment in each stock, the overall portfolio return for the month is equal to the average return for the six stocks. And what a month it was! From the close on January 4, 1991, to the close on February 1, 1991 (the first Friday of the month), the Unemotional Growth portfolio soared 22.11 percent. For many investors, that's a fine yearly return, but I warned you that 1991 was an exceptional year. After the recession the previous year, stocks really exploded in 1991. So if we had begun the year with $50,000, our portfolio would now be worth $61,055 going into the second month.

Let's see how things progressed in February. The top five stocks for February will be names familiar from January's rankings:

Stock (Symbol)	EPS	RS
Novell (NOVL)	99	99
American Power Conversion (APCC)	99	98
Intelligent Electronics (INEL)	99	98
Cordis Corp. (CORD)	99	97
Microsoft (MSFT)	99	97

Of the six stocks from January, one fell out of the rankings (Blockbuster Entertainment), which, given its lackluster January performance, isn't surprising. One of the stocks tied for the final slot in January (Costco Wholesale) remained in the sixth position for February, so you would have been perfectly justified to keep it instead of rebalancing to the five "official" Unemotional Growth stocks, but for the sake of consistency in my model, I included only the top five, since there was a clear-cut group of five in February.

Continuing the fine January performance, Novell picked up another 11.67 percent in February, American Power Conversion added 13.89 percent, Intelligent Electronics gained another 16.38 percent, Cordis returned 12.04 percent, and Microsoft gained 5.92 percent. (Incidentally, Costco Wholesale gained 9.57 percent if one had opted to keep six stocks.) The average for the five stocks in February, then, was a gain of 11.98 percent. Because of the way compounded growth works, this 11.98 percent gain isn't simply added to the January gain of 22.11 percent for a total of 34.09 percent. The February gain started from the value at the end of January, compounding the growth. Our $50,000 grew to $61,055 in January, but that entire $61,055 was invested for February. So the 11.98 percent gain equaled an additional $7,314.39. Our portfolio total after February, then, would have been $68,369.39. Compared with our original $50,000, that's a gain after only two months of 36.74 percent. The beauty of any such investment approach is that the long-term gains are cumulative. The entire balance is reinvested each time, so subsequent growth is even more powerful.

On to March. The rankings are very much the same in March as they have been since January. The top five were:

Stock (Symbol)	EPS	RS
Intelligent Electronics (INEL)	99	97
Novell (NOVL)	99	97
Cordis Corp. (CORD)	99	95
Microsoft (MSFT)	99	94
Costco Wholesale (COST)	99	92

Again, one stock from the previous month's group has fallen out of the rankings (American Power Conversion). And Costco Wholesale, which has been sitting in the sixth slot for the previous two months, slides into its place. For the first three months of 1991, then, you'd have had to replace roughly one stock per month (which requires two trades). If you weren't concerned too greatly with keeping each position identically weighted at the start of each month, you could get by with far fewer trades than the ideal model requires, of course. Replacing one stock every month would only require twenty-four trades per year—a much less onerous prospect than fifty or sixty, especially at today's minuscule commissions through deep-discount brokers.

Once again in March, the performance was impressive, another double-digit monthly return of 12.01 percent. The individual stocks performed like this: Intelligent Electronics lost 1.48 percent, Novell gained 14.43 percent, Cordis gained 19.83 percent, Microsoft gained 4.26 percent, and Costco Wholesale added 23.02 percent. Working from a portfolio total after February of $68,369.39, March's gain of 12.01 percent represents a profit for the month of $8,211.16. After the first quarter of 1991, the original $50,000 would have grown to a total of $76,580.55, a gain of 53.16 percent. (I told you 1991 was an astonishing year!)

Over the next three months, the model came back to earth a bit, with three successive losses of 7.20 percent, 0.50 percent, and 0.39 percent. By the year's halfway mark, the model was nevertheless still significantly ahead for the year. The $50,000 starting stake would have been worth $70,435.64, a gain after six months of 40.87 percent. Over the final six months, however, the model returned to its winning ways and posted successive monthly gains of 9.67 percent, 6.92 percent, 11.43 percent, 16.21 percent, 2.95 percent, and 13.63 percent. In a single wonderful year, the model portfolio had recorded a gain of 150.23 percent. Our original $50,000 investment at the beginning of 1991 would have grown to $125,115 by the first Friday of 1992. And all it required was the timeliness rankings from *Value Line* and the earnings per share (EPS) and relative strength (RS) rankings from *Investor's Business Daily* once each month.

Each investor who uses such an approach, of course, will have to decide how often to rebalance the weightings of each position in the portfolio. My model calculations assume that there is a full update and rebalancing every month, but for practical purposes, that isn't always realistic. The example of Costco Wholesale from 1991 shows how being too rigid can generate a lot of trades around the edges of the system that are unnecessarily costly. Selling a stock that slips to number six in the rankings, only to buy it back the following month if it regains the fifth slot, is frivolous, so use your judgment to decide whether a called-for adjustment makes sense. Also, buying or selling a few shares of a stock you already hold, just to bring its weighting in your portfolio into perfect balance, is another costly maneuver you're probably better off skipping.

This is not to say, however, that you should extend such fine-tuning around the edges to which stocks to include on a larger scale. If you start second-guessing the rankings as a whole and substituting freely, you might be better off abandoning the rankings altogether in favor of a much more hands-on analysis of individual stocks. Such an alternative is not a poor plan by any means, but it does call for a much greater commitment of time and much more experience in financial analysis to make such decisions well. Many of the readers of The Motley Fool, especially those with some time and experience to carry research much further than these screens require, will use the Unemotional Growth screen, not so much as a model to copy in its entirety, but as an idea-generating list of stocks that they will then research further for possible investments in their portfolios. As Fools, we're all for this independent-thinking approach, but we recognize that it calls for certain commitments not every investor can make. But whether you're using the Unemotional Growth approach as your entire growth-stock strategy, or simply a launching point for much more individualized financial research into the companies it suggests are potential winners, it's a terrific system for narrowing the thousands of candidates competing for your savings down to a manageable list of top-rated possibilities. Use it as you feel it fits your own investing needs and talents the best.

As I mentioned earlier, one of the concerns for many investors contemplating the use of the Unemotional Growth approach is the cost of trading on such an aggressive schedule. Even at deep-discount rates, it's important to keep an eye on trading costs as a percentage of the total portfolio to make sure you're not giving away too much of your hoped-for profits in commissions to your broker.

If you recall, a general rule of thumb is that one's trading costs should be kept under 2.5 percent of the total portfolio value each year. Let's say that in most months, the Unemotional Growth model requires you to replace one stock, and in a few months, two stocks are replaced. Such a rotation schedule would run approximately thirty trades per year. At the low end of the deep-discount broker rate range, that will run a minimum of $300 a year. At a bare minimum, then, you'll need to commit $12,000 to this strategy to keep trading costs under our benchmark. If the rankings prove more volatile or you're paying more per trade than $10, you'll probably have to start with somewhat more, perhaps even $20,000.

As for taxes, the majority of gains using such an aggressive approach will be short-term profits (on stocks held less than one year). As such, they'll be taxed at whatever your ordinary income tax rate is, not the more favorable long-term capital gains rates. If you're in one of the higher tax brackets, you have to keep an eye on this issue as another hidden cost. It's virtually impossible to generalize about the effects of taxes on one's returns, given the diverse nature of federal and state income tax rates, but, nevertheless, it's an issue every investor has to be aware of.

A word of caution about taxes, however. Don't choose your investment strategy simply based on what the total tax liability might be. The amount of taxes you pay to Uncle Sam isn't the important issue; the real issue is your after-tax return. If you end up paying more taxes with one strategy, but also end up with a larger gain as well, that's still a better plan than accepting a smaller after-tax return, even though you may be saving on your tax bill next April.

One method many readers of The Motley Fool have adopted as a measure to control trading costs (alas, it does nothing to help with the potential tax bite) is to lengthen the holding cycle for their Unemotional Growth portfolios from one month to two or three months. As you can see from the brief example of the month-to-month changes in the 1991 historical returns, the composition of the stocks included in the top rankings each month isn't particularly volatile. And logically, of course, there's a good reason for this short-term stability. As the earnings per share screen is one of our primary tools, and companies only report updated earnings results once per quarter, it's to be expected that the EPS ranking in *Investor's Business Daily* will remain relatively stable between quarterly earnings report seasons. By updating every quarter instead of every month, especially for investors who are on the borderline of having enough money to commit to this strategy and its potential costs, it is possible to reduce the number of trades required each year without affecting the basic premise of the strategy significantly. At the request of several of our online readers, I ran a limited historical test using a quarterly cycle rather than a monthly update and the results were still very good. In the periods I checked, the returns for the quarterly model only underperformed the monthly model by a few percentage points per year, suggesting that for very cost-conscious investors, the trade-off between slightly lower returns and lower trading costs may be a worthwhile consideration.

The most likely way to save on trading costs, however, is in the rebalancing of each position. My historical model assumes, of course, that at the beginning of each month, all stocks are reweighted equally. Actually implementing that procedure, however, leads to a lot of trading that is simply unjustified. In order to test the theory, I didn't want to let any single stock of a five-stock group exert an undue influence on the results by letting it grow unchecked. The returns in a terrific period would be exaggerated in the model's favor that way, and, likewise, the returns in a weak period for an overweighted stock would understate the effectiveness of the model in selecting an entire group of stocks.

In real-life investing, however, you're not going to make such fine adjustments frequently if doing so costs you too much in additional trading costs (both commissions and spreads). As I explained earlier, the idea behind rebalancing one's positions is to keep the risk attached to any single position spread evenly among the whole portfolio. You want to avoid one stock dominating the entire group lest a meltdown in that stock ruin your entire portfolio return. So use the theory about rebalancing in a real-world context. Don't bother rebalancing the positions every time you update your holdings. It's possible that the rotation cycle will take care of most of your rebalancing concerns as stocks cycle through your portfolio over the course of a year. When and if a stock starts to grow beyond reasonable boundaries, however, consider rebalancing it at one of your regularly scheduled updates. That way, each month, if you only need to replace one stock, you're faced with two trades rather than six (two trades to replace the one stock and four more trades to rebalance the held-over positions precisely). A little flexibility on this aspect of the model will not only save you quite a bit in trading costs, but will also help protect you against the risk of any one stock having an undue influence over the entire portfolio, especially with a group as concentrated as the five-stock Unemotional Growth screen.

Another risk management topic with the sometimes volatile Unemotional Growth screen that comes up frequently in our online discussions on The Motley Fool's message boards is the technique of using sell-stop orders to abandon ship if things look bad. Just to reprise, the most common type of sell order is when you call your broker (or place an order electronically) to sell a stock "at the market." That means you want to sell the stock right now and you'll take whatever the prevailing market price is at the time your order is executed, usually within a few seconds. A sell-stop order, though, is designed to be a safety net of sorts. It's an order placed with a broker to sell a stock position, not right this minute, but in the event that the stock price slides to a price predetermined by you. For example, if you own a stock currently trading at $50 a share and you've decided that you won't accept a loss greater than $10 a share (20 percent below where the stock currently trades), you can place a sell-stop order that instructs your broker to sell the stock immediately if it trades at or below $40 a share. Keep in mind, that's not a guarantee you'll be able to get $40 a share. If the stock plunges rapidly on bad news, for example, it may drop right through $40 to a lower level without ever trading at your specified price. The order will be executed the first time the stock trades at or below your limit, even if that price is significantly lower than your limit price. That said, in most cases, stop-loss orders are filled at or very near the price you specify. Sounds like a great insurance policy, doesn't it? Using them can be a great way to limit your potential losses while your potential gains are still limitless, right? As you might suspect, it's never that easy.

The crucial question if you're to use sell-stops as a regular part of your investment strategy is where to place them. Do you choose a fixed percentage loss for each stock below the purchase price? Do you adjust the stop-loss if the stock price rises, to lock in your gains on the way up? What percentage should you use? Should you use some kind of technical analysis like a moving average of the stock's price over the last 50 or 200 days to set the stop-loss level? Or some more esoteric technical indicator from complicated charting techniques? There are as many possibilities as there are proponents of sell-stop orders. But I have yet to see a simple and effective way of setting sell-stop orders that actually saved more money than it ultimately cost the investor.

William O'Neil, in his longtime best-seller *How to Make Money in Stocks*, discusses the use of sell-stops as part of his method called C.A.N.S.L.I.M., a technique very much in the price-momentum camp of investing. O'Neil advocates buying only a small number of stocks and then watching them like a hawk on a daily basis. He advocates setting sell-stop orders at 7 percent below one's purchase price for the stock. His reasoning is that everyone makes mistakes in picking stocks. He wants to get out of his mistakes immediately and look elsewhere for another stock.

Other theories suggest a somewhat looser level, say 15 percent or even 20 percent below one's purchase price, and then perhaps one should keep adjusting the sell-stop higher every time the price of the stock increases, perhaps 20 percent or 25 percent below whatever the most recent highest price was.

Many months ago, I, too, was caught up in the desire to find a sell-stop approach that would protect my portfolio against mistakes or huge downturns in the market. The memory of October 1987 is still fresh in many investors' minds, even a decade later. My thinking was that surely I could find some way to have saved some of that massive loss in a single month, or saved at least a portion of the losses in some of the worst stock picks over the decade's history for Unemotional Growth. Even cutting the losses at 25 percent for the worst performers might raise the overall returns a couple of percentage points per year. And over thirty years or so, you know how much even a couple of percentage points per year can mean to compounded growth. And in my mind, it was a marvelous theory. In practice, though?

Several months ago, a group of regular readers in the Foolish Workshop message board on our America Online site picked up the enthusiasm I had for developing some sort of sell-stop program for the Unemotional Growth model and began a systematic test of a variety of sell-stop systems on a long list of stocks included in the model's history. Looking at each day's range of high and low prices for a stock, one can re-create the sequence of events over many months to see what the actual effect of a sell-stop discipline might be. If your sell-stop discipline is that no loss can be larger than 15 percent from the stock's purchase price, you have to check every day's prices (not just closing prices in the newspaper, but the daily highs and lows) to see if the stock ever traded at that level during the period you would have been holding it.

The big danger with sell-stops is the very painful whipsaw that I mentioned earlier. Anyone who's ever used sell-stops for any length of time knows about being whipsawed. A stock you own starts to slide, so you place a sell-stop order to protect yourself against a big loss, only to see your stop triggered and the very next day the stock recovers and continues on to new highs. It's one of the most frustrating feelings you can imagine, and it happens all too often. It doesn't matter if the stock closed the month 50 percent higher; if your sell-stop was triggered somewhere along the way during the month, your discipline would have sold you out of the position and someone else made money on the big gain, not you.

What the research study compiled by this group pointed out is that at almost every percentage level, sell-stops cost investors more in the losses associated with getting whipsawed (both the actual loss at the time of the sale and the opportunity loss when the stock goes back up without you) than it saved them in protection against those occasions when a stock decision really was poor and the position fell apart. In other words, stops were lousy protection in the historical test. Simply holding the stocks throughout the whole period proved more profitable, even with the many bad stocks every investor will buy at some point and the market weakness in 1987 and again in 1990 and 1994, than any sell-stop discipline we could devise that wasn't extremely loose (30 percent to 40 percent below one's purchase price, at which point you have to wonder, Why bother?).

The volatility of many stocks, especially the more aggressive stocks that often grace the Unemotional Growth rankings, makes tight sell-stops especially impractical. Some of the more famous computer-related stocks, for example, can have daily swings of 10 percent or more as part of their normal patterns. Can you imagine trying to manage 7 percent sell-stop losses with such stocks? You might have picked a real winner and yet get stopped out the very next day because of the stock's volatility.

Like any attempt at market timing, what sounds wonderful in theory isn't always helpful in practice, and sell-stops are no exception. Everyone can point to examples where a sell-stop has saved him a bundle. But there are just as many examples where they've cost investors a bundle. Over the long run, I haven't seen a sell-stop approach that works well enough to justify the added complexity and cost of the extra trading. If someone develops one that is demonstrably useful, I'm all for it. But I've given up that particular quest for now after seeing the results of our own research into the topic. Take your lumps when they come, confident that if you're using a winning strategy, the long-term results will take care of themselves.

There you have it, Foolish reader, the completely unemotional strategy for identifying a group of potential growth-stock champions once a month (or once a quarter). Whether you use it as a model unto itself for your portfolio or as a starting screen for further Foolish research into the individual companies, it's a way of eliminating guesswork and self-doubt from the equation and greatly cutting the time you must spend on managing your investment portfolio if you want to invest directly in stocks rather than in mutual funds.

Unemotional Growth Models' Monthly Performance,

Top 5

Year	Jan.	Feb.	March	April	May	June
1987	20.25%	6.06%	3.97%	1.09%	5.82%	3.18%
1988	-13.58%	13.92%	-0.08%	10.20%	2.00%	4.03%
1989	16.89%	-3.66%	6.63%	11.51%	17.61%	-1.55%
1990	-0.61%	0.82%	4.39%	-0.37%	2.85%	-0.76%
1991	22.11%	11.98%	12.01%	-7.20%	-0.50%	-0.39%
1992	11.20%	-7.59%	-3.88%	-10.92%	3.64%	-4.44%
1993	15.11%	-2.65%	-0.19%	10.13%	6.03%	-0.35%
1994	3.57%	6.48%	-5.79%	-2.24%	-3.47%	-4.40%
1995	3.74%	11.79%	6.47%	1.38%	5.57%	25.54%
1996	18.10%	7.25%	13.91%	9.92%	14.31%	-4.66%
1997	-8.55%	-9.44%	-10.81%	18.35%	9.27%	11.32%

Top 10

Year	Jan.	Feb.	March	April	May	June
1987	20.27%	6.32%	5.25%	-3.01%	6.41%	1.02%
1988	-10.32%	14.01%	-1.17%	6.53%	0.70%	7.08%
1989	8.61%	0.62%	6.07%	7.87%	10.07%	-3.76%
1990	-8.02%	0.50%	8.38%	-1.48%	12.75%	-1.02%
1991	21.84%	8.93%	14.34%	-4.13%	1.53%	-3.85%
1992	7.32%	-3.05%	-3.47%	-7.01%	1.42%	-4.31%
1993	14.87%	-3.24%	0.90%	3.02%	7.54%	3.31%
1994	2.01%	0.40%	-4.09%	0.11%	-5.14%	-7.09%
1995	6.37%	8.70%	-0.06%	3.97%	6.11%	23.73%
1996	9.81%	3.31%	7.53%	6.63%	8.95%	-1.36%
1997	-3.08%	-8.26%	-8.30%	10.76%	7.73%	8.90%

January 1987 Through August 1997

July	Aug.	Sept.	Oct.	Nov.	Dec.	Total
4.23%	−2.41%	13.09%	−37.48%	−6.12%	22.77%	**21.32%**
−5.40%	−9.25%	8.23%	−3.29%	−2.26%	5.17%	**6.25%**
5.41%	5.92%	22.20%	7.01%	3.26%	−7.57%	**86.53%**
−17.50%	−7.51%	−3.83%	1.14%	24.76%	−1.58%	**−3.06%**
9.67%	6.92%	11.43%	16.21%	2.95%	13.63%	**150.23%**
7.81%	2.83%	6.26%	17.35%	6.51%	7.90%	**38.44%**
−1.91%	−1.06%	2.37%	−1.36%	1.01%	5.19%	**35.52%**
2.90%	4.98%	−3.47%	12.00%	−3.51%	−1.41%	**4.14%**
−0.10%	11.04%	−6.38%	8.59%	−5.63%	−13.10%	**53.43%**
−0.38%	−4.94%	11.24%	−5.04%	6.24%	2.32%	**87.95%**
8.21%	1.20%					**16.45%**
				Total 1987–96		**3,186%**
				CAGR 1987–96		**41.80%**

July	Aug.	Sept.	Oct.	Nov.	Dec.	Total
6.98%	1.75%	7.23%	−35.61%	−7.63%	28.54%	**25.21%**
−6.89%	−5.28%	8.14%	−2.75%	−2.29%	4.02%	**9.42%**
6.71%	3.03%	12.33%	−7.99%	2.92%	−2.01%	**51.79%**
−17.43%	−7.27%	−4.98%	−0.30%	18.29%	−2.32%	**−7.68%**
9.75%	1.15%	1.72%	12.97%	4.48%	16.11%	**119.79%**
7.71%	1.90%	5.24%	15.19%	5.48%	10.96%	**41.15%**
1.67%	2.30%	1.27%	−0.39%	−0.26%	2.56%	**37.76%**
0.82%	6.68%	−1.91%	6.10%	−2.86%	1.05%	**−4.77%**
1.59%	5.58%	−6.42%	9.72%	−10.57%	−12.41%	**36.07%**
−3.42%	−2.17%	10.22%	−7.12%	8.70%	−0.07%	**46.87%**
8.45%	0.66%					**15.66%**
				Total 1987–96		**1,462%**
				CAGR 1987–96		**31.63%**

Summary

One more time, let's lay out the steps used to determine the Unemotional Growth stocks.

- Begin with the 100 timely stocks from the *Value Line Investment Survey* (located on page 27 of the weekly "Summary and Index").
- Look up each of these 100 stocks in the latest issue of *Investor's Business Daily* and record both the earnings per share (EPS) and relative strength (RS) rankings for every stock. You'll find these rankings just to the left of the company's name in the daily stock tables. (A timesaving hint: Don't bother recording anything for stocks that have an EPS ranking under 90; they won't be in your elite group at the end.)
- Sort the stocks in descending order by the earnings per share ranking. You're likely to have many with rankings of 99 or 98, so use the relative strength (RS) ranking to break ties where needed.
- Select the top five (or ten) and purchase in equal-dollar amounts (not equal-share amounts).
- One month later, evaluate the stock list again and adjust your portfolio as necessary, selling any stocks no longer on the Unemotional Growth list, adjusting any positions if necessary to maintain a reasonable position balance, and buying the new stocks on the list. (Remember that it's optional whether you adjust the weighting of each position as you update. Rebalancing less frequently can save quite a bit in trading costs.)

Now that you understand both the longer-term Unemotional Value and shorter-term Unemotional Growth cycles, which should you use? Or can you put them together? In part 4, "Putting It All Together," I'll suggest some ways you can use the models in tandem, take you through a full sample year, and then in part 5 address a series of related questions that are frequently asked in our online forum. Still with me, Fool? Let's wrap these models into a neat package and let you get started on your unemotional investing career.

PART FOUR

Putting It All Together

In parts 2 and 3, I outlined a pair of investment models with different strategic focuses, Unemotional Value and Unemotional Growth. The Unemotional Value approach is designed to identify out-of-favor giants, blue chip stocks from the Dow Jones Industrial Average that are down on their luck relative to the rest of the thirty stocks in the average. The strategy calls for holding these stocks a minimum of one year (or perhaps eighteen months in order to take advantage of the new tax laws), allowing the stocks time to recover. Over the long haul, such an approach has come close to doubling the annual returns of the major market indices Wall Street professionals struggle to match. The second strategy, Unemotional Growth, is an earnings momentum approach, designed to identify those companies that are producing earnings on the bottom line that are better than those of almost all other companies, and which should continue their winning ways in the coming months and quarters. Again, a winning strategy, which over the last decade, at least, has blown the top off the returns meter, posting annualized gains of better than 40 percent a year since 1987.

One drawback common to both strategies, of course, is that they only select a handful of stocks each. Using either one in isolation means adopting a portfolio strategy that's extremely concentrated in a few stocks. With that kind of high concentration, the risk of any single stock blowing up and devastating the entire portfolio is much higher than with a more diversified portfolio. As I mentioned previously, with five stocks, if one of them gets cut in half by a catastrophic event, 10 percent of your entire portfolio would be gone at a single blow. With ten stocks, that concentration risk is halved. A 50 percent decline in a single stock would then only represent a 5 percent loss for the overall portfolio.

An obvious solution would be to combine the two strategies into a ten-stock portfolio. Not only does this diversify the holdings in number, reducing the individual stock risk to the portfolio, but it also marries two different strategies that can work well as complementary approaches. Investment strategies go in and out of fashion on Wall Street almost faster than hemlines rise and fall. One quarter, traditional value investing may be favored. Another quarter, earnings momentum (often called growth investing) may be in vogue. The labels themselves are a bit unhelpful because no investor buys a stock he doesn't feel would be a good *value*, and, likewise, every investment is presumably chosen to achieve *growth*. For better or worse, however, mainstream investing seems to be divided into two camps, which get labeled value and growth. The Unemotional Value and Unemotional Growth approaches incorporate those names, not so much for a lack of imagination on my part (something I can be accused of in all too many areas), but to give an indication of the kind of approach each is. Used together, though, each approach acts as a balance for the other. When value investing is stagnant, growth investing may be enjoying a resurgence, and vice versa. Using both strategies allows one to falter for a while without hurting overall returns because the other strategy is likely to be succeeding. That way, not only are both successful in the long run, but the combination of them helps to smooth out the peaks and valleys along the way. And there's a lot to be said for sleeping well at night!

If you wish to use both strategies, then, do you simply split your investment money in half and invest it equally in each of the portfolios? That's one way to do it and no one could ever fault you for it. But there are some other concerns you may want to consider in deciding how to weight the two strategies in your own portfolio.

Conventional wisdom, the kind you'll often hear from the talking heads on the cable business news channels and from full-time financial planners, tells you that as you get older, you can't afford as much risk as when you were young and spry. When you're young, a loss in the market isn't supposed to be as devastating because (1) you have more working years ahead of you to make up for the loss, and (2) you probably don't have as much invested when you're young, thus the magnitude of the loss is reduced. So conventional wisdom tells you to start pulling out of the stock market as you approach retirement and switch the bulk of your assets toward fixed-income investments where the principal is protected. A formula you'll often hear is that you should subtract your age from 100 and that's the percentage of your investments that should be invested in the stock market, with the rest in bonds or other fixed-income instruments. For example, a thirty-year-old would have only 30 percent in bonds and the rest in stocks. A retired investor at age seventy would have 70 percent in bonds and only 30 percent exposed to stocks.

As you know from reading part 1, Fools don't have a lot of patience with conventional wisdom. Besides settling for much lower returns by pulling out of the market, the ravages of inflation can make a long retirement a financial nightmare if your money is in fixed-income investments. The worker who retires at sixty today is still looking at a possibility of two, even three or four, decades through which time he'll need his investments working for him, not just marking time with inflation.

So let's turn conventional wisdom on its head. Instead of pulling money out of the market as you get older in favor of historically weaker investment alternatives, let's use good old conventional wisdom's formula a different way. I've already suggested in part 1 that even a retired investor should remain fully invested in the stock market, but I do think such an investor might get more conservative with his investment style within the stock market. Using the subtract-your-age-from-100 formula, let's come up with a different way of looking at the problem. Take your age, subtract it from 100 (round off to the nearest ten if you like), and that's the percentage of your stock portfolio you should consider being more aggressive with, perhaps in an approach like Unemotional Growth. The rest should be in a more conservative approach like Unemotional Value. If you're forty, for example, you might consider being more aggressive with 60 percent of your portfolio and put 40 percent into the core holdings represented by Unemotional Value.

As you age, then, you gradually shift the weighting of your portfolio from more aggressive stocks to more conservative ones, but you never pull out of the stock market altogether. Even in your retirement, your portfolio should be able to keep growing beyond your annual spending requirements and your investments should sustain you indefinitely. If you start saving and investing early enough in life, the percentage of your portfolio you'll have to pull out to finance your spending needs in retirement each year will be small enough that even if the market goes through a protracted bear market of several years, your financial position should remain secure.

Once you've determined how you wish to split your money between the two approaches, you must still decide how to administer the split weightings. For example, a forty-year-old investor with $50,000 to invest might opt to put $20,000 (40 percent) into Unemotional Value stocks and the other $30,000 (60 percent) into Unemotional Growth stocks. How many stocks from each model should he buy?

There are two possibilities for determining how to split up your money. Perhaps the easiest is simply to decide how many stocks from each model you want to hold and then always include that many, regardless of the amount of money being invested with each strategy. If our hypothetical forty-year-old investor decides he always wants five Unemotional Value and five Unemotional Growth stocks, he would take the $20,000 earmarked for Unemotional Value and split it evenly among the top five stocks in the current rankings, $4,000 in each stock. And the $30,000 he has set aside for Unemotional Growth would also be split up five ways, $6,000 each in the top-ranked Unemotional Growth stocks. As he gets older, the percentages and the dollar amounts would change, of course, but he's always going to hold five Dow stocks (Unemotional Value) and five aggressive growth stocks (Unemotional Growth).

Another method is to keep the dollar value going into each stock even, but to change the number of stocks one would buy from each category. For example, our forty-year-old investor wants to invest 40 percent in Unemotional Value and 60 percent in Unemotional

Growth, but he wants to keep the dollar amount invested in every stock the same in order to keep the risk evenly distributed. With a ten-stock portfolio, the other alternative is to buy four Unemotional Value stocks and six Unemotional Growth stocks, each stock weighted with the same investment amount. An older investor, for instance, might buy six or seven Unemotional Value stocks and only three or four Unemotional Growth stocks as a way of shifting the balance of his portfolio toward the less volatile Dow stocks, while always holding ten equally weighted positions.

Either method can work, so choose a system that works for you in splitting your money between the different strategies. In fact, ten stocks isn't a magic number (although it's easy to work with). If you prefer a little more diversity, there's nothing wrong with holding fifteen or twenty stocks. (When you start getting beyond twenty stocks, as an individual investor, you're probably trading performance for the extra diversity. You will get most of the diversity you'll ever need in the first fifteen to twenty stocks if they don't all represent the same industry. Beyond that simply adds unnecessarily to trading costs.)

A Year in the Life

To show you how this kind of portfolio management style can work, let me present an extended example, a full year in the life of a joint Unemotional Value / Unemotional Growth portfolio. To make things simple, let's assume a fifty-year-old investor, Ivan T. B. Rich (say it slowly with your best Dracula voice). Ivan came into 1996 with a portfolio worth $100,000.

Ivan wants to keep everything simple, so he'll buy ten stocks, five each from the Unemotional Value and Unemotional Growth rankings, investing $10,000 initially in each stock. The Unemotional Value stocks, of course, are not adjusted at all throughout the year. The original five choices are left alone until the beginning of 1997. The Unemotional Growth stocks, however, are to be adjusted each month. For the sake of simplicity, I'm going to omit trading costs from this sample year, but Ivan is electronically savvy enough that he's opted for a deep-discount brokerage account with an Internet-only broker, so his cost per trade is only $10. If you're worried about those costs for the sample, we'll pretend Ivan mailed a check to his broker each month for the amount of that month's commissions and we'll call it even.

January

Time to get started. A new year is beginning and Ivan has $100,000 to invest for 1996. Even though 1995 was a great year for stocks, Ivan won't be deterred. He believes in staying fully invested through weak and strong markets rather than attempting the futile task of timing the markets. With the $50,000 Ivan has set aside for the five Unemotional Value stocks, here's what he bought for 1996 ($10,000 in each stock):

International Paper (IP)
Chevron (CHV)
Caterpillar (CAT)
Minnesota Mining & Manufacturing (MMM)
DuPont (DD)

And to begin the year, January's five Unemotional Growth stocks (also $10,000 in each) were:

Cisco Systems (CSCO)
PeopleSoft (PSFT)
HBO & Co. (HBOC)
Linear Technology (LLTC)
Applied Materials (AMAT)

Instead of rebalancing every position every month (as our hypothetical model did), Ivan will take the more practical route of rebalancing a position that remains in the Unemotional Growth section of the portfolio only when it gets grossly out of line with the values of the other four stocks. (With the average position being 20 percent for each of the five stocks, a level for any one stock of 30 percent or 35 percent of the total value might be an appropriate danger signal.) That will keep trading to a minimum, saving both hassles and money. For the rest of the year, though, the Unemotional Value stocks are off-limits; in fact, we won't even look at them over the course of the year. We'll simply focus our monthly attention on the $50,000 invested in the Unemotional Growth half of the portfolio. Off we go. Ivan's placed his orders and we have a month to watch.

February

January was a great month for Ivan's Unemotional Growth stocks! Here are the values per stock after the first month. Remember that he started with $10,000 in each one:

Cisco Systems (CSCO)	$11,818
PeopleSoft (PSFT)	$11,814
HBO & Co. (HBOC)	$12,050
Linear Technology (LLTC)	$12,535
Applied Materials (AMAT)	$10,821
Total Value	$59,038

A $9,000 profit in a single month! That represents a gain of over 18 percent in January alone for the Unemotional Growth half of the portfolio. Don't expect too many months like this, but it's certainly a great way to launch a new year.

For February, two stocks need to be replaced. Linear Technology and Applied Materials both disappeared from the rankings, to be replaced by KEMET Corp. and Micro Warehouse. Ivan left the other three stocks alone, sold Linear Technology and Applied Materials, and split the proceeds ($23,356) between the two new stocks. Head to that winter resort and check back at the beginning of March.

March

February turned out to be a decent month overall, despite a loss in one stock (KEMET Corp.). Here are the values for each position as Ivan heads into March:

Cisco Systems (CSCO)	$12,727
PeopleSoft (PSFT)	$12,945
HBO & Co. (HBOC)	$13,583
KEMET Corp. (KMET)	$10,009
Micro Warehouse (MWHS)	$14,078
Total Value	$63,342

A gain in February of more than 7 percent gives him a profit after two months of better than $13,000 (26.68 percent) so far in 1996 on this part of his portfolio. Obviously, that's not a bad *year* in many cases, so Ivan thanks his good fortune, but he doesn't look for an exit. He forges on. There is now a little disparity between the largest and smallest positions, but the largest is just 22 percent of the portfolio while the smallest is still 16 percent, so the imbalance isn't enough to cause Ivan to rebalance any positions quite yet. To the choices for March! Again in March, two stocks require replacement, the poor performer in February (KEMET Corp.) and, surprisingly, the solid performer from last month (Micro Warehouse). This happens on occasion, however, as new earnings reports come out and the *Value Line* timeliness rankings shift. The other three stocks (from the original January selections) remain in the group. So, time for Ivan to sell two stocks and reinvest the proceeds ($24,087) in his two new holdings, JLG Industries and Parametric Technology. It's starting to get warmer; clean the rust off your golf clubs and start getting that putting stroke back into form.

April

March was another strong month, mostly thanks to newcomer JLG Industries' explosive 42 percent gain for the month. Here are the balances going into April:

Cisco Systems (CSCO)	$13,566
PeopleSoft (PSFT)	$13,542
HBO & Co. (HBOC)	$14,759
JLG Industries (JLGI)	$17,084
Parametric Technology (PMTC)	$12,990
Total Value	$71,941

A big gain for March of better than 13 percent gave Ivan a profit of nearly $22,000 (43.88 percent) after just one quarter of 1996—a phenomenal start to any year. The largest position is 24 percent of the total value and the smallest is 18 percent of the total, so no radical adjustments are called for yet. Let's pick up the April rankings. In

April, Ivan faces one of those dilemmas the investor faces when trying to save money on trading costs. All five of the March stocks remain in the top six positions in April's rankings, with a new stock, Oxford Health Plans, appearing with them in the top six positions. Should Ivan replace a stock that's still in the sixth position because a new one has shown up, or is this unnecessary fiddling around the edges of the rankings? There's no perfect answer, of course. If you're following the rankings precisely, you would make the switch, but as Ivan is already cutting costs by not rebalancing every month, he's likely to stick it out with his current five stocks rather than make a switch for that minor adjustment in the rankings. (As it turns out, both the stock he would have replaced, Parametric Technology, and the new stock, Oxford Health Plans, had similar gains in April, so the decision didn't affect the returns significantly.) So, throughout the April showers, Ivan held the same five stocks he had in March.

May

April turned out to be another fine month for Ivan's holdings, with all five stocks posting respectable gains. (Don't forget that 1996 was a good year for the overall stock market. Nevertheless, the S&P 500 was only up by about 5 percent through the first four months, so the success of the Unemotional Growth stocks during the same period can't simply be written off to that annoying cliché, "A rising tide floats all boats.") Here are the values for Ivan's holdings heading into May:

Cisco Systems (CSCO)	$14,160
PeopleSoft (PSFT)	$15,648
HBO & Co. (HBOC)	$16,470
JLG Industries (JLGI)	$18,982
Parametric Technology (PMTC)	$13,850
Total Value	$79,110

Another near double-digit gain in one month (9.97 percent) brings Ivan's four-month profit to $29,110 (58.22 percent). So how are Ivan's Unemotional Value stocks doing? Nope, not allowed to look yet—eight months to go before what they've done matters to us. Let's look at the Unemotional Growth rankings for May. As with

April, all five of Ivan's current stocks are still in the top six or seven slots for May, so rather than make unnecessary trades around the edges, Ivan's going to keep costs low and stick with what he already has. The flowers are blooming, Ivan's got his golf handicap back down into single digits, and his portfolio's having a heck of a year. Will it continue? There's no way to tell, of course, so his best course of action is to stick with his strategy—unemotional investing.

June

It's beginning to get monotonous, isn't it? Each month another terrific gain? Well, Ivan doesn't think so and he loves the results from May. Here are the dollar values as Ivan heads into June:

Cisco Systems (CSCO)	$15,628
PeopleSoft (PSFT)	$17,471
HBO & Co. (HBOC)	$18,252
JLG Industries (JLGI)	$26,706
Parametric Technology (PMTC)	$16,087
Total Value	$94,144

Another mammoth month, with the group gaining 19 percent. JLG Industries continues on its tear with another 40-percent-plus gain in a single month. By now it's grown to 28 percent of the portfolio and is a large-enough percentage that Ivan needs to consider spreading some money around to even things up. If JLG Industries gets above 30 percent of the total, Ivan will make some adjustments. For June, the same stocks Ivan's been holding for a few months now are still all among the top six in the rankings so he makes no changes. Will June bring another nice gain and push the portfolio over the 100 percent profit mark in a remarkably short six months? (It stands at a profit of 88.29 percent after May.)

July

It finally happened. The consecutive winning streak ended after five months, but June's loss was very small and after such an amazing spurt was hardly unexpected. Here are the stock values after the first half of 1996:

Cisco Systems (CSCO)	$15,662
PeopleSoft (PSFT)	$17,282
HBO & Co. (HBOC)	$19,037
JLG Industries (JLGI)	$26,183
Parametric Technology (PMTC)	$14,969
Total Value	$93,133

After June's breather, Ivan's still resting on a gain of 86.27 percent after six months. Is June's dip a sign of things to come, or is it just a pause in an otherwise remarkable ascent? Let's see what July and the heat of the summer have in store. Again, no trades were necessary as all five of Ivan's stocks remained in the top six positions. (Incidentally, the sixth stock is still Oxford Health Plans. The rankings just haven't changed dramatically in the previous four months.)

August

After gaining more than 115 percent in the four previous months, JLG Industries finally lost its balance and dropped 11 percent in August. Stocks that go on amazing runs like this often give back quite a bit of their gains quickly as well, so it's important not to let one stock begin to determine the whole outcome for an entire portfolio. JLG Industries never did reach Ivan's danger zone where it was 30 percent or more of the total value, but it was close. And as the largest position, when it sheds 11 percent, the effect is felt a little more powerfully than if the stock had been weighted evenly with all the others. Letting winners ride, then, is a risky venture. While they're climbing, that compounded growth is terrific, but when they start to tumble, it can get ugly. JLG Industries is only off 11 percent, but there's no way to predict whether that's a portent or just a pause. Here are the values for the five stocks after July:

Cisco Systems (CSCO)	$15,628
PeopleSoft (PSFT)	$18,979
HBO & Co. (HBOC)	$18,894
JLG Industries (JLGI)	$23,303
Parametric Technology (PMTC)	$15,743
Total Value	$92,547

Two small consecutive monthly losses have reduced the year-to-date gain to 85.09 percent, but since this model is tied so closely to quarterly earnings reports, it's not unusual to see a third month follow in the same pattern of the previous two. What does August have in store? Once again, no trades were necessary, as all five of Ivan's stocks were still among the top six slots.

September

Another down month has Ivan beginning to question himself. This is the single hardest factor to overcome in investing. When things aren't going your way, it's natural to begin doubting and second-guessing your strategy. "Maybe it won't work any longer?" "Maybe there's something different this time?" All natural questions, of course, but also the quickest way to get yourself into trouble. Remember that styles of investment and segments of the stock market go in and out of favor rapidly. Be patient with a good strategy and let it do the work for you. After a third down month, then, here are the values in Ivan's Unemotional Growth half of the portfolio:

Cisco Systems (CSCO)	$14,929
PeopleSoft (PSFT)	$17,848
HBO & Co. (HBOC)	$15,293
JLG Industries (JLGI)	$20,947
Parametric Technology (PMTC)	$16,346
Total Value	$85,363

The loss of almost 8 percent in August dragged the year-to-date profit down to 70.73 percent, still nothing to bemoan, but certainly not as thrilling as the position Ivan was sitting in three months earlier. That's the nature of stock investing, however. If your progress advances three steps for every two you must retreat, though, you'll be a very happy investor in the long run. On to September. Perhaps a three-month retreat is all Ivan will have to endure. Again, no changes are necessary to the holdings for September.

October

Off to the races again for Ivan's holdings. While JLG Industries gave up another 3 percent, the other four stocks all bounced back with a vengeance, making September another impressive month. Heading into October and the final quarter of 1996, here's how Ivan's portfolio stands:

Cisco Systems (CSCO)	$18,740
PeopleSoft (PSFT)	$21,871
HBO & Co. (HBOC)	$18,679
JLG Industries (JLGI)	$20,291
Parametric Technology (PMTC)	$17,680
Total Value	$97,261

In one month, Ivan's portfolio regained all of the losses in the previous three months and then some. For the year, the Unemotional Growth portion of the portfolio is ahead 94.52 percent. (No peeking at the Unemotional Value portion yet.) The rankings for October finally call for a change. JLG Industries has slipped to the border of the rankings, and after four successive losing months (and one of them coming as the rest of the stocks were rising), it's probably a safe assumption that whatever momentum the stock carried when Ivan first bought it is long gone. So out with it and bring in a new stock in the top five spots, 3Com Corp.

November

October was another give-back month, but nothing significant. Here's how the five stocks looked heading into November:

Cisco Systems (CSCO)	$16,853
PeopleSoft (PSFT)	$23,380
HBO & Co. (HBOC)	$17,110
3Com Corp. (COMS)	$21,147
Parametric Technology (PMTC)	$16,713
Total Value	$95,203

Ivan's portfolio is still trying to bust through for a magic *double*, when one achieves a 100 percent gain or more in a single year, but he can't seem to get over the final hurdle. Can he do it in November? The rankings for November are beginning to change enough so that Ivan has to say farewell to two of his original stocks, Cisco Systems and HBO & Co. The proceeds from those two sales ($33,963) are split between his two new stocks, Tellabs and Papa John's International.

December

Thanksgiving brought Ivan a few more pounds to work off on the StairMaster, and a slight bounce-back from October's minor dip. Of the five stocks, three posted gains in October, with 3Com Corp. and Parametric Technology notching double-digit advances. Here are the values of Ivan's new holdings as he heads into the final month of 1996:

PeopleSoft (PSFT)	$23,254
3Com Corp. (COMS)	$24,594
Tellabs (TLAB)	$18,081
Papa John's International (PZZA)	$16,383
Parametric Technology (PMTC)	$18,799
Total Value	$101,111

Sound the trumpet, pop the corks, jangle your belled caps, Ivan crossed the 100 percent mark after eleven months. Ah, but can he keep the total there for one more month and record a *double* for the entire year? December's rankings require some more adjustments, though, with three stocks to be replaced. Ivan's sale of Tellabs, Papa John's International, and Parametric Technology netted him $53,263 to be split among the three new stocks, ENSCO International, Oxford Health Plans—back in the rankings again—and Mosinee Paper.

End of 1996

December was another mixed month, with three stocks advancing and two declining, but it was enough to record a fabulous year for Ivan overall. Here's how 1996 ended up for the Unemotional Growth portion of his portfolio:

PeopleSoft (PSFT)	$24,638
3Com Corp. (COMS)	$23,600
ENSCO International (ESV)	$19,282
Oxford Health Plans (OXHP)	$17,422
Mosinee Paper (MOSI)	$18,280
Total Value	$103,222

For the entire year, then, Ivan's Unemotional Growth half of the portfolio more than doubled, gaining $53,222 on an original investment of $50,000 (a return of 106.44 percent). Now all you sharp-eyed readers will notice that this return is a fair bit higher than the model's return for 1996 (87.95 percent). Keep in mind that the theoretical model followed the rankings precisely, holding six stocks if there were ties and assuming an equal dollar weighting at the beginning of each month. With a couple of stocks exploding for massive gains (such as JLG Industries did early in the year), by not rebalancing those positions each month, Ivan's results were slightly different. Sometimes such rebalancing works against you; other times, it helps you. Like all aspects of using such a ranking system, use common sense in making your decisions. Don't let a single stock grow too large for fear it will implode and ruin all your hard-won gains, but at the same time, don't panic and rebalance every time a single stock has a nice monthly gain. It may have several of them in succession. Strike a balance between the desire to spread risk and the goal of letting compounding work for you.

Now it's time to look at the other half of Ivan's portfolio. If you'll recall, each of the Unemotional Value stocks also began 1996 with $10,000. Here's how they ended the year:

International Paper (IP)	$10,927
Chevron (CHV)	$12,852
Caterpillar (CAT)	$12,521
Minnesota Mining & Manufacturing (MMM)	$13,437
DuPont (DD)	$13,574
Total Value	$63,311

The group returned 26.62 percent for the year, then. Add the two portfolios together and Ivan's portfolio grew from $100,000 at the beginning of 1996 to $166,533, for an overall return of 66.53 percent. I know, I know, I can hear it already. "But if he had skipped the Unemotional Value stocks and plowed everything into the Unemotional Growth stocks, he'd have $206,444 now. Isn't that the better option?"

Maybe, maybe not. Keep in mind that any one fabulous year can distort your view of a strategy. What if 1996 had turned into another ugly bear market like 1973 and 1974? Most stocks got smacked around pretty hard during that bear, with the indices losing close to 30 percent. Yet the boring Unemotional Value stocks actually recorded a gain during that two-year period. So some Dow ballast is a good thing to include as your portfolio's core, even though in stellar years the returns may not be as glamorous as with more aggressive approaches. In rough times, you'll be glad you threw your lot in with the Unemotional Value stocks as well. Besides, 26 percent in a single year is nothing to be crying about; it still bettered the Dow's return slightly.

Looking ahead, Ivan would take his $166,533 and reapportion it between his two strategies to begin 1997. Since he's using a fifty-fifty split, he would invest a little more than $83,000 in each of the two approaches for the next year. The whole process simply begins anew. The time when you update your Unemotional Value stocks (whether you opt for a twelve-month or an eighteen-month holding period) is a good time to rebalance all your positions so that you can begin fresh. It's also a good time to reevaluate the weightings you wish to use in the following year and make those adjustments as well. As you get older, you can pick a year in between two decades to switch, say from a 50 percent value/50 percent growth split to a 60 percent value/40 percent growth split. If you happen to be using a quarterly update for the growth portion, your update schedule will still coincide with your update for the value stocks each time, affording you a convenient chance to do the necessary rebalancing. Not all years will be as outstanding as 1996 was, of course, but whether the return was a 66 percent gain or a loss for the year, I hope you see now how you can mesh these strategies together as complementary parts of a single diversified portfolio.

PART FIVE

Frequently Asked Questions

Now that you have all the details for both models and some ideas about how you might use them together, I'd like to devote this final part of the book to answering some of the most frequently asked questions from readers in our online forums. This list will not be exhaustive, of course. Any time I think I've seen every possible new question regarding these approaches, a dozen new ones pop up in our message boards. The beauty of the online world is that it affords almost immediate interactive exchanges, not only between writers and readers, but among the readers themselves.

A number of times in recent months, readers with common interests have joined together to pursue a research project that we weren't able to undertake as a staff project (for example, the sell-stop research study I discussed in part 3). The most exciting result of all this interaction, however, is that we're able to keep testing ideas in public as a way of refining strategies and sharing the best and worst results of our tests. (Believe me, sometimes it's more helpful when a test completely bombs. Knowing what doesn't work is just as crucial as discovering what does.) So, if there are questions running through your mind about these models, let me try to anticipate some of them now. If I don't cover a question you've been pondering, just jump online and ask it in our message folder at The Motley Fool. You may be on to the next big research idea for us.

❧ When the stock markets are near or at all-time-high levels, is it really a good time to invest?

This is possibly *the* most frequently asked question I have received, especially with the impressive gains for stocks over the last three years. Back when I first began participating in The Motley Fool's online discussions (October 1994), the Dow Jones Industrial Average was just reclaiming new high territory around 3,800 to 4,000 after a correction for much of 1994. As the market continued to rise into 1995 and I began writing full-time for The Motley Fool, I was asked again and again about the stock market being too high. "Shouldn't we wait for the inevitable big correction before we invest?" At the time, I gave a very honest and accurate answer, again and again: "I simply don't know what the market's going to do from here over the short run, and neither does anyone else, despite what they'll tell you." I would then launch into an explanation of the history of the Dow Approach and how it has fared well in both strong and weak periods.

I'd also point out that part of that success, especially in weak markets, was because with the Dow Approach, one is *not* buying the whole "market" anyway, only a handful of individual stocks that already have a slight protective cushion by virtue of their out-of-favor status. They're likely to have already fallen somewhat and if the entire market sinks, they should have less room to drop farther.

But the most important point of all is that for Fools, market timing is simply irrelevant. There are no "buy points" for the Dow Dividend Approach. In other words, you can invest in this approach whenever you're ready, and while in the short run you may have good or bad luck, over the long run (and I mean decades here, not the Wall Street definition of long run, which can often be measured by how long it takes a cup of coffee to cool), what happens those first few days, weeks, even months isn't going to be a huge concern for you. Keep in mind that once you get into the market with the

Dow Approach (any approach, for that matter, as far as we're concerned), your whole strategy is to stay fully invested forever, even though you'll rotate in and out of different stocks over the years. If you're 100 percent fully invested all the time, there's absolutely no reason to attempt to time the market. These models are designed to take the last stitch of emotion out of the decision fabric. "Oh, the market dropped a hundred points today? Darn. When's our tee time, though?" "Oh, we're up fifty percent so far this year? Great! Now keep your head still on this putt, will you? We're two down and I don't want to lose five bucks to these chowderheads."

How did those market timers in late 1994 and early 1995 do, by the way? All of the bears sitting on the sidelines as the Dow approached 4,000 in late 1994 are still on the sidelines presumably, since we have yet to see the "big correction" they were calling for. And since then, the Dow Jones Industrial Average has more than doubled. Wham! More proof that market timing just doesn't pay over the long run.

Let me add a little story here for those of you worried about starting now, in order to illustrate the crucial value of the investor's best ally—time. Let's compare two college roommates, Ready Freddy and Slow Joe. Both of them graduated the same year and landed similar jobs with similar salaries, but Joe wasn't concerned about his retirement right away. Freddy, though, couldn't wait to start saving some of his new paycheck.

Each year of the decade from 1961 to 1970, Freddy invested $2,000 into an account that mirrored the Dow Jones Industrial Average. (For the sake of simplicity, let's assume it is a tax-deferred and commission-free account.) At the end of ten years, Freddy quit making annual deposits and simply let the account continue to grow along with the DJIA. His total investment over the ten years was $20,000.

Slow Joe, on the other hand, didn't start investing for retirement until a decade later. He began putting $2,000 a year into the same investment Freddy used, but Joe decided to make up for his late start and deposited $2,000 a year for *two* decades instead of Freddy's one, every year from 1971 through 1990. His total investment was $40,000.

At the end of 1996, Ready Freddy's account would have been

worth $680,540, while Slow Joe's would be worth only $521,793, despite the fact that Joe made twice as many deposits as Freddy. Now if we change those annual returns to take advantage of the Dow Dividend Approach, the gains are even more impressive. Slow Joe's $40,000 investment grew to $1,773,149. But Ready Freddy's $20,000 investment would have grown to $3,500,971.

The most remarkable fact is that the 1960s (the period of Freddy's ten deposits) was a lousy period for the Dow. At the end of Freddy's ten years of deposits, his total portfolio was only worth $21,626, as four of the ten years in the 1960s were losing years for the Dow. Nevertheless, having saved the $20,000 early in his career, Freddy was able to use the magic of compounding.

Even though he invested half as much money as Joe, and at a worse time in the market's history, Freddy's total portfolio grew significantly larger simply because he started so early. So, if you're worried about market timing and you're afraid your luck will be rotten, think of Ready Freddy. It pays in a big way to get an early start and to wait patiently for The Motley Fool's favorite harlequin —the Compounding Clown—to start his dance.

❋ Okay, I'm convinced not to play market-timing games once I'm invested, but since I'm just beginning, is there a "best" time of year to start? All of your models are tested from January. Will I get the same results if I start, say, in September?

In the short term, or in any given year, one time of the year may prove a better time of the year to invest than other times, but over the very long run, such variability tends to even out. One researcher into the Dow Approach, Dr. Mark Pankin, tested the model using each new month as a starting point, and confirmed that the approach is successful starting at any time of the year.

If there is any advantage to be had in starting at a particular time of the year, it appears to rest in the final weeks of November and the month of December. One possible explanation for this seeming anomaly may lie in the games Wall Street money managers play in order to keep their shareholders happy. At the end of each quarter, and especially at the end of each year, mutual funds and other institutional investors go through a process called "window dressing," where they adjust their portfolios to appear as they want them to at year end on the annual reports to shareholders. Often what this entails is dumping their weak stocks and adding whatever the year's winners have been so that shareholders see the names they recognize as having been hot that year among the holdings of their mutual fund. This, of course, is based on an assumption by the mutual fund industry that investors are stupid. "Hmm, let's see. The portfolio has Intel and Microsoft and Dell Computer and Coca-Cola, all great stocks this year. He must be doing a great job managing my money!" Never mind that the fund underperformed the S&P 500 for the year. As long as the portfolio looks good on paper, so the theory goes, the shareholders won't notice. Then the fund managers turn right around again in January or February and start buying back the dogs they just sold.

How does this affect the Dow stocks? If you recall, the Dow Dividend Approach stocks often get thrown out in the window dressing process because they are just the kind of recent *dogs* that Wall Street managers don't want the shareholders to see in their list of holdings. So late in the year, the prices for these stocks sometimes drop even a bit farther as the institutions shed them temporarily. For the Dow Approach investor, it's bargain time, getting the stocks even a little lower than usual. Overall, though, don't be concerned about trying to time your entry point during the year. Over many years, the differences are very small, and with the new tax laws pushing holding periods toward eighteen months instead of twelve, the difference may well disappear altogether. The best time to invest was yesterday. Today is the next best time and tomorrow the best after that. Start early.

※ But I'm still worried I'm going to invest at exactly the wrong time. How do I know that I'm not investing at a market "peak"?

You never know, of course, but I maintain that for a long-term investor, it's not a crucial issue. Jersey Gilbert published the results of a study in the September 1996 issue of *SmartMoney* magazine that analyzed the results for a hypothetical investor with the worst possible luck. Gilbert tracked the results for a poor soul who invested $10,000 at precisely the wrong time in each of four different years (the wrong time simply being the year's market peak for the S&P

500). The four dates were January 1973, January 1977, December 1980, and August 1987.

In all four cases, leaving the investment in the S&P 500, despite the immediate drop after each investment, would have produced a better long-term return than Treasury bills over the succeeding fifteen years (or eight years in the case of the 1987 investment). The 1973 investment would have taken the longest time to catch up to the T-bill investment because of the severity of the bear market in 1973 and 1974. It took 12.8 years to catch up. The other three "unlucky" investments all managed to catch up to their rival T-bill investments in far less time. (The 1977 investment took 5.9 years, the 1980 investment 4.1 years, and the 1987 investment 4.3 years.)

Let's say your timing is even worse, however. You managed to invest $10,000 each year since 1979 on precisely the worst day of the year (that is, the market's peak). Don't ask me how you could possibly be that unlucky, but let's say you were. That $160,000 investment ($10,000 for sixteen years) would still have grown to $540,000, compared with the T-bill portfolio, which would be worth less than $280,000.

Peter Lynch puts it another way in his latest book, *Learn to Earn* (Fireside/Simon & Schuster, 1995): "Starting in 1970, if you were unlucky and invested two thousand dollars at the peak day of the market in each successive year, your annual return was 8.5 percent. If you timed the market perfectly and invested your two thousand dollars at the low point in the market in each successive year, your annual return was 10.1 percent. So the difference between great timing and lousy timing is 1.6 percent." As long as you stay fully invested in stocks and keep saving as a lifelong activity, timing is irrelevant. And, of course, we hope and trust that you'll do better than the S&P 500 return while you're in the stock market, using Foolish strategies. It would be too Wise not to.

❖ I've heard that when a stock splits, it's a great buying opportunity. Should I try to buy stocks before or after they split? Does it mean I automatically lose half my money if I buy right before a split?

At least once a week, a reader in our online message board folders will ask for advice about buying a stock that has announced an impending split. Our Foolish take on stock splits is that they are nonevents. The only tangible thing that changes when a stock splits is a pair of arbitrary numbers, the price per share and the number of shares outstanding. The company hasn't changed. The company's revenues and growth haven't changed. The value of your investment if you already own the stock hasn't changed. Then what's the big deal?

Let's look at the mechanics of splits and why they take place. When a company declares a stock split, say a two-for-one split, on a set day, the number of shares outstanding doubles and each share is worth half of the presplit price. It's exactly like going to the cashier with a $20 bill and asking for two $10 bills. You still have $20; it just looks a little different. On the same day, whatever cash dividend the company regularly pays also gets cut in half, so the dividend yield (the dollar dividend divided by the share price) remains constant.

If nothing's changed, then why do companies split their stocks? It's a simple matter of psychology. When stock prices reach a certain level, companies feel that investors will become nervous about buying more shares, held back by the impression that the stock is "expensive." The theory is that an individual investor is more comfortable buying Hewlett-Packard at $60 a share rather than at $120. So the company splits the stock to keep the arbitrary share price in a "comfortable" zone.

How does a split affect the Foolish investor? There's no convincing evidence that stocks either go up or down in the short term because of a stock split, so we ignore split announcements in favor of more fundamental issues like earnings growth and clean balance sheets. There is one consideration with splits worth looking into, however—trading commissions. Depending on the type of brokerage account you have, the commission charge might change drastically when a stock splits. For example, if your broker charges commissions based on the price per share, your fee will be higher to purchase the stock before it splits since the price per share is at that point still quite a bit higher. If you have a broker who charges a fee per share, though, you'll pay more after the split because the equivalent dollar investment will buy more shares at the new lower price. This is another reason I recommend the deep-discount brokers for Foolish investors who make all of their own buy and sell decisions. If you pay a flat fee, regardless of the number of shares or the price per share, a split doesn't matter to you in the least.

Don't sweat stock splits. Despite what you may hear from some-one with a very short-term outlook, they don't mean anything if you're investing Foolishly—that is, with an eye on fundamental valu-ations and long-term growth.

❖ I've just graduated from college and don't have any savings. And my salary is so modest, I can't afford much right now. Am I just doomed to a puny retirement if I don't win the lottery?

Our original real-money online portfolios in The Motley Fool began with $50,000, which for many would-be stock investors may seem like a pipe dream. If you're fresh out of school and have a modest salary of, say, $20,000 a year, it may seem as if it's barely enough to live on, let alone save and invest for the future. But if you're Foolish, your future doesn't have to be bleak and spartan!

The only savings plan I've come across that makes any practical sense is a form of forced savings. People who tell themselves they'll save whatever is left at the end of the month never get around to saving anything. And it doesn't matter if you're making $20,000 or $200,000 a year, that holds true. You'll find your expenses expand automatically when you get a raise. The only way to guarantee that you'll save is to treat savings like any other mandatory bill, and preferably the first one you pay each month. If you can force yourself to skim a certain percentage off the top of every paycheck (5 percent to 10 percent of your take-home pay), you can still set yourself up for that easy-chair retirement you've felt was always going to elude you. And if you can make yourself pay the monthly deposit into your retirement fund, you don't have to think about saving anything else the rest of the month. You can relax and spend every other penny of what you earn beyond that 5 percent or 10 percent with the comforting assurance that you're taking care of your retirement painlessly.

Let's look at how it might work. Let's assume that you're thirty-five years away from retirement and you haven't yet got a penny put away. Your take-home pay now is $20,000 a year, or $1,667 a month. (It's better to work from your actual take-home pay because we all know what income taxes do to your gross salary.) You decide to pay yourself first and you commit $165 every month for retirement (just under 10 percent for this simple example).

If you are starting from scratch, one economical way to invest Foolishly would be using dividend reinvestment plans (DRiPs), where you can bypass brokerage commissions on long-term holdings (more on DRiPs later). Another way might be to begin with an S&P 500 Index fund. As your portfolio grows, you can branch out into other Foolish investments, such as the models discussed in parts 2 and 3 of this book. And if you're investing this money in a self-directed Roth IRA, the growth is completely tax-free when you begin to pull money out at retirement age. Let's assume you are able to average 13 percent annually on your investments (roughly the annual rate of return for the S&P 500 Index in recent decades). Broken down into a compounded monthly return, that's 1.02 percent per month.

So, you're putting away $165 a month and your portfolio grows at a compounded return of 1.02 percent a month (13 percent a year). At the end of the first year, you'd have a total of $2,116 in your retirement fund. Still a long way to go, but an excellent start. And, remember, if it's in a Roth IRA, it's completely tax-free growth.

Let's flash forward a few years at a time to see how your fund would grow at this same 13 percent annual return and monthly contribution of $165.

Beginning	$0
1 year	$2,116
5 years	$13,701
10 years	$38,889
15 years	$85,194
20 years	$170,322
25 years	$326,821
30 years	$614,532
35 years	$1,143,461

In thirty-five years, you can start from scratch and still build a retirement portfolio worth over $1 million simply by paying yourself first from every paycheck! The most important factors I've left out, of course, are that you should be able to exceed the return for the

S&P 500 over your investing career, and that you're not going to be bringing home a $20,000 annual salary forever. The numbers here assume that your monthly paycheck and savings contributions never change. As your salary increases, you'll save more, of course, even if it must be invested in a regular taxable account, and your retirement fund will grow even more rapidly.

If you're able to achieve gains of 18 percent, for example, well within the range of annual returns for the basic Dow Approaches over the past several decades, your final portfolio value wouldn't be $1,143,461, but rather $3,954,542! Nearly $4 million, tax-free, simply by stashing away $165 a month (less than $2,000 a year).

The point of all these numbers, of course, is that you don't have to be born rich to make yourself wealthy. But it does take a little discipline. No one will send in that 10 percent contribution each month if you don't. But if you can make yourself do it every month before you pay any bills or buy anything extra, you'll all but guarantee yourself a wealthy retirement without having to worry about it constantly or praying that the government will fix the Social Security mess and be there to help you when you're old. How Foolishly easy and self-reliant is that?!

▨ But what are my chances of retiring on Easy Street if I'm not twenty or twenty-five years old and haven't started saving yet?

A college buddy of mine called not too long ago when he found out what I do for a living these days. He wanted some advice. Well, that's not completely true—he wanted a miracle!

My buddy (I'll call him Mr. Animal to give you a picture of the kind of student he was in college) is roughly my age; he's thirty-five. He's finally settled into a decent job, somehow persuaded a lovely woman to marry him, and they don't have any children. (They aren't planning to, either. She says the Animal's enough of a child for her.)

They just bought their dream house and were able to lock in a nice fixed-rate thirty-year mortgage. They both work, but their combined income is fairly modest, and by the time they set aside an emergency fund, their investment account (which is parked in a money market IRA) totals $5,000. And with the new mortgage payment and their car loan, Animal doesn't see how they can save more than $100 a month in the future.

Is it hopeless for the Animals? Let's find out.

Let's take their $5,000 IRA and put it to better use in our favorite conservative retirement strategy—the Dow Approach (Unemotional Value). Since 1971, this approach has compounded at 22 percent a year, so let's use that return as our future possible rate. In addition, the Animals can invest another $100 per month in their IRA account, $1,200 a year. (Whether this goes into his or her account is for them to sort out!) For the sake of simplicity, let's assume the $100 a month sits idle in the IRA until the once-per-year adjustment. It could be put to better use, and I'll address some possibilities later, but for the simplicity of this scenario, let's assume it just sits.

Since the Animals want to retire at age sixty-five in thirty years (when their house is paid off), let's compound that IRA account for the full thirty years. When the banker hands the Animals the paid deed to their house, their retirement account will have grown to . . . wait for it . . . $4,068,087! That's right—$5,000 down and $100 a month for thirty years at 22 percent grows to just over $4 million. (Remember, though, there is no guarantee that this investing approach will continue to return 22 percent a year in the future.)

But wait!, I hear you object. Won't bread cost $50 a slice in thirty years? Ah, too true, inflation hound. So let's account for that, too. If we assume an annual inflation rate of 3 percent, that $4 million thirty years from now would be worth $1,796,390 in today's dollars. If at retirement, then, the Animals simply stick the whole shooting match into a vanilla S&P 500 Index fund averaging 12 percent a year, they'll be able to retire on an average annual *salary* of better than $215,000 in today's dollars—without ever touching the principal.

Or even better, if they remain Foolish and keep the money in the Unemotional Value strategy, they can retire on an annual average salary of more than $395,000 in today's dollars—considerably more than they ever made from their jobs! Needless to say, Animal was thrilled to hear this, but not nearly as thrilled as his wife, who has to keep explaining to her mother why she married this guy in the first place. Now she has the retort she's been looking for: "He's going to make me a millionaire!"

❧ Just how good a deal is the newly created Roth IRA account?

Swing batter! I couldn't ask for a fatter pitch than this one. Assuming Congress and future administrations leave the Roth individual retirement account rules alone, this could be the single greatest incentive to saving for Americans in my lifetime. And given the potential disaster facing the Social Security system, we Fools had better be prepared to support ourselves in retirement. Uncle Sam may well be hanging out the "Gone Fishing" sign by the time many of us are old enough to collect anything of what we've paid in over the years.

To remind you of the important details of the Roth IRA, it's a newly created alternative to the regular IRA account that allows taxpayers (meeting certain income limits) to invest up to $2,000 a year (after-tax dollars, you can't deduct this on your income tax return) into an account that then grows completely tax-free so long as you keep the account open for a minimum of five years and don't start pulling money out until age fifty-nine and one-half. Unlike the regular IRA, though, you can continue contributing to this account even past age seventy if you're still working.

Just look at the possibilities for a young couple who both work and maintain Roth IRAs. Even adopting a simple investment approach like stashing the $4,000 away in an S&P 500 Index fund each year ($2,000 each for both husband and wife), the results over a career are astonishing. Assuming 12 percent annual growth from age twenty to age sixty and steady contributions each year, this young couple would be sitting on a tax-free retirement fund of $3,436,570. But with the much more powerful Dow Approaches, it's possible that they could achieve returns of around 20 percent a year. (Keep in mind the simple four-stock Unemotional Value approach has returned 22 percent a year since 1971.) At 20 percent a year, our married couple would be sitting on a tax-free pile—$35,250,518! I don't know too many investors who couldn't retire comfortably on $35 million, do you? And the best thing is, you can keep letting the money compound tax-free while you pull out only as much as you need each year to enjoy your retirement.

I don't think I can stress this enough. For taxpayers who qualify for the new Roth IRA, it's possibly the best retirement vehicle available anywhere. Don't let this opportunity escape your attention, Fools!

❧ I've just come into a large sum of money that I want to invest. Should I break it up into chunks and invest it a little bit at a time to protect against a drop in the market?

I am not a big fan of dollar cost averaging a lump sum into the market. In fact, I don't really consider breaking up a lump sum into segments and investing them over time to be dollar cost averaging at all.

Dollar cost averaging is really a technique for regular new savings. If you're putting an equal sum of new money into a mutual fund each month, for example, when the market has gone up, you'll buy fewer shares than you buy when the market goes down. When you invest the same amount each month, regardless of the level of the market, you're keeping the average cost per share lower and avoiding the temptation to try to time the stock market.

Adding money to the market each month, of course, is one of my favorite lessons to teach investors. It's the way to build real wealth for anyone with discipline and time. I would rather see you invest in stocks, of course, but even using an index fund tied to a major market index (the S&P 500 Index or the Dow Jones Industrial Average) is a fine way to save regularly.

The problem with using such a time-delay approach with a lump sum, however, is that you put yourself on the wrong side of history. Any number of studies have cited the fact that the stock market goes up from 70 percent to 75 percent of the time. If you're holding money on the sidelines to avoid taking a loss right away, you're betting on an occurrence that only happens 25 percent to 30 percent of the time. The risk you're not considering in withholding portions of the lump sum is the opportunity cost of the market going up before you invest, which, as I've said, is more likely to happen based on the historical odds.

No one can tell you the market won't go down the day after you invest your new windfall, simply because absolutely no one can make such a prediction. The *gooroos* who are famous for being expert market timers are often living off the reputation from one or two accurate predictions. Scores of them are still hawking their newsletters and 900-number services based on predictions they might have been right about fifteen or twenty years ago. Do they publish their entire records over a couple of decades? Not likely. Funny how we never hear about the scores and scores of predictions that never came to pass! Even after some of the more famous experts have been wrong for years in a row, they keep boldly predicting the future. When they're finally right once, they crow "I told you so!" Doesn't help their clients any, does it? So don't get sucked into a futile market-timing game. If you have money to invest, get it to work for you as soon as you can and then let long-term investing strategies (including those in this book) do their stuff. The Compounding Clown can't dance without the most crucial element to all investing careers—time!

⌘ How do I know how well my investments are doing? What is the best way to track my results?

One of the key components of Foolish investing is accountability. If one looks at the mutual fund industry, for example, the Securities and Exchange Commission requires each fund to disclose its official historical returns in its prospectus and in advertisements, but there's no law requiring the fund to make much of those results as it tries to persuade the millions of fund investors to choose it over all the rest of the competing funds. You'd never know by the glowing marketing job the mutual fund industry does that 82 percent of the stock funds that have been around for the last ten years couldn't keep pace with the S&P 500 Index. What you will see are endless claims to being number one in a certain category over a certain period. (The category and time period are usually in microscopic print.)

We're Number One!
(among mutual funds holding exactly 182 stocks between August 1, 1995, and August 5, 1995)

Inevitably, all mutual funds will have had one decent period when they've outperformed the market or their peers. And it's that period you'll hear about over and over again in advertisements. It doesn't matter if the fund trailed the market badly over a decade's time; if there was a single quarter or year when it had a stellar performance, you can rest assured that's the period the marketing department will hype. It's not illegal, of course, and with some digging, the reader can get the whole story. But the marketers are banking on the odds that most readers are either in a hurry, or aren't quite sure what to look for, or both. So the readers end up believing the spirit of the ads (that the fund is a winner), even though they only have part of the story.

Fortunately, like golf, investing can be measured objectively. A golfer who shoots three under par has done a fine job, even if his style is unorthodox and he hit five trees along the way, only to see his ball get lucky bounces. His score is his score, and it can be compared to another golfer's round on the same course on the same day. If you shoot 69 and I shoot 75, you played better. All the justifications in the world don't change the fact that you'll be taking home the trophy and I'll be buying the drinks at the nineteenth hole.

For investments in the stock market, we also have an objective *par*—the major market indices. You can choose either the Dow Jones Industrial Average or the S&P 500 Index for your comparative benchmark; it makes little difference as the two indices move very much in lockstep over long periods of time. The S&P 500 Index has become the de facto industry standard for institutional investors, despite the longer history of the Dow Jones Industrial Average, if for no other reason than it is designed to represent a somewhat broader spectrum of the overall stock market.

To be completely accountable, then, you should have a way to measure your portfolio's progress (or even the progress of an individual stock) against the S&P 500 Index. To do that, you'll need to understand a few mathematical formulas (nothing too complex) that will allow you to check your progress at any time. Incidentally, there are a number of fine commercial software applications for home finance that will track your investments as well, but I've found that an inexpensive financial calculator and a basic spreadsheet program like Microsoft Excel supply me with everything I need to track my investments. If worse comes to worst, you can even get by with <gasp> paper and pencil!

The first formula you'll need is the simple equation for calculating total return. This can be used to see how well an individual stock has done, or an index like the S&P 500, or even your entire portfolio, over one period in time. For example, if you bought a stock at $25 a share and it's now trading at $41 per share, how much has it gained?

$$\frac{\text{Current value } - \text{ Original value}}{\text{Original value}} = \text{Total return}$$

In this case, then, the total return equals the current value ($41) minus the original value ($25), or $16 per share, divided by the original value ($25). That equals 0.64, or 64 percent.

$$\frac{41 - 25}{25} = 0.64$$

The same formula can be used with total investment amounts. And this is particularly helpful because you can include all your trading costs in the dollar amounts to get a completely accurate picture of your returns. For example, if you invested $1,014 in a stock (including the commission to buy it) and received $1,235 for the stock upon its sale (again, after commission), your gain would have been 21.8 percent.

$$\frac{1,235 - 1,014}{1,014} = 0.2179$$

To measure how good or bad such a return is, though, you need to compare it to the return for the index over the identical time frame.

For instance, let's say on January 1, 1997, your portfolio was worth $25,000 and the S&P 500 was at 740.74. On September 15, 1997, your portfolio is worth $29,000 and the S&P 500 Index is at 919.77. Have you had a good year so far? Let's check. To get your portfolio return, subtract the original value ($25,000) from the current value ($29,000), leaving $4,000. Now divide that by the original value to get the percentage gain: $4,000 divided by $25,000 equals 0.16, or 16 percent. For eight and a half months, that's a pretty fair return. You should celebrate and start circulating your résumé among Wall Street firms, right? Well, hold on. The S&P 500 Index grew from 740.74 to 919.77 in the same eight and a half months. What kind of gain is that?

$$\frac{919.77 - 740.74}{740.74} = 0.2417$$

The stock market was up 24.2 percent during the same period your portfolio gained 16 percent, so even though it's been an above-average period by historical standards, you have a slightly less positive perspective on the growth of your own portfolio, given the market's even better performance. The S&P 500 Index is an especially good test against which to pit your returns because you know that if you simply can't beat it, you can easily join it by investing in an index fund. That's a comforting thought to fall back on if you find yourself on the wrong end of the index too many years in a row. Of course, if you're using the strategies we teach in The Motley Fool, we fully expect you to beat the S&P 500 over the long run, even if you have an occasional period where the index bests your returns. It's similar to baseball in that it's not the individual game that means everything; it's the sum total of all the games that determines who gets to play in the World Series. Don't get too wrapped up in individual years' victories or defeats, but keep track of your progress over the life of your investing career. You will be surprised how your long-term Foolish results will fare compared with the mutual fund managers who command seven-figure salaries for their professional management services. "Accountability evermore," quoth the Fool.

❖ But what if I am testing a portfolio I've held over four or five years? How can I calculate an annualized return to see how I'm really faring?

That's the drawback of the total return formula; it doesn't take time into account, so its uses are somewhat limited. To add time into the equation, the picture gets understandably a little more complex. (You'll want a calculator for this one unless you're really good at exponents. If you're not sure what an exponent is, $15 or $20 for a basic calculator might be money well spent.) The equation for annualized returns will include the time horizon (in years) so that, regardless of how long or short the investment period is, we can project an annualized return based on what has occurred.

Annualized return = (Current value / Original value) $\wedge$ (1 / Years) − 1

Let's say our portfolio started the year at $15,000 and after five months has gained 12 percent for a total value of $16,800. If we plug those values into the formula for annualized returns, we'll be able to see what our portfolio would achieve for a full year at this rate.

(16,800 / 15,000) $\wedge$ (1 / 0.4167) − 1 = Annualized return

The figure 0.4167 is the number of years represented in the problem. We're dealing with less than one year in this example (five months divided by twelve months). Now let's work through the numbers:

$16,800 divided by $15,000 equals 1.12. And 1 divided by 0.4167 equals 2.4. So our formula now looks like this:

1.12 $\wedge$ 2.4 − 1 = Annualized return

NOTE: The $\wedge$ symbol denotes an exponent. You can plug the equation into a spreadsheet just as I've listed it here and the calculation should work correctly. If you have a calculator that will perform square roots and fractional roots, the directions will guide you in the process for raising a number to a specific power. In this example, you're raising 1.12 to the 2.4 power, then subtracting 1 from the result. The reduced formula now looks like this:

1.3125 − 1 = 0.3125 (or 31.25%)

In other words, your annualized return based on the five months is roughly 31 percent. If it had taken two years to achieve that 12 percent total return, though, instead of five months, your annualized return would be significantly lower. Here's the formula using a two-year time horizon:

(16,800 / 15,000) $\wedge$ (1 / 2) − 1 =
1.12 $\wedge$ 0.5 − 1 =
1.0583 − 1 = 0.0583 (or only 5.83% per year)

This formula is extremely important in wading through the hype you'll often see in marketing campaigns for mutual funds or newsletters in the industry, where the headlines will proclaim huge total gains over a certain period.

Our Portfolio Up 1,000%
(over the last 25 years)

It sounds impressive, doesn't it? After all, if you had invested $10,000 with the manager, your total value today would be $110,000. But throw that claim in the accountability hopper and you'll find out the return is actually pretty weak, trailing the historical returns for the market indices.

($110,000 / $10,000) $\wedge$ (1/25) $- 1 =$
11 $\wedge$ 0.04 $- 1 =$
1.1007 $- 1 = 0.1007$ (or 10.07% per year for the 25 years)

Use this formula when you need to calculate an annualized return for any starting and ending value over a specific time period. This result is also called the compound annual growth rate.

There's an important distinction to be made between an average return and the compound annual growth rate. Let's look at a series of five consecutive annual returns for a sample portfolio.

Year 1	25%
Year 2	-7%
Year 3	14%
Year 4	75%
Year 5	-10%

If you take the simple average by adding the five values together and dividing by five, the result is an average (or mean) return of 19.4 percent. But such an average rate of return does not account for the sequence of the individual annual returns and how the compounding of an actual portfolio achieving these returns would be affected by the sequence. For that, you need to calculate the compound annual growth rate.

Let's say this model began with $10,000. After year one's gain, the total is worth $12,500. The second year brought a loss of 7 percent of that new total value, bringing the total down to $11,625. Year three's gain brings the total to $13,253. Year four's big gain brings the total to $23,192. And year five's loss drops the final total to $20,873. Now let's calculate the compound annual growth rate (annualized return). We know the starting value ($10,000), the ending value ($20,873), and the time period (five years):

$(20,873 / 10,000) \wedge (1/5) - 1 =$
$2.0873 \wedge 0.2 - 1 =$
$1.1586 - 1 = 0.1586$ (or 15.86%)

The annualized return of 15.86 percent is quite a bit lower than the simple average return of 19.4 percent. Using such a simple average gives you a misleading sense of how your portfolio is really doing. If you had, in fact, been getting an annualized return of 19.4 percent, your total value at the end of the five years would have been $24,267 instead of the $20,873 we actually had—a considerable difference. Know the difference then between a claim of a simple average and a compound annual growth rate. (Fortunately, the mainstream firms in the investment industry all use compound annual growth rates in their publications and advertisements. They often call them annualized returns, but they mean the same thing.)

🟫 Those formulas are great when you only have two values (the starting and ending values), but I add money to my portfolio every month. Do I have to track each new savings deposit separately, or is there some way I can calculate an overall return for my portfolio to compare against the S&P 500?

Now you're getting to a more difficult calculation. Glad you asked!

The biggest accounting difficulty arises if you add or subtract money from your account during the course of the period that you wish to measure. Both the total return and compound annual growth rate equations assume a single deposit and no cash flow during the period being tested. If you add regularly to your account (as we hope you do as lifelong savers) or withdraw money to pay for living expenses during retirement, et cetera, you need to use a much more complicated approach to measuring your annualized returns. You can't simply add up the total of all your deposits and use that as the original value in our previous equations, because each deposit and withdrawal is on a different time horizon from the rest. It makes for a much more complicated calculation—one that's all but impossible to do easily by hand.

Fortunately, financial software programs like Quicken and many spreadsheets include a function that can accommodate you (internal rate of return). These functions measure the time value of the cash flows into or out of your portfolio and generate an overall annualized return for all of the additions and withdrawals as a single portfolio. (You may have to hunt for the feature that works best in your spreadsheet software. The XIRR function in Excel is what I use, but it took some work to find it. It did not appear in the original standard group of functions, but going to the Tools menu, selecting Add-Ins, and then checking the box called Analysis ToolPak added the XIRR function to my main list of financial functions options.)

Using that function, you simply set up a two-column spreadsheet. In the first column, list the dates of every cash deposit or withdrawal to your account. In the second column, list the amount for each transaction (make sure to include a negative sign for withdrawals to distinguish them from deposits). You don't have to list the dates and amounts of dividends or stock splits because those are part of the portfolio's growth, not new money you're adding or money you're withdrawing to buy that villa on the seventeenth green. For your final entry, use today's date and your total portfolio value as the amount. (Enter this total amount with a negative sign as if you were withdrawing everything, even though you're not really taking out any money.) The function wizard will ask you to identify the spreadsheet cells you used for the dollar values and then the cells for the dates, and, *voilà*, it automatically calculates your annualized return. (It will probably appear as a decimal value that you can either translate yourself or format within the spreadsheet to print out as a percentage value.)

Here's an example of a portfolio where the investor starts with $1,000 and invests another $1,000 each month for two years. At the end of the two years, the value of the portfolio equals $29,250. The spreadsheet you set up will look like this:

Date	Amount
1/1/95	$1,000
2/1/95	$1,000
3/1/95	$1,000
4/1/95	$1,000
5/1/95	$1,000
6/1/95	$1,000
7/1/95	$1,000
8/1/95	$1,000
9/1/95	$1,000
10/1/95	$1,000
11/1/95	$1,000
12/1/95	$1,000
1/1/96	$1,000
2/1/96	$1,000
3/1/96	$1,000
4/1/96	$1,000
5/1/96	$1,000
6/1/96	$1,000
7/1/96	$1,000
8/1/96	$1,000
9/1/96	$1,000
10/1/96	$1,000
11/1/96	$1,000
12/1/96	$1,000
12/31/96	($29,250)
Return	**20.2%**

The internal rate of return function calculated the overall annualized return for this portfolio at a very strong 20.2 percent. Using that figure, the investor can then make a meaningful comparison to the annualized return for the S&P 500 Index over the same stretch to see whether he's keeping pace with the industry benchmark or not. For those of you who make monthly deposits into your stock portfolio (or deposits on any schedule, in fact, regular or not), or make regular contributions to mutual funds in a retirement account through your employer, using this kind of calculation for the internal rate of return will keep a running tally for you at all times of how you're doing for the long haul. Each time a new statement arrives from your broker or fund company, all you have to do is update the spreadsheet by adding your most recent deposit (and its date) and update the final date and total amount. The annualized return is recalculated for you automatically. Ain't technology grand?

Once you set up such a spreadsheet a time or two, it's simple and extremely helpful, especially if you make regular additions to a retirement fund. My wife's 403(h), for example, receives an automatic monthly deposit taken directly out of her paycheck. By listing those monthly deposits (which change by a few dollars every time her salary changes) and using the XIRR function, I'm able to tell immediately how her retirement account is doing relative to the S&P 500 over the same period. It only takes about five minutes to update each quarter when her new statement arrives. The same goes for our regular stock portfolio, to which we add cash on a regular basis. No myths, no fudged numbers, full accountability, the Foolish way to keep track!

⌗ You mention frequently that we should save regularly (even monthly). But how can I add small monthly amounts to a stock portfolio without getting eaten alive by trading costs each time?

You're absolutely right that trying to add small amounts each month directly to your stock portfolio can be a very costly proposition if you're not careful. With no-load (no sales commission) mutual funds, it is a simple task. You simply send the fund company a check each month (or even have it automatically drafted from your bank account), and at the close of business on the day your check arrives, the fund company exchanges the money for an equivalent number of shares. It doesn't cost you a thing and it allows you to add regularly, in almost any amount. (Some funds do have minimum requirements for additional dollar investments, but they're generally very low, $50 or $100, perhaps, if anything.)

If you're investing in a four-stock Unemotional Value approach, though, even if you're sending in $1,000 per month, the minimum trading cost of $40 to buy four new stocks each month would eat up 4 percent of your monthly savings amounts. That's simply not an acceptable arrangement. So let's look at a number of savings alternatives you may consider if you wish to add new money to your portfolio regularly and keep trading costs reasonable.

I've mentioned dividend reinvestment plans (DRiPs) on a number of occasions. It's time to explain precisely what they are and how you might use them. DRiPs are plans administered by the individual companies themselves or banks that they hire to allow existing shareholders to reinvest the quarterly dividends automatically into more shares of company stock instead of receiving the dividend as a cash payment. If you own Exxon, for example, and would like to keep adding to your position instead of getting that quarterly cash payout, you can enroll in the company's dividend reinvestment plan and all future dividends will go toward buying additional shares until you leave the plan or sell your total position in the stock. One difference between mutual funds and common stocks is that, typically, one cannot buy fractional shares of a common stock through a traditional broker. With mutual funds, you send in whatever dollar amount you wish and you're credited with exactly as many shares as that amount will afford, to thousandths of a share. That is, if you mail in $500 and the mutual fund's net asset value (its price per share) is $45.36, you will receive 11.023 shares of the mutual fund. Buying stocks through the traditional brokerage route, you must buy them in whole numbers. In the DRiP plans, however, you'll get those fractional shares through your automatic reinvestment because you're buying directly from the company, not through a broker.

Perhaps the biggest advantage of dividend reinvestment plans is an arrangement most of the companies have with shareholders whereby the shareholder can send in additional money directly to the company to buy more shares without having to go through a traditional broker. The plans vary from company to company, but many companies charge nothing for this service. So if you add money each month to your favorite stocks, you can bypass brokerage commissions altogether. In fact, some companies even offer their shares to members of the DRiP at a reduced price, giving shareholders something of a built-in return in exchange for their long-term loyalty.

To enroll in a company dividend reinvestment plan, it usually requires that you own at least one share of the stock (a few companies require more shares). And there are a number of ways to acquire that single share to get you started. One is to get a relative or friend who already owns stock in the company to transfer one share to you

(you'll have to pay him for the share, of course, unless it's going to be a gift). Then, once the share is registered in your name, you can join the DRiP directly. Another way is to buy your initial share or shares of a company through one of the deep-discount brokers. At $10 to $15 for the trade, this is a relatively minor one-time cost. However, many brokers charge an additional fee to register the share(s) in your name and send you the certificate. Then you can enroll in the dividend reinvestment plan directly and buy additional shares without fee from the company when you decide to invest in the future. A third way is to purchase the first share through one of the commercial services set up to serve DRiP investors. One such organization is called the MoneyPaper (1-800-388-9993). The MoneyPaper is a monthly publication devoted to the companies offering dividend reinvestment plans. For a subscription fee, you'll receive a guide to the companies, the monthly newsletter, and other services aimed at getting you started with purchases of the individual stocks. As of this writing, the MoneyPaper is also offering Foolish readers a special discount, so if you call to find out more, be sure to tell them you're a Fool.

Having said all of this about dividend reinvestment plans, I should caution you about them as well. I think DRiPs are *not* a good idea with the Unemotional Value approach, and they would be impossible with the Unemotional Growth approach (for timing reasons, obviously, but also because many of the stocks that appear in the Unemotional Growth rankings do not pay dividends). The reason I don't advise using DRiPs with the Dow Dividend Approaches is because they are not particularly flexible. When you send in money to a DRiP, it will get invested on the company's timetable, not immediately after arriving. If the company's investment schedule is particularly rigid, your money can sit idle for up to a month before it actually gets invested. But even more of a problem with the Dow Dividend Approaches is that you may well be selling a stock only nine months or so after receiving your first quarterly dividend check. If the stock rotates out of the Dow Dividend Approach portfolio after a single year (as roughly half of the stocks each year will), you're forced to set up and cancel dividend reinvestment plans every year to keep your money in the current group of Dow stocks. One alternative, perhaps, is always to keep a DRiP open once you've started it. When it came time to sell a stock according to the Dow Dividend Approaches, you would sell all but one share and leave that share idle until the next time that stock appeared in the rankings. I think this is a bit of a paperwork hassle, however, for an approach that's beautiful in part because of its sheer simplicity.

Dividend reinvestment plans are really best, in my view, for stocks you plan to hold for many years, not ones you may well rotate out of one year after buying. If you're buying General Electric or Coca-Cola or another market dominator, for example, and plan to hold it indefinitely as a core segment of your portfolio, then DRiPs become a very good, economical way to invest additional funds. Send off your checks each month to your favorite stocks and save a fortune on monthly commissions. For example, if five years ago, you had begun investing $50 each month through a dividend reinvestment plan with Travelers Group, you would have acquired over 135 shares of the stock (accounting for all stock splits). In fact, you would have more than that because of dividends, but even ignoring the dividends, the growth is impressive. Those 135.431 shares were worth $8,981 on September 15, 1997. Only $3,000 of that was money you would have invested. The other $5,981 was the result of price growth. (Using the XIRR function to calculate the internal rate of return, that comes out to an astounding 46 percent a year.) The irony here is that you would have been able to achieve this growth using a dividend reinvestment plan and bypassing any commission charges levied by brokers like Salomon Smith Barney, which just happens to be a division of Travelers Group. Profiting from the brokerage industry without having to pay its fees. A delicious irony.

Not all stocks will grow consistently the way Travelers Group has over the last five years, of course. But if you have some core holdings you wish to add to regularly, consider dividend reinvestment plans. If you'd like to learn more about DRiPs, one of the country's foremost experts on them is Chuck Carlson. He's written a number of fine books about DRiPs, including *Buying Stocks Without a Broker, No Load Stocks,* and *Free Lunch on Wall Street.* You can also learn more about DRiPs at The Motley Fool Web site (www.fool.com).

❊ If I want to add regularly to my Dow Approach portfolio, though, what *do* you recommend?

The easiest way, but not the most productive, is simply to sock away your regular savings deposits in some other investment vehicle until the calendar comes around again and it is time to update your Dow portfolio. At that time, you can add the new money to the total to be invested for the next cycle. For example, if you're working with a five-stock Dow portfolio that begins with $2,000 in each stock ($10,000 total), let's say that during the ensuing year, you are able to save an additional $500 per month. At the end of the year, if your original portfolio has grown by 20 percent, it would now be worth $12,000. Add to that the additional $6,000 (plus any interest) you saved throughout the year and you would begin the next year with approximately $18,000. That would mean you would invest roughly $3,600 in each of the five stocks.

You have a number of options regarding where to park the additional monthly funds, however. The simplest may be to mail them directly to your brokerage account. Each account has an accompanying cash component that is generally invested for you automatically in a money market account of some kind. When you receive quarterly dividend payments, this is where your broker parks them unless you instruct otherwise. Sending the monthly checks to your broker would get you some minimal interest, they would be virtually as safe as in a guaranteed bank account, and they would be conveniently in place when you're ready to adjust your holdings at the end of your Dow portfolio cycle. The problem, of course, is that the money is sitting all but idle, earning a very low interest rate compared with what it might be earning elsewhere.

Another option is to maintain an account with an S&P 500 Index fund, which would allow you to add money monthly at no commission charge. During the year, the monthly checks you've added would at least keep pace with the major market index. Historically, that would be a much better return than a money market account, although not quite as attractive as the returns achieved by the Dow Approaches. (You may have to shop around for an index fund that will allow you to start with a relatively small amount. You want as much money as possible at work for you in the Dow Approach, so each year when you update your Dow holdings, you would all but drain the index fund to shift that money into the next year's list of Dow stocks. Shop around for an index fund that will work well within that plan.)

Yet another alternative would be to run multiple groups of Dow stocks, starting at different points throughout the year. For example, you may want to buy four Dow stocks in January, another four in April, then again in July and October. By running multiple Dow portfolios, you're getting new money into the favored Dow stocks relatively quickly instead of having to let it sit idle for most of the year. It's true that such a plan increases the trading costs because you're managing what amounts to several portfolios simultaneously, each with its own set of regular updates and trading costs. But with the deep-discount trading costs as low as $40 to $60 per year for each portfolio, the added costs may well be justified by the higher returns you should achieve over time by putting the money to work more quickly in the best stocks available.

If you opt to run multiple Dow portfolios, always buy whatever stocks are currently in the rankings at the time of each new purchase, regardless of what you may have purchased just three or six months previously. The goal is always to invest in the stocks that represent the best relative values today. Undoubtedly, you will end up investing in some stocks that you already hold in other groups. Don't let that concern you. Just keep careful track of when you purchased what so that when it comes time to update, you'll be selling the correct stocks and will be able to qualify for the best capital gains distinctions. Don't be concerned if your several portfolios are not the same size. They're all components of the same master portfolio. You're just giving yourself four open windows through which you can add new money every year without unduly running up commission costs. As always, test your own situation against our benchmark guide that suggests you keep annual trading costs under 2.5 percent of your total portfolio value. You may find that for now, running two Dow groups, staggered six months apart, is all you can afford. You can always add new groups later if you find you can afford them and they'll help you with your savings plans. Make the possibilities suit your own needs.

▨ Are there any other methods you like for adding money regularly?

(Another hanging curve, just waiting to be parked in the center-field bleachers.) Why, yes, there is another, and thanks for asking! This final option is one I happen to like better than all of the previous options I've discussed here, but before I explain any further, I also need to mention that it is a bit more advanced and does require one to accept a higher level of risk. In my opinion, though, it's a risk well taken. I'm talking about using a conservative level of margin leverage with your Dow portfolio.

I mentioned in part 1 that I recommend that all taxable accounts should be opened as margin accounts rather than solely as cash accounts, even if you never plan on using the margin alternative. (Sorry, IRAs are not eligible for margin investing.) Investing on margin is simply borrowing a portion of your total investment from your broker. The loan is then paid back as new cash comes into your account, either through dividend checks you receive, new cash you add, or from the sale of any stocks in your portfolio. There's no time frame on the loan. You simply pay interest on the outstanding margin balance each month for as long as you owe money to your broker. There are limitations, of course.

In the 1920s, the margin requirement was only 10 percent. That is, if you wanted to buy $10,000 worth of stock, you were required to put up a minimum of $1,000 of your own money and could borrow the other 90 percent. This excessively liberal margin rule, in the opinion of many historians, contributed greatly to the excesses that ultimately resulted in the great stock market crash of 1929. Today, the margin requirement is 50 percent, meaning at least half of any investment must be funded with your own capital. My own belief is that such a level is still too speculative for a long-term investor and I prefer to see Foolish investors keep any margin balances under 20 percent of their total portfolios.

What's margin good for? Basically, the use of margin is a way of adding some extra return to your portfolio if you believe the stocks you own will achieve a greater return than the cost of borrowing the money in the first place. For example, if you have to pay an annual interest rate of 8 percent to your broker on the margin balance, but you earn 20 percent on the stocks you bought with the borrowed funds, you've made a tidy profit by borrowing the money. Let's look at an example with dollar amounts so you can see how it works.

Suppose you have $20,000 to invest. If you borrow another $5,000 from your broker, you can invest the whole $25,000 in your favorite stocks. Of the $25,000, 80 percent of it is your money and the other 20 percent is borrowed from your broker. (That ratio is considered to be 20 percent on margin.) If your $25,000 investment grows by 20 percent, the value of the stocks in your account at the end of the year will be $30,000. But you still owe your broker the original $5,000 loan plus interest. If the interest rate is 8 percent, you would owe $400 in interest plus the original $5,000, leaving you a grand total of $24,600. That represents a 23 percent gain over your original investment of $20,000, even though your actual portfolio return was only 20 percent. The increase in your profit came from borrowing extra money at a rate less than you were able to earn by putting that money to work.

Before we go a step farther, though, you need to see the flip side. While using margin leverage can exaggerate your gains, it can also exaggerate your losses, so it does increase your level of risk. For Dow investors, though, this has been a calculated risk well worth taking over the last several decades. There have only been a handful of losing years for the Dow Approaches since 1971, and none of them was a severe loss. With that kind of consistency of results, the use of a conservative level of margin leverage seems reasonable.

Let's look at a sample using the actual annual results for the Unemotional Value Four since 1971. We'll assume a complete turn-over each year, at which time you would pay off the loan and all the interest before starting in the next year with a new group of stocks. We'll maintain a constant level of margin borrowing, 25 percent of the actual portfolio value at the beginning of each year. (If you borrow 25 percent of your actual portfolio value, you are investing 80 percent of the total with your own money and 20 percent with borrowed funds. For example, 25 percent of $20,000 is $5,000. That $5,000 loan is 20 percent of the invested total, $25,000.) We'll also assume a constant margin interest rate of 8 percent. In reality, margin interest rates can fluctuate, of course, as the economy changes. Currently, brokerage rates charge just under 7 percent to more than 9 percent. Shop around to find the best deal for the amount of money you anticipate borrowing. The rates at many brokers fluctuate based on the amount you borrow (see the section on choosing a broker in part 1).

Year	Start	Return	Total
1971	$ 20,000	19.89%	$ 23,978
1972	$ 23,978	24.91%	$ 29,951
1973	$ 29,951	25.74%	$ 37,660
1974	$ 37,660	5.30%	$ 39,656
1975	$ 39,656	68.71%	$ 66,904
1976	$ 66,904	36.92%	$ 91,605
1977	$ 91,605	5.32%	$ 96,479
1978	$ 96,479	9.89%	$ 106,020
1979	$ 106,020	9.99%	$ 116,612
1980	$ 116,612	45.47%	$ 169,635
1981	$ 169,635	−4.63%	$ 161,781
1982	$ 161,781	39.50%	$ 225,684
1983	$ 225,684	41.74%	$ 319,885
1984	$ 319,885	6.38%	$ 340,294
1985	$ 340,294	22.85%	$ 418,051
1986	$ 418,051	27.30%	$ 532,179
1987	$ 532,179	20.07%	$ 638,987
1988	$ 638,987	13.62%	$ 726,017
1989	$ 726,017	15.28%	$ 836,952
1990	$ 836,952	−17.61%	$ 689,565
1991	$ 689,565	81.61%	$1,252,319
1992	$1,252,319	29.94%	$1,627,263
1993	$1,627,263	26.22%	$2,053,931
1994	$2,053,931	4.72%	$2,150,877
1995	$2,150,877	30.58%	$2,808,615
1996	$2,808,615	24.34%	$3,492,232

First the comparison. The investor above begins with $20,000 in 1971, investing in the four-stock Unemotional Value approach without any margin leverage. He adds nothing during the ensuing twenty-six years and simply rotates into the new stocks each year. At the end of 1996, his portfolio would have grown to $3,492,232. Not bad, eh? The above table shows the annual growth of his portfolio.

But compare that result with his neighbor, who began in 1971

Year	Start	Borrow	Invest
1971	$ 20,000	$ 5,000	$ 25,000
1972	$ 24,573	$ 6,143	$ 30,716
1973	$ 31,732	$ 7,933	$ 39,665
1974	$ 41,308	$ 10,327	$ 51,634
1975	$ 43,218	$ 10,805	$ 54,023
1976	$ 79,473	$ 19,868	$ 99,341
1977	$ 114,560	$ 28,640	$ 143,200
1978	$ 119,887	$ 29,972	$ 149,858
1979	$ 132,310	$ 33,077	$ 165,387
1980	$ 146,186	$ 36,546	$ 182,732
1981	$ 226,351	$ 56,588	$ 282,938
1982	$ 208,724	$ 52,181	$ 260,904
1983	$ 307,606	$ 76,902	$ 384,508
1984	$ 461,948	$ 115,487	$ 577,435
1985	$ 489,549	$ 122,387	$ 611,937
1986	$ 619,586	$ 154,896	$ 774,482
1987	$ 818,628	$ 204,657	$1,023,285
1988	$1,007,628	$ 251,907	$1,259,535
1989	$1,159,024	$ 289,756	$1,448,781
1990	$1,357,218	$ 339,304	$1,696,522
1991	$1,031,316	$ 257,829	$1,289,145
1992	$2,062,760	$ 515,690	$2,578,451
1993	$2,793,493	$ 698,373	$3,491,867
1994	$3,653,191	$ 913,298	$4,566,489
1995	$3,795,665	$ 948,916	$4,744,582
1996	$5,170,645	$1,292,661	$6,463,306

with an identical $20,000 and who invested in precisely the same stocks over the ensuing twenty-six years. The only difference is that he used 20 percent margin leverage (borrowing an additional 25 percent of his portfolio value at the start of each year at a cost of 8 percent interest). At the close of 1996, instead of sitting on a very impressive $3.5 million, our margin investor's portfolio ballooned to more than $6.6 million.

Precisely the same stocks, precisely the same original investment, but more than $3 million in extra profits because of a conservative level of margin. Instead of the annualized growth rate of 21.96 percent our first investor achieved, our margin investor achieved an

Return	Subtotal	Interest	Total
19.89%	$ 29,973	$ (400)	$ 24,573
24.91%	$ 38,367	$ (491)	$ 31,732
25.74%	$ 49,875	$ (635)	$ 41,308
5.30%	$ 54,371	$ (826)	$ 43,218
68.71%	$ 91,141	$ (864)	$ 79,473
36.92%	$ 136,017	$ (1,589)	$ 114,560
5.32%	$ 150,818	$ (2,291)	$ 119,887
9.89%	$ 164,679	$ (2,398)	$ 132,310
9.99%	$ 181,910	$ (2,646)	$ 146,186
45.47%	$ 265,821	$ (2,924)	$ 226,351
−4.63%	$ 269,838	$ (4,527)	$ 208,724
39.50%	$ 363,962	$ (4,174)	$ 307,606
41.74%	$ 545,002	$ (6,152)	$ 461,948
6.38%	$ 614,275	$ (9,239)	$ 489,549
22.85%	$ 751,764	$ (9,791)	$ 619,586
27.30%	$ 985,916	$ (12,392)	$ 818,628
20.07%	$1,228,658	$ (16,373)	$1,007,628
13.62%	$1,431,084	$ (20,153)	$1,159,024
15.28%	$1,670,154	$ (23,180)	$1,357,218
−17.61%	$1,397,765	$ (27,144)	$1,031,316
81.61%	$2,341,216	$ (20,626)	$2,062,760
29.94%	$3,350,439	$ (41,255)	$2,793,493
26.22%	$4,407,434	$ (55,870)	$3,653,191
4.72%	$4,782,027	$ (73,064)	$3,795,665
30.58%	$6,195,475	$ (75,913)	$5,170,645
24.34%	$8,036,475	$(103,413)	$6,640,401

annualized rate of 25.02 percent. Those extra three percentage points a year, when compounded over two and one-half decades, make a world of difference, don't they?

❊ But how does margin come into play in my monthly savings plan?

Ah, now that's where the real beauty of margin leverage comes in. Let's take an example to show how you can use margin as a cost-effective savings tool as well as helpful leverage to juice up your long-term returns. If an investor has $20,000 to invest, but also adds

$500 a month as a regular savings plan, he can start the year by borrowing $5,000 on margin, investing the entire $25,000. Then, as he sends his new $500 a month to his broker, the monthly deposits simply go into paying off the margin loan balance early. By the end of ten months, his monthly $500 checks will have paid off the $5,000 loan and whatever interest he might owe will probably have been covered by his quarterly dividend payments. With his final two monthly deposits of $500 to end the year, he'll simply be building up a slight cash position with which to start the next year. When he updates his portfolio to start the new cycle, he can do the same thing —borrow money on margin, knowing his monthly savings additions will pay the loan down during the course of the year.

There are a couple of advantages in using this plan as both a savings vehicle and a cost-savings strategy. First, we know that a long-term conservative yet powerful investment strategy like the Dow Approach is ripe for the use of a conservative amount of leverage. The typical gains are more than double the cost of borrowing the money from a broker, so the increase in total return for your portfolio can be significant. Second, since you are planning to add money to the portfolio regularly, you are paying the loan down relatively quickly, which both reduces your extra risk in having a margin balance and saves on the interest expense compared with a margined portfolio where you make no savings deposits. And, finally, because your savings deposits are being put to work before you even deposit them, you don't have to bother with a complicated strategy to invest that additional money each month. It's already at work for you in the stocks you bought at the beginning of the year. You only have to make one set of trades per cycle (no need to run multiple portfolios) and you don't have to bother with idle money or index funds as a parking place for your new money. All you do each month is send the check to your brokerage account and it is automatically deposited against your margin balance. Even though it's somewhat more sophisticated in theory than the other methods for dealing with new money, in practice, using a conservative level of margin leverage is actually the simplest to administer.

Let's look now at a single year's cycle using this type of an approach. At the start of the year, we have an investment value of $30,000. Sticking to our limit of 20 percent on margin, we would borrow $7,500, giving us a total of $37,500 to put into our favorite Dow stocks for the next year (or eighteen months if you're trying to capitalize on the new tax laws). We will be adding $500 a month to our account and our margin interest rate is 7 percent annually (or 0.565% per month). The following table takes us through each month, showing the margin balance, the interest charges, and the monthly deposits.

In January, you begin the year with the new loan balance of $7,500 and you have no monthly deposit. (I am assuming you would have added the $500 for January to the total as you started the year.) You didn't receive any dividend payments. (For simplicity, I'll assume all the dividend payments arrive together in March, June, September, and December. I've calculated the dividend amounts based on an estimated 3 percent dividend yield on the original investment total of $37,500.) The interest charge that accrues in January is $42.38, bringing your margin balance to $7,542.38.

The next month, your first $500 deposit is received, reducing your margin balance to $7,042.38. The interest charge for February ($39.79) is tacked on and your new balance is $7,082.16.

In March, you send in another $500 and receive your first quarterly dividends, worth $281.25 (one quarter of the 3 percent dividend yield for the year). That reduces the loan amount to $6,300.91. Add in the interest charge for March ($35.60), and the balance is $6,336.51.

And so on, each month throughout the year. Every time you deposit a monthly check, it reduces the balance on the margin loan. By the end of the year in this example, the margin loan has been reduced to $1,173.98. In the meantime, the $37,500 you invested back in January has appreciated by 18 percent, let's say. Your portfolio of stocks is worth $44,250 and you still owe the broker $1,174. Your net worth, then, is $43,076. Not bad, considering one year ago it was only $30,000. Between regular savings, the growth of your investments, and the leverage you achieved through a conservative level of margin borrowing, you were able to increase your portfolio by 43.6 percent in a single year.

Don't let the small margin balance at the end of the year bother you. That will get paid off immediately as you sell stocks to adjust your holdings for the new year. And if you're planning to continue

Month	Beginning Balance	Savings Deposit	Dividends Received
January	$7,500.00		
February	$7,542.38	$500.00	
March	$7,082.16	$500.00	$281.25
April	$6,336.51	$500.00	
May	$5,869.49	$500.00	
June	$5,399.83	$500.00	$281.25
July	$4,644.67	$500.00	
August	$4,168.09	$500.00	
September	$3,688.82	$500.00	$281.25
October	$2,923.99	$500.00	
November	$2,437.69	$500.00	
December	$1,948.64	$500.00	$281.25

saving regularly using this strategy, you would be borrowing a new amount to begin the following year anyway. If you're more comfortable knowing that you're going to have the whole margin loan paid off before the end of the year, determine how much to borrow at the beginning of the year by how much you plan to add to your portfolio each month. As long as the total amount you borrow at the beginning of the year doesn't exceed 25 percent of your actual portfolio value, you will be keeping the margin ratio under 20 percent. (Example: Borrowing an additional 25 percent on a $50,000 portfolio is $12,500. Of that total of $62,500, the borrowed portion is only 20 percent, while the $50,000 starting amount is 80 percent of the total. That ratio is considered "20 percent on margin.")

Brokers all have maintenance requirements for margin investors. If for some reason you're heavily leveraged, say 50 percent on margin and 50 percent invested using your own money (the legal maximum today), and then the market declines sharply, you're likely to trigger a margin call. If the amount of your total investment that you actually own (your equity) drops below the broker's required limit, you'll either have to add more cash to bring your balance up to that level or sell some of the stocks in your portfolio to pay back some of the loan. (Since the market swooned to trigger such a call, selling back stocks while they're down is a doubly bad idea.) So keeping your margin limit at 20 percent or less, as I've suggested, all but eliminates

New Balance	Margin Interest	Ending Balance
$7,500.00	$42.38	$7,542.38
$7,042.38	$39.79	$7,082.16
$6,300.91	$35.60	$6,336.51
$5,836.51	$32.98	$5,869.49
$5,369.40	$30.31	$5,399.83
$4,618.58	$26.09	$4,644.67
$4,144.67	$23.42	$4,168.09
$3,668.09	$20.72	$3,688.82
$2,907.57	$16.43	$2,923.99
$2,423.99	$13.70	$2,437.69
$1,937.69	$10.95	$1,948.64
$1,167.39	$ 6.60	$1,173.98

the possibility of getting such a margin call, especially with the somewhat less volatile stocks we select in the Dow Approaches. Like any borrowing instrument, margin can be wonderfully powerful when used intelligently. When it's abused, however, it's an invitation to disaster.

▓ Aren't there any mutual funds using the Dow Approach? That would make monthly investing easy.

Traditional diversified mutual funds simply can't be concentrated in such a small number of stocks. The Securities and Exchange Commission rules for investment companies prohibit such funds from investing more than 5 percent of the fund's total assets in any one stock. So at a bare minimum, mutual funds must hold at least twenty stocks. Many hold hundreds of stocks at a time. The individual investor isn't limited by such rules, though, and can easily focus on four, five, even ten Dow stocks, avoiding the diluting effects of having to hold so many stocks.

Many major brokers do, however, offer unit investment trusts featuring five- or ten-stock versions of the Dow Approach. A unit investment trust is similar to a mutual fund in the sense that it pools together money from a multitude of investors and invests the total as a single portfolio in these stocks. There are two crucial differences, however, between funds and unit investment trusts. A trust is designed with a fixed time horizon, during which time no trading is done. This period has typically been a year, but with the new tax laws, some trusts are being redesigned to incorporate an eighteen-month holding period. No new investors can enter the trust during that period, and to pull your money out early can result in some hefty penalties.

The other major difference between funds and these trusts, and it is a difference that baffles me, is the cost structure. The average cost ratio for stock mutual funds is around 1.5 percent of the fund's assets per year. That covers the manager's fee, marketing costs, administrative costs, trading costs, whatever the fund needs to operate. Many funds, especially the index funds, are significantly more economical, some charging fees under $1/2$ of 1 percent per year. Yet these unit investment trusts, which are unmanaged portfolios—buying stocks one time according to a formula like the Dow Approach, which takes all of fifteen minutes to calculate—charge anywhere from 2.5 percent to 3.0 percent per year in fees. Most of them charge a 1 percent fee up front when you enter the trust, and then spread the remainder of the fee out over the last several months of the trust's duration. Some trusts will waive the up-front 1 percent fee if you roll your investment over into a new trust when the original one expires. But if you add new money at that time, as all saving Fools should do, whoops, there goes your exemption on the up-front fee. With today's deep-discount brokerage accounts, I don't see any advantage to these unit investment trusts. It only costs $40 to $60 in trading costs per year for a four-stock Dow portfolio. (When you update, two of the four stocks usually require replacement. That requires four trades. If you have to adjust the balances in the remaining two stocks, that can require two more trades. A typical year, then, requires from four to six trades.) With an account as small as $2,000, the range of trading costs is 2 percent to 3 percent. And from there, each year the cost percentages would decline, since the total trading costs are a fixed dollar amount at the deep-discounters. For example, when your portfolio hits $10,000, your total trading costs for the year, doing it yourself at a deep-discounter, would still only run $40 to $60. Compare that with the unit investment trust fees of 2.5 percent to 3.0 percent ($250 to $300). Why pay a couple of hundred dollars *and* lose control of your money for the next year when you can purchase the same investments in your own account, maintain complete control, *and* pay only a fraction of the costs? The unit investment trusts are simply another sign that the Wall Street Wise are hoping to keep the individual investor ignorant and dependent on their services. (Yes, Fools, the king really is naked.)

⌘ If these models are so terrific, why doesn't everyone use them? Once the news about them gets out, won't they get too popular and become less effective?

Let's take the Dow models first. The strategy to buy the highest-yielding companies among America's biggest and bluest of the blue chips isn't new. Investors, both institutional and retail, have known about it for a long time and have used it successfully. But there are several factors that should keep it from ever becoming too popular. First, these are among the largest stocks traded publicly. The volume of shares traded in these stocks daily is enormous. Even if all of the Fools using this approach came together to make their trades on the same day, we'd barely make a dent in the trading volume of these giants. And with investors buying different Dow stocks at different times of the year as the rankings fluctuate, we have virtually no chance of affecting the movements of these stocks. Second, there's a reason this strategy is sometimes called the Dogs of the Dow. No one really wants these stocks, which, of course, is why they're good bargains for us. From a purely emotional standpoint, would you have wanted to buy Exxon right after the *Valdez* accident? Would you have been first in line to buy shares of Union Carbide after the Bhopal disaster? It takes a disciplined strategy to buy stocks that look awful to everyone else. And, third, let's face it—it's boring to buy widow and orphan stocks (or, as my mother calls them, blue-hair stocks) and then sit on your hands for a year or eighteen months. Most investors are in the market through mutual funds, so they don't have an active say in where their investment dollars are placed. But those investors who do take an active role in choosing their own stocks either get their information from a traditional broker (and few brokers who are compensated based on commissions are going to recommend such a low-turnover strategy) or are excited about finding the next small-cap star performer and too emotional to stick with such a disciplined and slow approach. It's hard to see this strategy ever becoming too popular. One poor year for it and the marginally committed investors using it will proclaim the approach dead and disappear from the Dow arena. Human nature being as emotional as it is, this approach goes against the grain, which is why it's so consistently successful.

As for the Unemotional Growth approach, too many people following it could indeed have an adverse effect on some of the smaller stocks that appear in the screen, simply because of their reduced liquidity compared with the enormous Dow stocks the Unemotional Value approach selects. But there's no way to measure such an effect, unfortunately. Since part of the approach is geared to momentum (earnings momentum as well as price momentum), I expect the Unemotional Growth model will perform in cycles as momentum-style investing goes in and out of favor. We noticed such a phenomenon in our online discussions of the approach in early 1997. When I first announced my research results, there was quite a stir in the Foolish Workshop for such a simple approach that had achieved such mammoth gains over the previous decade. Not surprisingly, the model hit a rough patch early this year, right after the excitement about the 1996 performance hit a new peak, and the model portfolio plunged over 26 percent in the first three months of the year. Almost immediately, our message folder, which had hosted what had been a vibrant and excited discussion, became a ghost town. By the end of March, the discussion had all but disappeared as investors went looking for the needle in yet another haystack. Since March 1997, the portfolio has rebounded fairly dramatically, up 58 percent in the months from April through August. Despite the model's name, there aren't many genuinely *unemotional* investors who will stick with a discipline in tough times. That single fact is what gives me reason to doubt the models will ever get too popular for their own good. Each new weak stretch will weed out the uncommitted and emotional investors and leave the garden free for those who are sticking to a long-term discipline.

▩ Where to from here?

I think of this book as a starting point for further Foolish research rather than as a final destination. The online community is such an exciting source of ideas and free information (some bad, much very good) that I fully expect the research we've begun in our Foolish Workshop and throughout the forum to foster more such models in the coming years. As more and more electronic sources of historical data become available, we will continue to test theories about what drives stock movements with an eye toward useful tools for the individual investor. For too many years, the individual investor was at a huge disadvantage to the professional money managers. Data weren't available, research was limited to professional access only, and the costs of managing a private portfolio were prohibitive. All of that has changed in recent years and the playing field is rapidly being leveled. Whether you use the screens laid out in this book as models for your own portfolio, or simply as launching points into your own fully Foolish financial analyses, is unimportant. The crucial factor is that now we are able to share our findings immediately with a world-wide interactive community of investors—the largest investment club ever. No longer is the individual investor obligated to support the Wall Street Wisemen in order to prepare for his financial future. Fool on!

No ascent is too steep for mortals. Heaven itself we seek in our Folly.
—HORACE

✕ ACKNOWLEDGMENTS

This book would never have been written had it not been for the vision of two brothers who lured me away from academe (it didn't take much coaxing, if truth be told) into the burgeoning world of Folly. Tom and David Gardner, founders of The Motley Fool, took a chance on me when they had no compelling reason to do so, and all the more remarkable was the fact that they hired me to write for The Motley Fool, having never met me in person and knowing that my training was in literary theory rather than in financial analysis. Such is the way of cyberspace.

But an even more profound gratitude goes to my real teachers in this financial game—the thousands of readers who have challenged me, assisted me, taught me, and experimented with me as the theories in this book grew from little more than hunches into full-blown research studies. Because of the forum built by the Gardners and the countless readers who visit The Motley Fool on America Online and the World Wide Web each day, I'm privileged to be part of the largest and most talented investment club in the world.

More directly related to this book, my thanks go to Jim

O'Shaughnessy, author of three terrific investment books, for his generous gifts of time, guidance, and introductions into the world of publishing. His encouragement and help were the primary motivations behind my effort to get this project down on paper.

Once the idea crystallized, though, it was a team of people who made the process smooth when I didn't have a clue about how to proceed. Special thanks go to my agent at ICM, Suzanne Gluck, who took my proposal and in the course of a whirlwind week turned it into a real project; to Bob Mecoy, my editor at Simon & Schuster, who remained calm, encouraging, and enthusiastic every time I panicked; and to Pete Fornatale, his assistant, who kept me continually supplied with information and endless new titles to read when I couldn't face writing another page. One of these days, I may actually get to meet them all in person and thank them properly.

And, finally, my heartfelt thanks go to my family: especially my parents, Joe and Barbara Sheard, my wife, Cynthia, and my son, Brenden. They demonstrated amazing faith in me as I left one career path, so close to a major milestone, and began walking down a different and altogether unmapped one. Who could have predicted even five years ago that this is what I'd be doing today? Yet the journey's been rewarding in ways more profound than those which can be tallied on any brokerage statement.

INDEX